Why Do You Need This New Edition?

If you're wondering why you should buy this new edition of *Writing Poems*, here are 8 good reasons!

The eighth edition's content has been refined and offers a more selective group of poems for discussion.

1 Dozens of new poems have been added to *Writing Poems*, including poems by the following poets: Yasser Abdel-Latif, Kim Addonizio, Gwendolyn Brooks, and Stephen Dunn.

2 The selections in "Poems to Consider" continue to be both classic and contemporary works, and the eighth edition includes many younger poets from a wider range of ethnicities, cultural backgrounds, and aesthetic approaches.

3 The "Poems to Consider" section in each chapter has been trimmed to a more manageable five to six selections, helping to make the eighth edition more concise and selective.

4 The discussions on rhythm in Chapter 3 have been refined and clarified so students will have just the essentials to get started; more complex terms have been moved to Appendix II.

5 Fresh exercises in the "Questions and Suggestions" sections have been included throughout to inspire student poems.

6 A new appendix includes useful questions for discussing and revising poetry that can help support a class or workshop and that students can use on their own.

7 The compartmentalized structure of the eighth edition makes it a flexible teaching tool, allowing instructors to teach the book's chapters in any sequence that suits their own pedagogy.

8 A new lower price makes *Writing Poems* an affordable choice as well as an excellent resource for creative writers.

PEARSON

WRITING POEMS

Eighth Edition

Michelle Boisseau
University of Missouri–Kansas City

Hadara Bar-Nadav
University of Missouri–Kansas City

Robert Wallace
Late of Case Western Reserve University

Pearson

Boston   Columbus   Indianapolis   New York   San Francisco   Upper Saddle River   Amsterdam
Cape Town   Dubai   London   Madrid   Milan   Munich   Paris   Montréal   Toronto
Delhi   Mexico City   São Paulo   Sydney   Hong Kong   Seoul   Singapore   Taipei   Tokyo

Acquisitions Editor: Vivian Garcia
Executive Marketing Manager: Joyce Nilsen
Production Manager: Jennifer Bossert
Project Coordination, Text Design, and Electronic Page Makeup: Integra
Cover designer: John Callahan
Cover image: Elena Ray/Shutterstock
Senior Manufacturing Buyer: Dennis J. Para
Printer and Binder and Cover Printer: R.R. Donnelley/Crawfordsville

For permission to use copyrighted material, grateful acknowledgment is made to the copyright holders on pp. 226–230, which are hereby made part of this copyright page.

Library of Congress Cataloging-in-Publication Data

Boisseau, Michelle
    Writing poems / Michelle Boisseau, Hadara Bar-Nadav, Robert Wallace.—8th ed.
        p. cm.
    Includes index.
    ISBN-13: 978-0-205-17605-2
    ISBN-10: 0-205-17605-4
    1. Poetry—Authorship. I. Bar-Nadav, Hadara. II. Wallace, Robert. III. Title.
    PN1059.A9W34 2012
    808.1—dc22

                                                    2011012277

1 2 3 4 5 6 7 8 9 10—DOC—14 13 12 11

ISBN-13: 978-0-205-17605-2
ISBN-10: 0-205-17605-4

For Tom and Anna
and
for Scott George Beattie

CONTENTS

PART I: FORM   21

2 | VERSE   23

3 | MAKING THE LINE (I)   41

4 | MAKING THE LINE (II)   59

5 | THE SOUND (AND LOOK) OF SENSE   77

PART III: PROCESS   177

10 | FINDING THE POEM   179

BEFORE DESIGNING
THE COURSE

A Preface to the Teacher

Poets learn from poets. As in the earlier editions of *Writing Poems*, the eighth edition embraces this crucial idea: Clues for how to write new poetry can be found in the work of past and contemporary poets. In the poems of others, beginning poets apprehend the possibilities for their own work, joining a tradition of great poets even as they begin to write their own new poems.

Because reading poems stimulates and guides the writing of poems, this book acts as a handy anthology (heavily weighted with poems written in the past twenty years), a friendly guide for the student, and a backup for you as the teacher. The book thoroughly covers fundamentals such as lineation, imagery, and metaphor so that you can spend more class time focusing on your own students' poems, responding to the issues that their poems pose, and illustrating what poems have to teach them about craft.

New to This Edition

Our aim in the eighth edition has been to refine the book's content and offer a more selective group of poems for discussion.

- Dozens of new poems have been added to *Writing Poems*, Eighth Edition, including poems by the following poets:

Yasser Abdel-Latif	Terrance Hayes	Mary Ruefle
Kim Addonizio	Bob Hicok	Jamie Sabines
Deborah Bogan	Heather McHugh	Ruth Stone
Gwendolyn Brooks	Simone Muench	Stefi Weisburd
Victoria Chang	Aimee Nezhukumatathil	Dean Young
Stephen Dunn	D. A. Powell	Kevin Young
Paul Guest	Spencer Reece	

- The selections in "Poems to Consider" continue to be both classic and contemporary works, and the eighth edition includes many younger poets from a wider range of ethnicities, cultural backgrounds, and aesthetic approaches.
- The "Poems to Consider" section in each chapter has been trimmed to a more manageable five to six selections, helping to make the eighth edition more concise and selective.

- The discussions on rhythm in Chapter 3 have been refined and clarified so students will have just the essentials to get started; more complex terms have been moved to Appendix II.
- Fresh exercises in the "Questions and Suggestions" sections have been included throughout to inspire student poems.
- A new appendix includes useful questions for discussing and revising poetry that can help support a class or workshop and that students can use on their own.
- The compartmentalized structure of the eighth edition makes it a flexible teaching tool, allowing instructors to teach the book's chapters in any sequence that suits their own pedagogy.
- A new lower price makes *Writing Poems* an affordable choice as well as an excellent resource for creative writers.

Enduring Features

- A wealth of writing exercises that prompt students to write their own poetry.
- An anthology of approximately one hundred and fifty classic and contemporary poems, offering students a diverse selection of examples, illustrations, and inspiration.
- Throughout the book, discussion of the writing process that emphasizes the crucial role of revision.
- Focused sections within chapters (for example, "Line," "Meter," "Syllabics," "Repetition") that offer instructors the flexibility of teaching in discrete units.
- Poets' quotations integrated throughout the text that provide inspiration and illumination to beginning and advanced students.
- Comprehensive coverage and a practical student-friendly approach to help instructors teach a successful and dynamic course.

Acknowledgments

We wish to thank the following instructors who reviewed the eighth edition's manuscript during its development: Melissa Chichester, Mott Community College; Heidi Czerwiec, University of North Dakota; Matthew Boyd Goldie, Rider University; Patricia Colleen Murphy, Arizona State University; Brad Summerhill, Truckee Meadows Community College; and Marianne Taylor, Kirkwood Community College.

—M.B. and H.B.

A Note from the Publisher

Supplements Available with *Writing Poems*, Eighth Edition

A Student's Guide to Getting Published (ISBN: 0-321-11779-4)

This clear and concise "how-to" guide takes writers of all genres through the process of publishing their work—including the considerations of submission, how to research markets, the processes of self-editing and being edited, and how to produce a "well-wrought manuscript," among other useful and practical information. Available at no additional cost when value-packed with *Writing Poems*.

A Workshop Guide to Creative Writing (ISBN: 0-321-09539-1)

This laminated reference offers suggestions and tips for students to keep in mind in a workshop situation—both as participant and presenter. Blank space is provided for students to record additional guidelines provided by their instructor. Available at no additional cost when value-packed with *Writing Poems*.

The Longman Journal for Creative Writing (ISBN: 0-321-09540-5)

This journal provides students with their own personal space for writing. Helpful writing prompts and strategies are included as well as guidelines for participating in a workshop. Available at no additional cost when value-packed with *Writing Poems*.

Responding to Literature: A Writer's Journal (ISBN: 0-321-09542-1)

This journal provides students with their own personal space for writing. Prompts for responding to fiction, poetry, and drama are integrated throughout. Available at no additional cost when value-packed with *Writing Poems*.

Glossary of Literary and Critical Terms (ISBN: 0-321-12691-2)

This handy glossary includes definitions, explanations, and examples for more than 100 literary and critical terms that students commonly encounter in literature classes. Available at no additional cost when value-packed with *Writing Poems*.

Related Titles

Poetic Form: An Introduction (ISBN: 0-321-19820-4)

Written with humor and wit by David Caplan, this guide aims to convey the pleasures of poetry—a sestina's delightful gamesmanship, an epigram's barbed wit, a haiku's deceptive simplicity—and the fun of exploring poetic forms. Each chapter defines a particular verse form, briefly describes its history, and offers examples. Writing exercises challenge students to utilize the forms in creative expression. Covering a wider range of forms in greater detail and with more poetic examples than similar guides on the market, it provides enough material to thoroughly introduce the language's major forms while allowing flexibility in the classroom.

Re:Verse: Turning Towards Poetry (ISBN: 1-405-83616-4)

This book, aimed at people just starting to study literature, takes nothing for granted but opens poetry up to all in a way that makes it both exciting and fresh. Examples are taken from a balanced combination of traditional writers such as Keats, Wordsworth, Blake, and Shakespeare and modern poets such as Seamus Heaney, Jackie Kay, and Benjamin Zephaniah.

1

STARTING OUT
An Introduction

This was a Poet—It is That
Distills amazing sense
From ordinary Meanings—

—EMILY DICKINSON

Poetry is nearly as old as humanity itself. Poems are so interwoven with the human story that we can follow their origins into the dimmest reaches of our roots. Not long after we began to structure the sounds that we could make into language, we began tinkering with that language, making it memorable, making poems. The earliest generations of poets made discoveries with language and form and invented new poems, as did the generations that followed, all the way down to us. People from cultures all over the globe trace their origins through poems. From Iceland to Cameroon, on makeshift tables in apartment complexes, around campfires on windy plains, in some five thousand human languages, people use poems to express who they are, what they believe, what they have done, and, most of all, what it feels like to be alive.

Ezra Pound urges poets to "make it new." What strikes one era as innovative and exciting may strike a later generation as worn and dated. To make it new, a poet must be familiar with poetic forms and styles of the past and present; you can know what remains to be written only if you already know what exists. As T. S. Eliot puts it, the poet "lives in what is not merely the present, but the present moment of the past, unless [the poet] is conscious, not of what is dead, but of what is already living." The poet must take to heart the enduring poems of the past.

Writing poems combines what the poet knows of poetry's craft and possibilities with the unique characteristics she or he brings to the adventure—new subjects, new attitudes, new insights: "a place for the genuine," as Marianne Moore says. Each poet must learn and relearn how to write his or her own poems. Learning to write poetry means exploring. It means not only recording what you think or feel but investigating those thoughts, digging deep, striving for a new shivery understanding. Howard Nemerov wryly defines writing poems as a spiritual exercise "having for its chief object the discovery or invention of one's character," a statement that hints at the challenge of writing successful poetry.

A course called "Creative Writing" might better be called "Experimental Writing." Faced with the daunting specter of a blank page, the poet may feel intimidated by the injunction *be creative; create.* But being told to *experiment, to try something out,* can be freeing and even exhilarating. Poet Ann Lauterbach asserts that the "willingness to risk failure seems essential. To risk failure one needs a sense of unfettered play, the play that would allow a failure to become useful for the next attempt...." Even on a bad day when all you can seem to do is thrash around with a stubborn poem, you *can* experiment. Reorder a few words, find words that are more precise, shift punctuation, shape an arresting sentence, and form it into the first line of a poem. What might the poem's next line say?

The poem you end up with may not be what you had expected—and all the better. We experiment in order to surprise ourselves, to find out what we don't know, to clarify what we're trying to discover. Each experiment teaches us how to pose a problem more sharply, how to comprehend more thoroughly what we are looking for. The great German poet Rainer Maria Rilke in his *Letters to a Young Poet* offers this advice:

> Being an artist means: not numbering and counting, but ripening like a tree, which doesn't force its sap, and stands confidently in the storms of spring, not afraid that afterward summer may not come. It does come. But it comes only to those who are patient...*patience* is everything!

Writing—trying to dig up one's deepest feelings, perceptions, and ideas—will always be an intimate, vulnerable activity. You may be hard on your poems, but go easy on yourself.

We learn to write poems from reading (and rereading) poems we like, those poems that inspire us to write poems in the first place. That's how poets trained themselves before creative writing courses, and that's how they still learn. Elizabeth Bishop's advice to an aspiring poet in the 1960s still holds today:

> Read a lot of poetry—all the time....Read Campion, Herbert, Pope, Tennyson, Coleridge—anything at all almost that's any good, from the past—until you find out what you really like, by yourself. Even if you try to imitate it exactly—it will come out quite different. Then the great poets of our own century—Marianne Moore, Auden, Wallace Stevens—and not just 2 or 3 poems, each, in anthologies—read ALL of somebody.

When you meet poems that speak to you, in this book or elsewhere, see what else by those poets you can find in your bookstore, in the library, in journals, or on the Internet. Buy their books and read the literary journals in which they publish. These poets will help you realize places your own poems might go.

And as you write, make sure you're having fun. Keep your sense of humor lively, as the poet Sharon Bryan (B. 1943) does in this celebration of words:

 ## Sweater Weather: A Love Song to Language

Never better, mad as a hatter,
right as rain, might and main,
hanky-panky, hot toddy,

hoity-toity, cold shoulder,
bowled over, rolling in clover,   5
low blow, no soap, hope

against hope, pay the piper,
liar liar pants on fire,
high and dry, shoo-fly pie,

fiddle-faddle, fit as a fiddle,   10
sultan of swat, muskrat
ramble, fat and sassy,

flimflam, happy as a clam,
cat's pajamas, bee's knees,
peas in a pod, pleased as punch,   15

pretty as a picture, nothing much,
lift the latch, double Dutch,
helter-skelter, hurdy-gurdy,

early bird, feathered friend,
dumb cluck, buck up,   20
shilly-shally, willy-nilly,

roly-poly, holy moly,
loose lips sink ships,
spitting image, nip in the air,

hale and hearty, part and parcel,   25
upsy-daisy, lazy days,
maybe baby, up to snuff,

flibbertigibbet, honky-tonk,
spic and span, handyman,
cool as a cucumber, blue moon,   30

high as a kite, night and noon,
love me or leave me, seventh heaven,
up and about, over and out.

Bryan's poem develops by mining the riches of English idiom, by staying alert to associations that the sounds and images suggest. The poem leaps from one phrase to the next, so that the double "l" sounds in "shilly-shally, willy-nilly," in line 21 lead to more "l's" repeated in the following stanza, which lead to an echoing of "o" followed by short "i" sounds:

roly-poly, holy moly,
loose lips sink ships,
spitting image, nip in the air

Often student poets start out writing a poem with a firm idea in mind about what they want to say, approaching the poem as if it were to be developed logically, like an essay or report. Starting a poem with a fixed notion, however, can quickly frustrate you because what you wanted to say inevitably changes as it is translated to the page. If instead of holding on to an initial idea, you relax your grip on the poem and concentrate on the words as they come—paying attention to how an image or a sound suggests others—you can let the poem develop more naturally and in unexpected directions. And in the end you'll have more fun—an excruciating fun, perhaps, but a real engagement with language and discovery. Robert Frost once said, "No surprise for the poet, no surprise for the reader." If in writing the poem, the poet doesn't find out something new and stay curious about where a poem might lead, why would a reader? Good readers—teachers, peers, a writing group (even one online)—are also essential. They keep us honest. We may convince ourselves that the poem we have labored over says brilliantly what we mean it to say, but an objective reader will test those convictions. As you listen closely to what other readers have to say about your poems—and as you articulate your readings of other poets' work—you develop the critical skills necessary to revise your own poems. "All criticism is autobiography," Oscar Wilde wrote. Helping others revise their poems can help you teach yourself and is a great way to build community while sharing insights about the craft of poetry.

Word Magic

The joy that painters find in pushing around paint, poets find in playing with words, as Sharon Bryan's "Sweater Weather" demonstrates. You may find it helpful to picture the words of your poems as paint—you can choose, change, blend, and layer them. Because we use words in our everyday lives—buying a burger, answering the phone—we sometimes forget what power they wield. As far back as we can look, humanity has tested and sharpened that power. The oldest poems we have are the spells, prayers, curses, and incantations that accompanied the magical rites of ancient cultures. Words blessed apple trees and warriors' weapons, healed boils, cast out demons, and drove away swarms of locusts. Through chants, ancient people sanctified the newlyweds' first bed, celebrated a birth, cursed the rich and powerful, strengthened medicinal herbs, and sent the dead to the next life.

Like all effective poems, magic spells are precise. It's the specificity of *toe, wool, tongue,* and *blindworm* that stirs the repulsive potion of *Macbeth's* witches:

> Eye of newt, and toe of frog,
> Wool of bat, and tongue of dog,
> Adder's fork, and blindworm's sting,
> Lizard's leg, and howlet's wing—
> For a charm of pow'rful trouble.   5
> Like a hell-broth boil and bubble.
> Double, double, toil and trouble,
> Fire burn and cauldron bubble.

Like Bryan's "Sweater Weather," Shakespeare uses sound to help him create. The word "spell" itself suggests how potent words are. As part of a curative for various ailments, ancient peoples often literally spelled out a charm—something like a physician's prescription. An old charm in England against rabies called for writing down the spell on a piece of paper and feeding it to a mad dog. As part of a magic formula, soothsayers often spelled out in a triangle the occult word "abracadabra," and so evoked the essential power of language, the ABC's.

Though we may not admit it, the power of words directs our lives. Certain words remain taboo, and though we all know them, we try to avoid them in public. We use magical words in church, in court, and when we quarrel. With pledges, oaths, and vows, people become wives, husbands, partners, nuns, physicians, presidents, witnesses, and citizens. In uttering the words, we cross a threshold; we are not precisely the same people as before we pronounced them.

The ancient forms of language itself, its glacial mass and lightning flash, give shape to every new thought and discovery that our poems can make. Poets need not concern themselves too directly with the sources of poetry's magic. It is enough to know that when writing well, we may tap into this energy just as we flip on a light without considering how the power came from plants and animals that lived eons ago and from which, through dynamos and copper wires, ancient light arrives at the lamp on our desk.

Diction

Diction, or word choice, is one of the poet's greatest tools. By choosing the *exact* word, not merely something close, the poet convinces and draws a reader into a poem. Through shrewd attention to the **denotative,** or literal, meaning of words, the poet makes explicit the world of the poem. A word used unwittingly, such as *liquidate* for *melt,* can quickly confuse and even ruin a poem. Poets take every advantage words can offer; while working on the drafts of his poem "Among School Children," Yeats accidentally substituted "a *mess* of shadows" for "a *mass* of shadows" and immediately recognized the subtler possibilities that accompanied his choice.

As you write, you will find a good dictionary valuable, not only for checking spelling and usage but also for locating a word's etymology (the history of its development). Such etymologies can lead you to a word's **connotative** meanings—its figurative meanings—as well as the overtones and nuances that a word or phrase suggests. For example, because the etymology of *nuance* leads back to *nue,* or cloud, a "nuance" can be likened to the subtle shading and dip in temperature a cloud gives the landscape of a poem. And because poems operate in relatively small spaces, the layers that lie beneath the surface—the poems' **implications**—have profound importance. A good thesaurus (the name comes from the Greek word meaning "treasury") can lead to scores of synonyms for a word. Substitutions for the verb *eat* include *attack, banquet, bite, breakfast, chaw, chew, chow down, cram, devour, digest, feast, feed, gnaw, gobble, gorge, ingest, inhale, masticate, munch, nibble, nosh, peck, pick, pig out, scarf, swallow, taste,* and *wolf.* Looking at the etymology of the word will take us to *gradual destruction* and *wearing away* as well as to *preoccupy* and *engross.* The omnivorousness of English—which has taken in words from many languages—offers us opportunities to convey exactly what we mean and to articulate and refine our most elusive ideas and feelings.

In making your poems, try to rely on precise nouns and verbs—language's bones—rather than on modifiers that qualify your meaning. Loading modifiers onto your poems won't make them seem more appealing, just overdecorated, like a room crammed with too many knickknacks. Consider the difference between "She walked away furiously" and "She stomped off," or between "The day was very hot" and "The day sweltered." A well-chosen verb is more effective and visceral than a tacked-on modifier. Beware of adverb overload.

When choosing words, balance their meaning and nuances with how they fit the situation or attitude of the poem. If a love poem declares, "Let me integrate my life with yours," we will question the speaker's seriousness or wonder why the lover has chosen the tone of a job application. The character of a poem's diction (e.g., formal, informal, neutral, colloquial, vulgar) helps establish the **tone,** a poem's attitude toward its subject. Sometimes an odd word provides exactly the sense and surprise the poet is after. Consider, for instance, Louise Glück's "coagulate" in "The Racer's Widow" (p. 32) or Robert Hayden's (1913–1980) "austere and lonely offices" in the last line of this poem:

 ## Those Winter Sundays

Sundays too my father got up early
and put his clothes on in the blueblack cold,

then with cracked hands that ached
from labor in the weekday weather made
banked fires blaze. No one ever thanked him.   5

I'd wake and hear the cold splintering, breaking.
When the rooms were warm, he'd call,
and slowly I would rise and dress,
fearing the chronic angers of that house,

Speaking indifferently to him,   10
who had driven out the cold
and polished my good shoes as well.
What did I know, what did I know
of love's austere and lonely offices?

The denotative meaning of "offices" is "tasks or duties," but the word's con-notations remind us of the authority and responsibility we might associate with fatherhood. The word also carries great psychological weight. In choosing "offices" Hayden registers ambivalence; the son feels remorse for belatedly recognizing his father's efforts, and yet the son, despite what he knows, still feels emotionally distant. Some deep pain still haunts him, and the more formal diction of the last two lines helps to suggest the gravity of his loss. Notice, also, how much the simple word "too" placed in the first line tells us; *every* day, even on the day of rest, his father labored for his family.

As we write our own poems, we might be tempted to resort to **clichés**—stale, familiar words, phrases, and metaphors. In fact, our first drafts may be loaded with them, as the most obvious and cliché expressions are often the first to arise. As Hayden's poem demonstrates, however, the language of poetry pays attention; by its nature a cliché does not. You can test for a cliché by asking yourself whether the word, phrase, or image you are using is particular or generic. If you're writing about a rainbow, do you see a real rainbow with all its translucence, transience, and tenuousness? No rainbow looks exactly like another. Or do you see the commercial artist's generic sentimental symbol: neat little arches lined up according to the spectrum in flat, unreal colors?

Another test for a cliché is to ask yourself if you really know what the word, phrase, or image means. Isn't *hated her with a passion* redundant? If you say you're eating *humble pie,* what's in that pie? Does it have anything to do with the deer innards the king's huntsmen ate instead of the choice venison reserved for nobility? Also, ask yourself if the phrase provokes a physical sensation or only a general impression. A poem should be able to use every suggestion available to it. Does *light as a feather* capture the ticklish, wispy barbs? Be careful not to confuse clichéd and formulaic writing with idiomatic writing. *Idioms* are expressions that have become fixed in a language as constructions deemed natural. English speakers say, "I am going *to* Italy," not, as in other languages, "I am going *in* Italy." Tampering with idiomatic expressions doesn't freshen language; it makes it sound clumsy and laughable.

Clichés aren't a neutral form of truth; they're truth frozen into fraud.

—William Logan

Each era has its own stale formulas; our special curse includes *phenomenal, hard-liner, cut and run, download,* and *poetry in motion.* Poetry often generates a kind of cliché all its own, **poetic diction**—fancy or contrived language that gets used and reused until it becomes dull and tries a reader's patience. American poets of the 1960s and 1970s had a particular affinity for *stone, dark, alone, dance,* and titles that included gerunds such as *rising, diving,* and *spinning.* The words *o'er* for *over, ere* for *before,* or *thou* for *you* were the poetic clichés of an earlier time, and using them now makes a poet sound stilted and goofy as a cartoon.

Clichés often coincide with **abstractions**—vague words that generalize experience or perception. Words such as *love, beauty, sadness,* and *joy* lack the electricity of precise language, which can help you communicate more clearly to your reader. As an experiment, try taking a poem of your own and circling all the abstractions. Then replace the abstractions with precise language. "God is in the details," said the architect Mies van der Vohe. His statement suggests the power of **concrete,** or specific language, what Ezra Pound called the "luminous details."

Syntax

Syntax is the structure of phrases, clauses, and sentences. The word *syntax* comes from the Greek *syn* ("together") and *tassein* ("to arrange"): "to arrange together." Also from *tassein* comes the word *tactics,* suggesting the value of syntax to the poet in deploying forces. Syntax is the muscle of poetry.

The syntactical qualities of good writing in general apply to poetry, and include these principles:

1. Use active voice.
2. Vary sentence structure.
3. Use unusual syntax only when appropriate to meaning.
4. Avoid antiquated and high poetic diction.
5. Use parallel structures for parallel ideas.
6. Place main ideas in main clauses and subordinate ideas in subordinate clauses.
7. Put modifiers next to the nouns they modify.
8. Control tense and subject–verb agreement.
9. Set the most significant part of a sentence at the end.
10. Break any rule that makes you sound ludicrous.

If you're unsure about syntax, devote some time to learning it. A writing guide such as Strunk and White's classic *The Elements of Style* can help, as well as an ear attuned to the ways poems marshal meaning and emotion through language.

In "Sweater Weather: A Love Song to Language," Sharon Bryan overcomes the informal rule against using sentence fragments by aligning the celebratory phrases in a parallel list. Her careful coordination of the phrases keeps us from getting tangled in fragments, and her interplay of the poem's sounds helps it cohere and progress. For example, in the last two lines, "love me or leave me, seventh heaven, / up and about, over and out" (lines 32–33), the phrases are balanced, allowing the "o," "e," and "v" sounds to resonate and hold the parts together. The sentence fragments support the poem's rollicking rhythm.

In the first stanza of "Those Winter Sundays," notice how Hayden deploys his sentences to create a startling emotional impact. Following the four-and-a-half-line opening sentence that lists the father's chores ("Sundays too my father got up early / and put his clothes on in the blueblack cold..."), the son delivers a short sentence that comes like a heavy blow: "No one ever thanked him." The brevity of admission helps us feel how little effort—even to express thanks—the other family members took. Try rewriting that stanza—either combining both sentences into one long sentence or breaking them apart into a series of short ones—and you'll quickly see how Hayden's syntax bears the responsibility for much of the poem's emotional depth.

Syntax is a poem's muscle; flexing or relaxing those muscles lends the poem its strength and agility. Deborah Ager's "Night in Iowa" (p. 13) compresses the landscape of a place, of an entire night, into a mere four lines filled with detail, mystery, and longing. And through his deft handling of the sentence in this poem, Henry Taylor (B. 1942) creates the impression of relentless, runaway action:

 Barbed Wire

One summer afternoon when nothing much
was happening, they were standing around
a tractor beside the barn while a horse
in the field poked his head between two strands
of the barbed-wire fence to get at the grass   5
along the lane, when it happened—something

they passed around the wood stove late at night
for years, but never could explain—someone
may have dropped a wrench into the toolbox
or made a sudden move, or merely thought   10
what might happen if the horse got scared, and
then he did get scared, jumped sideways and ran

down the fence line, leaving chunks of his throat
skin and hair on every barb for ten feet
before he pulled free and ran a short way   15
into the field, stopped and planted his hoofs
wide apart like a sawhorse, hung his head
down as if to watch his blood running out,

almost as if he were about to speak
to them, who almost thought he could regret   20
that he no longer had the strength to stand,
then shuddered to his knees, fell on his side,
and gave up breathing while the dripping wire
hummed like a bowstring in the splintered air.

Taylor manages all twenty-four lines of the poem through one sentence, driving home a sense that nothing can keep the horse from the accident. The main girders on which the poem is built are the independent clauses "they were standing around" and "then he did get scared." Working off of these seemingly innocuous clauses Taylor constructs the conditions under which the horse is driven to his unstoppable end. The many imbedded phrases and subordinate clauses (such as "while a horse / in the field poked his head," "when it happened," "what might happen if," and "who almost thought he could regret") suspend the horse's death and allow the reader to hope such an event will not be inevitable. The shorter phrases of lines 22 and 23 mimic the horse's jerky movements at the end ("then shuddered to his knees, fell on his side, / and gave up breathing) and are counterbalanced by the poem's final subordinate clause: "while the dripping wire / hummed like a bowstring in the splintered air." The horse is dead, but the air continues to hum with the sound of barbed wire. Notice, too, the dazzling, concrete language throughout the poem.

A few words on grammar and mechanics: Sometimes inexperienced writers labor under the delusion that knowing grammar might dry up their creative juices. But not knowing the rules will dry up your readers. To paraphrase Byron, easy writing makes hard reading. As a carpenter knows when to use a particular screwdriver and a cook when to use garlic, good writers know the tools at their disposal, and don't, for instance, use a semicolon in place of a colon. Proofreading your poems is essential. Though we don't notice correct spelling, a poem blotched with misspellings distracts the reader and destroys the illusion of the poet's control. When a poet steps on stage with an unzipped fly, the audience won't be paying attention to his or her poems.

Pruning and Weeding

Like a coiled spring, much of a poem's power comes from its compression. We don't mean that all poems should be epigrams or that a poem should be cramped and written in robot-speak. Cutting out all the articles or prepositions in a poem doesn't make it tighter, just wooden. But the poet should follow the principle of not using two words when one will suffice. Don't state the obvious but show enough that the reader can gather a strong impression.

What I want is a poem which is an act of Will: chiseled, bony, all ivory tusk.

—Lucie Brock-Broido

Notice in "Those Winter Sundays" how we feel the son's sense of regret and longing even though he doesn't overtly state these emotions. *Show* the experience of the poem to your readers rather than telling them how to feel or think. If your language is precise and clear, your readers will understand without the need for your heavy hand. Ernest Hemingway notes that when thoroughly engaged in a subject, the writer can leave out certain obvious or implied things, and the reader "will have a feeling of these things as strongly as though the writer had stated them. The dignity of movement of an iceberg is due to only one-eighth of it being above water." Subtlety of this sort is rarely achieved in early drafts and so compression usually takes place during revision. By constantly sifting the words and gauging each sentence, the poet allows what lies beneath the surface—the implications—to propel the poem. Often a poem goes wrong when the poet overlooks what a word or sentence pattern implies. Getting words down on the page, like poking seeds into the ground, is just the first step. The seeds may sprout, but unless the gardener prunes and weeds, the garden will become a choked mess. This is why so many poets think of poetry as *an art of revision.*

As you play around with a poem, look for redundancies, for what you can clear out of the way. Cynthia Macdonald advises students to think of what she calls the "Small Elephant Principle." We don't need to state that an elephant is big; your readers will assume this is the case. If the elephant is small, however, that's worth mentioning. Apply this principle as you weigh choices such as "winter snow," "black hole," or "delicious chocolate cake."

Tightening the poem, seeing what can be dropped, can make the elements of a poem more dramatic, powerful, and urgent. Take a look at this poem that Wilfred Owen (1893–1918) wrote from the trenches of World War I. He was killed in France just before the armistice.

 Dulce et Decorum Est

Bent double, like old beggars under sacks,
Knock-kneed, coughing like hags, we cursed through sludge,
Till on the haunting flares we turned our backs
And towards our distant rest began to trudge.
Men marched asleep. Many had lost their boots   5
But limped on, blood-shod. All went lame; all blind;
Drunk with fatigue; deaf even to the hoots
Of tired, outstripped Five-Nines° that dropped behind.

Gas! Gas! Quick, boys!—An ecstasy of fumbling,
Fitting the clumsy helmets just in time;   10
But someone still was yelling out and stumbling,
And flound'ring like a man in fire or lime...
Dim, through the misty panes° and thick green light,
As under a green sea, I saw him drowning.

In all my dreams, before my helpless sight,   15
He plunges at me, guttering, choking, drowning.

If in some smothering dreams you too could pace
Behind the wagon that we flung him in,
And watch the white eyes writhing in his face,
His hanging face, like a devil's sick of sin;   20
If you could hear, at every jolt, the blood
Come gargling from the froth-corrupted lungs,
Obscene as cancer, bitter as the cud
Of vile, incurable sores on innocent tongues,—
My friend, you would not tell with such high zest   25
To children ardent for some desperate glory,
The old Lie: Dulce et decorum est
Pro patria mori.

8 Five-Nines: 5.9-inch caliber shells.   **13 misty panes:** of the gas mask.

The soldier's death by mustard gas makes a compelling case against the motto—popular during World War I—from the Latin poet Horace: "Dulce et decorum est pro patria mori," translated as, "Sweet and fitting it is to die for one's country."

Owen's drafts of the poem (the originals are held in the British Library) show how he coaxed this vivid picture from his material. In early drafts, he labored over these lines, which appeared just before the startling second stanza:

Then somewhere near in front: Whew...fup, fup, fup,
Gas shells? Or duds? We loosened masks in case,—
And listened. ~~Nothing~~. Far rumouring of Krupp.
          ~~crawling~~ swoosh stung
Then ~~sudden~~ poison[s] ~~hit~~ us in the face.

This version shows the anxious soldiers listening for sounds that might indicate gas shells detonating and the poisonous gas drifting down on them. After fiddling with the lines for a while, Owen crossed all of them out; obviously he saw that beginning the stanza abruptly with "Gas! Gas! Quick, boys!" made the menace fiercer. The soldiers are suddenly engulfed.

It's sometimes helpful to imagine the poem you are working on as a raft. It must be held together tightly and carry only what is necessary, or it will sink. Slack writing (wasted words, wasted motions) hinders the smooth movement of a poem. As Anton Chekhov notes: "When a person expends the least possible movement on a certain act, that is grace." Not all poems should be short, nor as short as this poem by Ezra Pound (1885–1972) that, from a thirty-five-line draft, was whittled down to a two-line poem. But every poem should be as short as possible, each choice of phrase, word, and punctuation mark deliberate and thoughtful. Every mark in your poems should be a conscious choice for a specific effect.

In a Station of the Metro
The apparition of these faces in the crowd;
Petals on a wet, black bough.

Writing such a short poem can be extremely difficult and risky. As in any poem, each word must really count. The images in Pound's poem in themselves suggest apparitions. The shortness of the poem reinforces the sense of ghostly apparitions, and the poem reveals itself to be about image and absence. In poems like this, or in other short poetic forms such as haiku, each word carries extra weight. Here is another short poem; this one by Deborah Ager (B. 1971):

Night in Iowa
Nimbus clouds erasing stars above Lamoni.
Jaundiced lights. Silos. Loose dogs. Cows
whose stench infuses the handful of homes,
whose sad voices storm the plains with longing.

Notice how much Ager packs into each line. In so short a poem, each line virtually becomes its own poem.

Clarity, Obscurity, and Ambiguity

No one champions **obscurity** for its own sake. "It is not difficult to be difficult," Robert Francis quipped. If what you are saying is worth saying in a poem, nothing can be gained (and everything can be lost) by obscuring it. Yes, poems that handle complicated issues may be demanding. All the more reason to be as scrupulously clear as you can. Readers will not find a poem more compelling if they have to slosh through a swamp, especially if the final result proves unworthy of their effort. You may feel what you have to say seems too obvious to state directly, but don't confuse clarity with the underdeveloped, the mundane, or the unexamined; clarity can carry the most complex thoughts.

In this poem, Wallace Stevens (1879–1955) pokes fun at naysayers who simplistically insist, "The world is ugly, and the people are sad," and blind themselves to the universe's marvels.

Gubbinal
That strange flower, the sun,
Is just what you say.
Have it your way.

The world is ugly
And the people are sad.

That tuft of jungle feathers,
That animal eye,
Is just what you say.

That savage of fire,
That seed,   10
Have it your way.

The world is ugly
And the people are sad.

Each new metaphor for the sun—"strange flower," "tuft of jungle feathers," "animal eye," "savage of fire," "seed"—demonstrates the dazzling power of the ordinary. You won't find "gubbinal" in a lot of dictionaries (Stevens loved odd words); a "gubbin" is a small fragment. Ironically, through sentence fragments such as "That seed," Stevens makes a full case against clichéd thinking, against easy notions about the state of the world and the people in it.

Don't confuse obscurity with **ambiguity,** a poem's ability to offer more than one plausible reading at a time. The connotations of words, syntax, the multiple meanings that line breaks suggest, the implications of its images, the strength of its metaphors, its use of allusion, its shape and sound—every aspect of a poem enriches and creates poetry's depth and resonance so that we return to a poem again and again, drawing more from it each time.

Beginning poets learn that clarity is demanding, for what may seem obvious to the poet may be anything but obvious to the reader. Student poets may squirm as class discussions about their poems lead to vastly different or even bizarre conclusions about what they meant. Sometimes this means the poet has work to do to clarify the poem. However, sometimes the fault lies with readers who don't pay close enough attention and so miss a signal. A poem of multiple layers lends itself to multiple readings. Responsible readers try to make sure that their reading of a poem accounts for its many layers and possibilities. It's unfair to ignore the diction, tone, or other signals a poem gives about how it should be read in order to make a single narrow reading work. In "Gubbinal," we do a great disservice if we ignore the exuberance of images such as "tuft of jungle feathers" and conclude that Stevens *literally* meant "the world is ugly and the people are sad."

Sometimes obscurity enters a poem accidentally, through a confusing sentence fragment, odd word choice, a pronoun that doesn't refer to what the poet intends, or a sudden shift in time or location. When readings of a poem cancel each other out—or just lead in totally opposite directions—obscurity follows. Such obscurity can frustrate the reader, who may simply give up.

During discussions of your poem in class, you may feel pangs listening to others read your poem in ways you never imagined, but

Insofar as poetry has a social function it is to awaken sleepers by other means than shock.

—Denise Levertov

try to listen intently and consider each comment. Such readings can show you better how to direct your poem and may lead you to just the insight your poem needs. How wonderful to have a group of other active poets to help you with your work! As you reconsider your poem and revise it, be open-minded and willing to play with new ideas and suggestions; you can't twirl around the dance floor if you're staring at your feet. A list of questions that can help you revise on your own or respond to poems in a workshop appears in Appendix I.

Bear in mind that your readers will find things you did not intend, as well as things you did. With any poem, readers will bring their own associations and feelings. These will never be exactly like the poet's, just as one person can never hope to convey to another person the *exact* mental picture of a particular place. As long as the reader's version of your poem works alongside your own and doesn't undermine its basic intention or meaning, then the exchange works. Poetry is an art of communication. When readers bring themselves to a poem and make it truly their own, they are doing precisely what any poet hopes they will, making the poem come alive.

QUESTIONS AND SUGGESTIONS

1. Create an "authority list," that is, a list of things you are expert in and that make you unique. You might include items such as rock climbing, getting speeding tickets, being a child in a one-parent household, or cooking Mexican food. Return to this list for inspiration when you feel stuck and continue to add items to support your writing.

2. Take a poem you are revising and circle all the abstractions. Then replace as many abstractions as you can with concrete, specific language. How can words like *soul, joy, anger,* and *love* be expressed in concrete terms?

3. Take a poem you have written, and practice compressing it. Try cutting out all the adjectives and adverbs. Then try reducing the poem by about 25 percent. If you're feeling particularly daring, strike out every other line. (Remember to keep an open mind when you are revising; you can always save your best lines and put them back in later.) Now examine what you have left. Is a new poem developing? Try to pursue that poem, refine the diction, and rearrange the lines. Can you cut out 25 percent more? In which of your other poems can you use compression to make the language really sing?

4. Write a poem that uses at least four words from side "A" from the following list and at least one word from side "B." Make the diction choices

appropriate to the context. What happens to your poem when the more formal diction from side "B" enters the poem?

A	B
snow	carapace
leaves	apparition
gravel	obtuse
mountain	numinous
cloud	umbrage
water	placate
rain	molecule
ink	appraise

5. *For a group:* All group members should make photocopies of three poems they really love. Meet up with your group members and bring the poems, scissors, tape, and blank sheets of paper. Next, cut each poem into individual lines and phrases. In the center of a table, everyone should spill out his or her poem pieces and then use them to assemble new poems. Feel free to break the poem pieces into single words and adjust punctuation and capitalization as needed. When you have finished, read the poems aloud to each other and then type them up and continue to revise.

POEMS TO CONSIDER

Barter   2009
RAVI SHANKAR (B. 1975)

Possessed of some rudimentary detection skills,
I can spot a Rothko or a liar at twenty paces.
Can panfry dosas, walk on rooftops, misplace bills

in the most obvious places, clutter open spaces
with dog-eared books or newspaper clippings.   5
I've been known to win at cards or in most races,

like upon the blacktop during recess, zipping
to snatch a chalk eraser. Can speak, if soused,
in decent French, & remain adept at equipping

friends for a camping trip. Have even roused   10
flame from flint & steel, still know my knots
from clove hitch to bowline, & when housed

by a friend, I know enough that dinner's bought
by me. Could, if pressed, construct metafiction,
elaborate fun house mirrors of prose that cannot   15

be turned into a movie. Have worked construction,
broken floors with a jackhammer. Sold knives
one summer to suburban housewives, using diction

of tang & rivet. Can dispense a kiss that survives
the lips, solve algebraic equations, & score goals   20
in soccer. Say I've taken the shape of many lives.

Mule Hour   2009
TERRANCE HAYES (B. 1971)

Ma and me ride a blue mule into the South, where cockroaches
dream of the apocalypse and weep each sunrise bright as grief.
And crushed, their insides are milky as moonlight banked in cloud.
Because between nightfall and morning, the roaches crawl all over
Dominion in their secondhand shoes making deals with the angel   5
of exile, who does not call the Lord his master and is nobody's slave.
I'd like to call him, Father, the one wearing a vest of woven snakes,
but he will not answer, not in the storm which darkens our route,
not with the roach he keeps trapped in his mouth. Ma and me ride
a blue mule until its dumb heart gives out. She grips its tail and I   10
its ears and we drag it to the side of the road like a bag of garbage
on trash day, its muscles soft as cushion and its bones soft too,
like coil gone lazy in a couch, and we leave it burning with all
the humanity fire strips away. A blue stench rides Ma and me
deep into a dream of the South where the roaches weep   15
like the mules of slaves, where they are quiet as cows waiting
for slaughter, and if their backs shine like jewels in the field,
the roaches on parade, it's because they are bright in the rain
and filled with a wonder which cuts through them and the fields
they wander and the hands that pluck them from tobacco leaves   20
with the certainty of a blade. I want to live as the roach lives, without
a head or body, free on both sides of the grave, like my father
beneath a charmed umbrella spitting on the Lord before he walks away.

Famous

1982

NAOMI SHIHAB NYE (B. 1952)

The river is famous to the fish.

The loud voice is famous to silence,
which knew it would inherit the earth
before anybody said so.

The cat sleeping on the fence is famous to the birds   5
watching him from the birdhouse.

The tear is famous, briefly, to the cheek.

The idea you carry close to your bosom
is famous to your bosom.

The boot is famous to the earth,   10
more famous than the dress shoe,
which is famous only to floors.

The bent photograph is famous to the one who carries it
and not at all famous to the one who is pictured.

I want to be famous to shuffling men   15
who smile while crossing streets,
sticky children in grocery lines,
famous as the one who smiled back.

I want to be famous in the way a pulley is famous,
or a buttonhole, not because it did anything spectacular,   20
but because it never forgot what it could do.

Abstraction

2005

GEOFFREY BROCK (B. 1964)

It's coitus interruptus with the sweaty world.
It's the view from the window of the plane

As it gains altitude and the pines recede
Into forest—always it's the pull away.

The pull away from the darkness and the heat   5
Of a mother's bleeding body, toward cold light,

Toward names and language and desire and their
Majestic failures. It's love, it's death of love,

It's junk mail: see that blue truck shuddering
From my concrete curb, bearing this letter   10

For the Current Resident at your address?
And real death, too—the red-beaked gull we saw

Abstract a mullet from the surf and wheel
Across the iron-black sands of a nameless beach.

Reading Sonnevi on a Tuesday Night   2004
WAYNE MILLER (B. 1976)

A film of mist clings to the storm windows
as the thunder gets pocketed and carried away
in the rain's dark overcoat. A good reading night—

car wheels amplified by the flooded street,
leaf-clogged gutters bailing steadily, constant   5
motion beyond my walls echoing

my body's gyroscopic stillness. Sonnevi says
Only if I touch do I dare let myself be touched,
and that familiar and somewhat terrifying curtain

of reading slips around me, pinning sound   10
to the room's lost corners, pinning the room
to an emptying sky. I'm in the glacial grooves

of Sonnevi's words as he makes love
and listens to Mozart in a spare apartment,
now reawakens to her voice saying goodnight   15

so much that I couldn't sleep I was elated.
His world slips through the waterfall
of language and hovers here, on the other side,

in my apartment, where we listened to Monk
showering with the door open, soft-boiled eggs   20
by the pink light of the Chinese take-out,

made love against the footsteps of morning
commuters, smoked cigarettes on the fire escape
right up to the minute you left. Here,

we are in this continuousness—our lives   25
dissolved in the channels of written lines—
every word I've read was in me before I read it.

They're pulled from me like seconds
from the cistern of an unfinished life. Love's
endless weathering moves the body   30

of our words: we read to understand
we're not alone in it—*we carry one another,*
assuredly—
            though we do this alone.

PART

I

FORM

2

VERSE

When you open a book, you generally know whether you are looking at poetry or prose. Most poetry is written in lines, as verse; it has a fluid right margin. Prose is rectangular and comes in paragraphs. Prose fills the page from the left to the right margin that is set arbitrarily, *externally*, by the printer, not by the writer. The printer determines when a new line of prose begins, and the wider the page, the longer the line. Prose trains readers to ignore the movement from line to line. Poetry, however, demands that readers pay attention to that movement. When we write poems, we usually set out by writing verse, one *line* (versus one sentence) at a time. **Verse** is a system of writing in which the right margin, the line turn, is set *internally* by the poet. No matter how wide the page, the line remains as the poet intended. The poet, not the printer, usually determines the line breaks.

All verse, even what is called "free" verse, relies on measure or some other rationale or system by which the poet breaks lines. The choices may be trained or intuitive, but the nature of verse insists the poet consider and weigh each line and each line break.

This vital aspect of verse appears in the etymology of the word itself. *Verse* comes from the Latin *versus,* which derives from the verb *versare,* meaning "to turn." (The root also appears in words like *reverse,* "to turn back," or *anniversary,* "year turn.") As a noun it came to mean *the turning of the plough,* which creates a *row* or *line.* Thus, the English word *verse* refers to the *deliberate turning from line to line* that distinguishes verse from prose. In this age-old image, like the farmer driving ox and plough, the poet plants the seeds of sound and meaning row by row, guided by the line just written, aware of the line to come, and so enabling the cross-pollination that enriches the poem for a reader's harvesting.

The deliberate turning of lines is essential to verse. The rhythm of prose is simply the linear cadence of the voice, a flow patterned only by the phrases

I dwell in Possibility—
A fairer House than Prose—
More numerous of Windows—
Superior—for Doors—
        —Emily Dickinson

and clauses that are the units of sentences. In verse, however, the cadence of sentences also plays over the additional, relatively fixed unit of the **line.** Reading verse, we pause ever so slightly at line ends—even when no punctuation is there; this pause gives the line ending more emphasis than the words at the beginning and middle of the line. As such, it is important to pick strong words (nouns, verbs, etc.) as the last words in your lines. Controlling the dynamic nature of the line is central to crafting poems.

Line breaks may coincide with grammatical or syntactical units. Such breaks reinforce regularity and emphasize normal speech pauses, as in these passages from Wallace Stevens's "Metaphors of a Magnifico," which we will turn to shortly:

> Twenty men crossing a bridge,
> Into a village,
> Are twenty men crossing twenty bridges,
> Into twenty villages,

When the end of a line coincides with a normal syntactic pause (usually at punctuation), the line is called **end-stopped,** as in the preceding lines.

Line breaks also may occur within grammatical or syntactical units, creating pauses and introducing unexpected emphases.

> The boots of the men clump
> On the boards of the bridge.
> The first white wall of the village
> Rises through fruit-trees.

Coming at the end of a line, "clump" seems perhaps louder than it might if the word came at another position in the line. Lines such as this, which end without any parallel to a normal speech pause, are called **enjambed** (noun: **enjambment**). Generally speaking, end-stopped lines relax tension, and enjambed lines induce tension because of the sense of suspense they create for the reader.

These pairs of lines from Stevens's "Sunday Morning" are also enjambed, and contain an additional pause inside the line (illustrated by ‖):

> Deer walk upon our mountain, ‖ and the quail
> Whistle about us their spontaneous cries...
> At evening, ‖ casual flocks of pigeons make
> Ambiguous undulations as they sink...

This additional pause is called a **caesura,** a normal speech pause that occurs within a line. The caesura produces further variations of rhythm. The poet can create momentum in the poem that can underscore, counteract, even contradict what is happening within the poem by varying end-stop, enjambment, and caesura, and by playing sense, grammar, and syntax against them. Robert Browning draws us into "My Last Duchess" (p. 145) in the opening of the poem through his deft handling of pauses within and at the end of lines:

> That's my last duchess painted on the wall,
> Looking as if she were alive. ‖ I call
> That piece a wonder, now: ‖ Frá Pandolf's hands
> Worked busily a day, ‖ and there she stands.
> Will't please you sit and look at her? ‖ I said   5
> Frà Pandolf by design, ‖ for never read
> Strangers like you that pictured countenance,
> The depth and passion of its earnest glance....

In this poem, an Italian Renaissance duke is speaking to the envoy of another nobleman whose daughter the duke wants to marry. But before he negotiates for a new duchess, he is showing off a painting of his last, whom, we come to understand further into the poem, he has had murdered. Note how rarely the duke's speech is end-stopped; each line creates momentum that pulls the poem forward as the duke subtly justifies his cruelty. So powerful is the poem's drive forward and so deftly does Browning use enjambment, that many readers miss that the poem is rhymed in what we call **heroic couplets,** pairs of rhyming lines (as seen in "wall" and "call," "hands "and "stands," "said" and "read," etc.).

Line

The poet's deployment of lines accounts for a large part of what makes a poem a poem; as Paul Valéry put it, poetry creates "a language within a language." Consider this quatrain written by an anonymous sixteenth-century poet:

Western Wind

> Western wind, when wilt thou blow,
>   The small rain down can rain?
> Christ, if my love were in my arms
>   And I in my bed again!

In love and far from home, the speaker longs for spring, when he and his lover will be reunited. His speaking *to* the wind reinforces his isolation and loneliness. Both the wind and the "small rain" are personified. (**Personification** means treating something inanimate as if it had the qualities of a person.) Here, rain seems to

And the line comes (I swear it) from the breath, from the breathing of the man who writes....
—Charles Olson

share the speaker's impatience. Direct address to the wind also suggests that the exclamatory "Christ" in line 3 signals this poem is a prayer. The speaker's world is a world of forces—wind, rain, Christ—and his passion makes the human element a force among forces. The incomplete sentence formed by the conditional of lines 3 and 4 ("if my love") suggests the speaker's unsatisfied longing.

The compression of verse calls for staying alert—word by word, line by line—and paying attention in a way we rarely do with prose, which is habitually discursive and continues to add information, drawing us onward to what is next and next. Prose, like a straight line, extends to the horizon. Verse draws us in as it spirals into itself.

Poems make us alert to each line. Writing in verse creates a spatial dimension that prose cannot imitate. See how Wallace Stevens (1879–1955) manages his lines here:

 ## Metaphors of a Magnifico

Twenty men crossing a bridge,
Into a village,
Are twenty men crossing twenty bridges
Into twenty villages,
Or one man   5
Crossing a single bridge into a village.

This is old song
That will not declare itself...

Twenty men crossing a bridge,
Into a village,   10
Are
Twenty men crossing a bridge
Into a village.

That will not declare itself
Yet is certain as meaning...   15

The boots of the men clump
On the boards of the bridge.
The first white wall of the village
Rises through fruit-trees.
Of what was it I was thinking?   20
So the meaning escapes.

The first white wall of the village...
The fruit-trees....

Stevens lays out his lines as a kind of equation. Depending on one's perception we can have twenty men or one man, twenty bridges or one. Looked at from a distance, one might see a group of men moving over one bridge, but within the group each man crosses just one bridge. Stevens rearranges his lines within the stanzas to register these shifting perspectives, floating in the third stanza the word "Are" on a line by itself so that it acts almost as an equals sign. The stanza creates a simple formula, which the next stanzas question and toy with as Stevens explores how we arrive at meaning through images, and how images themselves move beyond meaning in order to move us. The short stanzas that close the poem register the stops and starts of the mind turning over possibilities, bringing in sensual images (the white wall and fruit trees) that seem to collapse thought. We are left with ellipses that linger suggestively, inviting our imaginative participation and perhaps sending us back to the poem's start.

Form

When we consider form, we delve deeply into the mystery of art. Balanced proportions please us. As children many of us delighted in arranging blocks in patterns, and we used rhythm to remember things such as "Thirty days hath September...." Form does not merely organize a poem's content—it *expresses* content. How a poem appears on the page is just as important as what it says.

We may think of poetic form as growing out of two kinds of strategies, metrical and nonmetrical. Both make good poems. As the poet Robert Lowell remarks, "I can't understand how any poet, who has written both metered and unmetered poems, would be willing to settle for one and give up the other." The two turn out to be far more alike than different, despite the oppositional, reductive terms sometimes used to refer to them: "closed" and "open," "fixed" and "free," "solid" and "fluid," or "organic" forms. Such terms tend to misrepresent the way poems are actually written. The process, in which scattered thoughts, phrases, images, and insights, and so on gradually come together into a poem, is always open, free, and fluid at the beginning and becomes, as the poet realizes the poem's form, finally closed, fixed, and solid. Hayden's "Those Winter Sundays" (p. 6) is ultimately no more organic, no less artificial, than "Western Wind." All poems are *made* things, and making requires a process, usually with many drafts.

As Paul Lake points out in "The Shape of Poetry," "The rules of formal poetry generate not static objects like vases, but the same kind of bottom-up, self-organizing processes seen in complex natural systems such as flocking birds, shifting sand dunes, and living trees." As Lake notes, the process of writing is not static, because the poet's ideas of what a poem is or might be—the poems he or she admires—enter the loop of feedback and revision. The poet inevitably borrows and varies, and so re-creates formal elements that occur in other poems. Whether in a traditional "fixed" form or in one the poet invented for the occasion, called a **nonce** form, in every successful poem the poet actively *achieves* the final form.

Poet Lyn Hejinian takes Lake's ideas about form one step further, pointing to the visual and spatial qualities of poetry in which both text and white space can become active components of a poem. She claims: "Writing's forms are not merely shapes but forces; formal questions are about dynamics—they ask how, where, and why the writing moves...." Hejinian posits: "Form is not a fixture but an activity." As you write and as you read through this book, consider the visual impact of poems and the energy lines and forms produce.

Space here won't permit a full discussion of the many kinds of traditional forms poets have used in English (a brief description of some of them appears in Appendix II). Particular ages seem to be drawn to certain kinds of poems. The 1590s saw a spate of sonnet sequences, and the early seventeenth century delighted in complex invented forms. The eighteenth century honed the heroic couplet. The Romantics were intrigued by the ode. Since early in the twentieth century, poets have increasingly pushed the rules of fixed forms, invented new ones, and turned to traditional forms that earlier poets had used, such as the blues (which originated in the African American South), the sestina (in twelfth-century France), and the pantoum (in Malaysia). Forms, like fashion, resurge and recede— but poets, those designers with words, rarely grow weary of the classics.

Knowing the possibilities of form guides and challenges a poet and provides breadth and vision as well as discipline. The sestina—with its repeated end words—seems particularly suited for poems of obsessiveness. The heroic couplet has proved a shrewd vehicle for balanced argumentation and for farce. The more forms you are familiar with and the more forms you try, the greater your flexibility when deciding how to structure your content or subject matter to greatest effect. Let the poem itself, not just the form, direct how the poem develops. And if the poem works best by breaking a rule, break it.

Every form started as an experiment on something that came before. There have been many exquisite unrhymed sonnets (see Henri Cole's "The Hare" on p. 138) and poems with irregular rhyme schemes (see Frost's "After Apple-Picking" on p. 87). However, such variations in form achieve the greatest impact when the forms are altered for specific effect according to the content.

In Sonnet 73, William Shakespeare (1564–1616) shapes the rhyming **quatrains** (groups of four lines) and **couplet** (a group of two lines) and uses them to find the shape of his material, similar to how a good interviewer probes a witness to create a clear picture. The sonnet form helps lay out and weigh the parts of the speaker's argument.

> That time of year thou mayst in me behold
> When yellow leaves, or none, or few, do hang
> Upon those boughs which shake against the cold,
> Bare ruined choirs° where late the sweet birds sang.
> In me thou see'st the twilight of such day   5
> As after sunset fadeth in the west,
> Which by-and-by black night doth take away,

Death's second self that seals up all in rest.
In me thou see'st the glowing of such fire
That on the ashes of his youth doth lie,   10
As the deathbed whereon it must expire,
Consumed with that which it was nourished by.
This thou perceiv'st, which makes thy love more strong,
To love that well which thou must leave ere long.

4 choirs: choir lofts.

The form of the **English sonnet** itself (see Appendix II for more on the sonnet) encourages Shakespeare to find the stages of his poem's argument (thesis and antithesis) and then to turn and call the argument into account (synthesis). The English sonnet is built of three quatrains of alternating rhyme that close with a couplet. The closing couplet often registers a turn, a twist, or a distillation of ideas or feelings presented earlier. (This turn in the sonnet is called a **volta**.) In effect, the form itself, with its various stages of argument, helps the poem's composition.

In the successive quatrains, Shakespeare's speaker compares his aging to a different period of time: to autumn, the dying of the year; to twilight, the dying of the day; and to glowing ashes, the dying of the fire. The three quatrains emphasize the three-step comparison. The couplet at the end, which marks a shift in tone, presents a kind of resolution to the problem offered in the quatrains. Form and content work together.

The order of the comparisons corresponds to the speaker's mounting anguish. The poem moves first from a bare winter daylight scene to a twilight scene, and then to a night scene, when a fire dies out. The progression from day to dusk to night emphasizes the image of night as "Death's second self" and possibly suggests night as the time one most fears dying. This shift in **temporal setting** (the time in which a poem takes place) is purposeful and helps us connect night with death. Each of the three images begins with a more positive tone than it ends with. The increasingly self-diminishing revisions in line 2 offer a clear example: "yellow leaves, or none, or few." The yellow leaves, like the "twilight" and the "glowing" of the fire, attempt an optimism that the speaker cannot maintain.

Another progression builds through the three images. In the first two quatrains we are out of doors, looking up at the tree and sky; in the last we have come indoors. This shift in **spatial setting** (the poem's physical location) leads us indoors and helps to suggest a darker and more confined space. Moreover, the constraint of the sonnet form itself matches the speaker's attitude. He addresses the trouble of aging only indirectly, through inanimate images, as if to hold its personal implications at a distance. But his apparent composure deceives.

Framed as a compliment to the person addressed, the closing couplet begins on a positive note: "This thou perceiv'st, which makes thy love more strong." But the next line betrays the speaker's fears: "To love that well which thou must leave ere long." The speaker connects his aging with his beloved leaving him. Throughout the poem, the speaker has expressed, not his self-image, but what he imagines to be his lover's image of him ("thou mayst in me behold," "In me thou see'st," and "This thou perceiv'st"). By "leave" in line 14 he need not mean more than "leave behind," but the phrase carries a painful sense of betrayal.

The brevity of the final couplet creates the force of the poem's closing. Within two lines, Shakespeare turns around an argument that had built up in twelve. The sudden shift in focus—which nevertheless stems from the preceding lines—creates part of the sonnet's tensions and one of the attractions that draws poets to the form. The sonnet registers the tensions of an argument, its proportions the power of a winning one: Because the couplet operates in a smaller space than the quatrains, it is more direct, immediate, and forceful.

The general proportions of the sonnet—a longer first part that is finished with a concise second—can be seen in many poems and forms of art. The action often comes to a head in the last twenty or thirty minutes of a movie. In a novel, the crisis typically happens in the penultimate or in the last chapter. Of course, satisfying closure requires subtlety. A story that suddenly ends with the central characters killed off will seem disappointing and melodramatic unless risk has been carefully woven into the plot.

Recollect the closing of Robert Hayden's "Those Winter Sundays": "What did I know, what did I know / of love's austere and lonely offices?" The final lines work like the closing of a sonnet. In a short space, they transport us to a higher plane of emotional recognition, from the speaker's memory of his father's thankless work, to his sudden remorse for his indifference to his father's acts of love.

Look at the delicate precision of content and the shrewd sense of proportion Whitman creates in this nonmetrical poem:

A Noiseless Patient Spider
WALT WHITMAN (1819–1892)

A noiseless patient spider,
I marked where on a little promontory it stood isolated,
Marked how to explore the vacant vast surrounding,
It launched forth filament, filament, filament, out of itself,
Ever unreeling them, ever tirelessly speeding them.   5

And you O my soul where you stand,
Surrounded, detached, in measureless oceans of space,
Ceaselessly musing, venturing, throwing, seeking the spheres to connect them,
Till the bridge you will need be formed, till the ductile anchor hold,
Till the gossamer thread you fling catch somewhere, O my soul.   10

The lines unreel loosely across the page, suggesting the long filaments the spider strings out into the wind when preparing to construct a web. The two stanzas—one for the spider, one for the soul's "musing, venturing, throwing, seeking"—shape the poem's central comparison.

Each stanza has five lines. Notably, the first line in each is shorter than the other four, as if to suggest the outward lengthening of the spider's filaments and of the soul's "gossamer thread." The form of the poem suggests the correspondence between spider and soul. The spider's activities, described in stanza 1, are neither explained nor resolved until the last line of stanza 2. The success of the soul's "gossamer thread," catching and anchoring, implies a similar success for the spider.

Through the two-part structure of his poem, Whitman unveils similarities between spider and soul and so discovers truths about them both. Notice the verbal echoes between various words in the two stanzas: "stood" and "stand," "surrounding" and "Surrounded," and "tirelessly" and "Ceaselessly." Similar links bridge the images, as in the contrast of small to grand scale with "on a little promontory," followed in stanza 2 by "measureless oceans of space." After "promontory" (a cliff jutting out into the ocean), the images of "oceans of space," "bridge," and "anchor" lend unity to the comparison. Like the spider's action, the poem's apparently random movement has a deeper, unifying purpose.

Like the closing couplet of Shakespeare's poem, Whitman's final two lines, parallel phrases that begin with "Till," signal the poem's culmination. After the soul's striving through the long sentences of the second stanza, it reaches completion as the thread catches. Grammatically, the poem could end with "somewhere," but such an ending would suggest indecisiveness. The strong sounds of Whitman's final exclamation, "O my soul," suggest the speaker's spiritual arrival. A poem's power depends less on a choice between being metrical or nonmetrical, or fixed or free, than on the poet's ingenuity and skill in taking full advantage of form.

Balance

By shaping and reshaping the form, the poet zeroes in on what the poem reveals, and brings those revelations to the reader. Careful attention to what is materializing on the page lies at the heart of writing a poem. By concentrating on the line you are writing, you can weigh it, judge it, see its implications, and let it help you discover something about what your poem might reveal: that discovery is what you're after. It needn't be earth-shattering; modest revelations can stun us. Close scrutiny of the developing line, particularly its sense of balance or imbalance, permits the poet to sense the places the poem might go.

In his essay "Listening and Making," Robert Hass points out the rhythmical imbalance in these lines from the opening section of Whitman's long sweeping "Song of Myself":

I lóaf and invíte my sóul,   3

I léan and lóaf at my éase ‖ obsérving a spéar of súmmer grás.   3/4

The numbers in parentheses at the end of each line above indicate the number of stresses per syntactic unit. The rhythm of the first line (three stresses) is essentially repeated by the first part of the second line (three stresses); but the second part not only extends the line but does so by *four* stresses. Hass adds, "Had Whitman written *observing a spear of grass,* all three phrases would be nearly equivalent...; instead he adds *summer,* the leaning and loafing season, and announces both at the level of sound and of content that this poem is going to be free and easy."

As a further example, Hass offers this brief poem by Whitman:

 A Farm Picture

Through the ámple ópen dóor ‖ of the péaceful cóuntry bárn,   3/3

A súnlit pásture field ‖ with cáttle and hórses féeding.   3/3

And háze and vísta, ‖ and the fár hórizon fáding awáy.   2/4

Each line has six stresses (marked with an ictus ´), divided by a light phrasal pause as indicated. The asymmetry of line 3 (2/4) effectively resolves the pattern (a 3/3 version of the line might not because it would suggest sameness). By shifting the pattern within the third line, Whitman releases the tension, letting the rhythm come to rest in the longer, four-stress phrase "and the far horizon fading away."

Looking even closer, we notice that lines 1 and 2 are not only linked by their parallel, balancing rhythms, but also make up one of the poem's two sentences; together they present the setting: the frame of the open barn doorway, the "cattle and horses feeding" seen in the distance.

> *From the first it had been like a Ballad. It had the beat inevitable. It had the blood.*
> —Gwendolyn Brooks

The asymmetry of rhythm in line 3 and the elongation created by the phrase "and the far horizon fading away," suggests the speaker is drawn to the uncertain and far-off landscape, because it represents possibilities either longed for or unrealized ("fading"). Perhaps he pauses from his work and looks out, his attention drifting beyond the animals to a distant, vanishing horizon.

In the previous examples, the end-stopped lines create a sense of steadiness and vague yearning. In this poem by Louise Glück (B. 1943), however, a number of lines break violently. Observe how the enjambment creates tension and interacts with the lines' often striking imbalance:

 The Racer's Widow

The elements have merged into solicitude.
Spasms of violets rise above the mud
And weed and soon the birds and ancients
Will be starting to arrive, bereaving points
South. But never mind. It is not painful to discuss   5

His death. I have been primed for this,
For separation, for so long. But still his face assaults
Me, I can hear that car careen again, the crowd coagulate on asphalt
In my sleep. And watching him, I feel my legs like snow
That let him finally let him go   10
As he lies draining there. And see
How even he did not get to keep that lovely body.

Look at how sentences break at line ends, then stop abruptly at the beginning of lines (e.g., "But still his face assaults/Me"), giving the rhythm an effect of jerking forward and then dead-ending, of careening around corners, like a car going out of control. The device of sharply turning the line also appears in "bereaving points/South," "discuss/His death," "on asphalt/In my sleep," and—going the other way—in "And see/How even he." The poem's rhythm seems quite off-balance, strategically so, especially in these lines:

For separátion, ‖ for só lóng. ‖ But stíll his fáce assáults   2/2/3

Mé, ‖ I can héar that cár caréen agáin, ‖ the crówd coágulate on ásphált   1/4/4

In my sléep. ‖ And wátching hím, ‖ I féel my légs like snów   1/2/3

That lét him fínally lét him gó   4

The repetition of "let him" in line 10 ("That let him finally let him go") has no punctuation, and so appears syntactically and frantically incoherent. The "snow-go" rhyme in lines 9 and 10 makes us aware the poem rhymes in couplets, in **slant,** or inexact, **rhymes** as seen by "solicitude–mud" and "ancients–points." The dissonance of slant rhyme heightens the sense of trauma.

The widow contradicts her claim that "It is not painful to discuss / His death." The lurching rhythm, wrenching imagery ("Spasms of violets"), and almost compulsive alliteration ("I can hear that car careen again, the crowd coagulate...") imply she is barely managing. These choices allow Glück to convey the widow's struggle, an ill-concealed emotional turmoil.

A quite different impression emerges from the rhythm of the following poem by Elizabeth Spires (B. 1952). The speaker, three months' pregnant, meditates languorously.

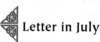 **Letter in July**

My life slows and deepens.
I am thirty-eight, neither here nor there.
It is a morning in July, hot and clear.

Out in the field, a bird repeats its quaternary call,
four notes insisting, *I'm here, I'm here.*   5
The field is unmowed, summer's wreckage everywhere.
Even this early, all is expectancy.

It is as if I float on a still pond,
drowsing in the bottom of a rowboat,
curled like a leaf into myself.   10
The water laps at its old wooden sides
as the sun beats down on my body,
a wand, an enchantment, shaping it
into something languid and new.

A year ago, two, I dreamed I held   15
a mirror to your unborn face and saw you,
in the warped watery glass, not as a child
but as you will be twenty years from now.
I woke, a light breeze lifting the curtain,
as if touched by a ghost's thin hand,   20
light filling the room, coming from nowhere.

I know the time, the place of our meeting.
It will be January, the coldest night
of the year. You will be carrying a lantern
as you enter the world crying,   25
and I cry to hear you cry.
A moment that, even now,
I carry in my body.

Through a strong sense of rhythmic stasis, Spires's poem presents a speaker at
ease. Of the twenty-eight lines, twenty-two are end-stopped; five of the seven
lines in stanza 1 are complete sentences. Scanning lines 1 and 2 shows:

Mў lífe slóws ănd déepéns.   3

Í ăm thírtў-éight, ‖ néithér hére nor thére.   3/3

Not only do the two phrases of line 2 repeat the three-stress pattern of line 1,
but, as the breves (˘) indicating unstressed syllables show, the pacing of the three
stresses in each phrase is the same. The poem ends with a similar balance:

Ă mómént thát, ‖ évén nów,   2/2

Ĭ cárrў ín mў bódў.   3

The poem closes with a regular pattern of stressed and unstressed syllables: the speaker is poised for the next stage.

Even in its use of enjambment, the poem is relaxed but not slack; note the break between lines 11 and 12, which connects full clauses. Caesuras usually occur midline, suggesting balance. Also, the enjambment of "shaping it / into something languid and new" seems quietly expressive, implying transformation. The imbalanced early caesura in line 19, "I woke," suggests the sudden waking to the wafting curtain.

Spires builds her poem in four seven-line stanzas. The balanced form evokes the order and serenity the speaker feels in the expectancy around and within her. It is July, the middle of the year, the middle of the summer, and she too is in the middle, "thirty-eight, neither here nor there." Anchored solidly in the present, she can contemplate how her life "slows and deepens" and can move through time. Her imagination climbs from the vivid present in stanza 1, to the drowsiness in stanza 2, to a memory of a dream a year or two ago in stanza 3, then arrives in stanza 4 at the anticipation of January, winter, a new year, and the child's birth: the future she holds within her. Each stanza contains a stage and yet leads naturally to the next, just as each part of her pregnancy leads naturally to birth. The form of the poem contains *and* creates its meaning.

QUESTIONS AND SUGGESTIONS

1. Take a poem you are revising, and make all the lines end-stopped. Then try enjambing all the lines. What various effects do you notice? Which of your own lines seem to work better as end-stopped or enjambed? Most poems have a mix of end-stopped and enjambed lines, depending on how best to support each line.

2. Here is a lineated poem printed as prose. Experiment with breaking the lines in various ways. What different effects can you create? (The original poem appears on p. 132.)

 The Empire in the Air

It was a fragile empire with knobs and wires, like a bomb. It lived in a blue suitcase in the airplane's belly. It had a little screen that flashed the time and the moments we had left, ticked them gently away. We laughed and sipped our drinks while the empire, wrapped in its inevitable wires, imagined the airplane splitting like a milkweed pod, the clothing that would burst from our broken suitcases into the air.

3. Notice how William Stafford uses stanzas to pace his poem "Traveling through the Dark" (p. 39). Consider how each stanza marks a different stage in the speaker's experience with the deer. Notice, too, that he lets the details show us how he feels rather than telling us directly. What effect does Stafford create by closing the poem with a shorter stanza? Write a poem of similar length and form about a speaker coming upon an animal unexpectedly, looking closely at it, and reacting in some way. Concentrate on letting the responses be suggested through the imagery.

4. Write a portrait of a person in sonnet form using Gwendolyn Brooks's "the rites for Cousin Vit" (p. 36) as a model. As you write your own sonnet, keep in mind how she uses sound and syntax, and how she uses the sonnet form and its argument (thesis, antithesis, synthesis) to shape her poem.

5. Glance through this textbook and look for poems in couplets, **tercets** (three-line stanzas) and **quatrains** (four-line stanzas). Why do you think these authors made those decisions? What do the poems in each of these stanza forms have in common? Choose a poem of your own that you aren't satisfied with and experiment with stanzas. Try breaking the poem into stanzas of two, then three, then four lines, and so on. Where might you cut or add lines to support your chosen form? If something *feels right,* you may have found a way to reawaken the poem.

POEMS TO CONSIDER

VI *the rites for Cousin Vit*   1949
from "The Womanhood"
GWENDOLYN BROOKS (1917–2000)

Carried her unprotesting out the door.
Kicked back the casket-stand. But it can't hold her,
That stuff and satin aiming to enfold her,
The lid's contrition nor the bolts before.
Oh oh. Too much. Too much. Even now, surmise,   5
She rises in the sunshine. There she goes,
Back to the bars she knew and the repose

In love-rooms and the things in people's eyes.
Too vital and too squeaking. Must emerge.
Even now she does the snake-hips with a hiss,   10
Slops the bad wine across her shantung, talks
Of pregnancy, guitars and bridgework, walks
In parks or alleys, comes haply on the verge
Of happiness, haply hysterics. Is.

Poŝtolka (Prague)   2002
CHRISTIAN WIMAN (B. 1966)

When I was learning words
and you were in the bath
there was a flurry of small birds
and in the aftermath

of all that panicked flight,   5
as if the red dusk willed
a concentration of its light:
a falcon on the sill.

It scanned the orchard's bowers,
then pane by pane it eyed   10
the stories facing ours
but never looked inside.

I called you in to see.
And when you steamed the room
and naked next to me   15
stood dripping, as a bloom

of blood formed in your cheek
and slowly seemed to melt,
I could almost speak
the love I almost felt.   20

Wish for something, you said.
A shiver pricked your spine.
The falcon turned its head
and locked its eyes on mine.

For a long moment I'm still in   25
I wished and wished and wished
the moment would not end.
And just like that it vanished.

Form

1981

HEATHER MCHUGH (B. 1948)

We were wrong to think
form a frame, a still
shot of the late
beloved, or the pot thrown
around water. We wanted   5
to hold what we had.

But the clay contains
the breaking, and the man
is dead—the scrapbook
has him—and the form of life   10
is a motion. So from all this
sadness, the bed being touched,

the mirror being filled,
we learn what carrying on
is for. We move, we are moved.   15
It runs in the family.
For the life of us
we cannot stand to stay.

What the Mosquito Gives

2007

AIMEE NEZHUKUMATATHIL (B. 1974)

You are the father of my father and I am the mosquito of the rain barrel.
I give to you three ripples of night water, one single white petal

of a frangipani tree. I give to you four limes to crush
into a spicy pickle sauce. A clasp of coconut gives me back

a day when you were alive, when you showed me the monkeyface   5
of the shell, the gallop in each clap. My sister is a tamarind

and I am the dusky husk covering her until she splits
open. You told my tiny red purse that it could hold

a whole elephant, a handful of pink scallop shells, two musky pods
of cardamom. I still have all those onion skin letters you wrote me.   10

The foreign stamps. The careful curls of your script, each letter
spaced wide enough for a six-year old to read on a porch

with her father, wiping his eyes with the back of his hand.

Traveling through the Dark   1960
WILLIAM STAFFORD (1914–1993)

Traveling through the dark I found a deer
dead on the edge of the Wilson River road.
It is usually best to roll them into the canyon:
that road is narrow; to swerve might make more dead.

By glow of the tail-light I stumbled back of the car   5
and stood by the heap, a doe, a recent killing;
she had stiffened already, almost cold.
I dragged her off; she was large in the belly.

My fingers touching her side brought me the reason—
her side was warm; her fawn lay there waiting,   10
alive, still, never to be born.
Beside that mountain road I hesitated.

The car aimed ahead its lowered parking lights;
under the hood purred the steady engine.
I stood in the glare of the warm exhaust turning red;   15
around our group I could hear the wilderness listen.

I thought hard for us all—my only swerving—,
then pushed her over the edge into the river.

Unconditional Election   2001
DAVID BAKER (B. 1954)

We have decided now to kill the doves
—November the third, nineteen ninety-nine—
who gather in great numbers in the fields
of Ohio, vast and diminishing,

whose call is gray and cream, wing-on-the-wind.   5
I lean from the deck to hear their mourning
cry, like the coo of a human union.
They persevere as song in the last days.

Or is it the wind I hear this morning,
crossing the great, cold lake, the hundred dry   10
miles of fields cut down to stubble and rust?
The rain gauge, hollow as a finger bone,

lifts to survey the stiffening breeze.
The boards of our deck are a plank bridge

hanging over nothing, the season's abyss.   15
When we decided not to have the child,

how could we know the judgment would carry
so far?—each breath, each day, another
renewal of our *no*. A few frail leaves
hurry now dryly in waves at my feet.   20

The doves have no natural predator,
so we will be their fate. We will prowl
the brown fields, taking aim at the wind,
or huddle inside in the lengthening dark.

It no longer matters who is right. Their cry   25
comes from both sides of the window at once.

3

MAKING THE LINE (I)

The universe is rhythmic. Light arrives from the sun in regular waves. The sounds of a passing car reach us in waves. Whether breathing, swimming, typing, texting, washing windows, or rowing a boat, our bodies naturally fall into a rhythm; we might pick up the pace, but we try to stay with a rhythm. Indeed, unrhythmic activity takes more energy and feels awkward and unnatural. When we hear another's voice, we tune in to the rising and falling rhythm of speech. We hear something very different when a person dashes from a house yelling, "Help me! Lord, help me!" than we hear when someone murmurs the same words as she slides a spoon into chocolate mousse. Poetry applies what we know about the natural rhythms of spoken language to make art.

Meter

To create a line with a regular rhythm, the poet takes advantage of some prominent element in the language and repeats it at regular intervals. Every language has its own distinctive cadence and from it develops ways of making lines rythmic. Latin poetry, for example, uses the duration of vowels, long or short, as the controlling element. Chinese, in which all words are monosyllabic, counts syllables. As it developed, poetry in English exploited how the language registers stressed and unstressed syllables. In making patterns of stresses, the poet creates a **meter,** which means measurement; in making a metrical line, a poet makes a **measure** of beats. We hear, even *feel,* the rhythm immediately. The linguist Derek Attridge says,

> Poetry *takes place* in time; its movement through time…is its *rhythm.* It should be read aloud whenever possible, and even when read silently it should take up the same amount of time that reading aloud would give it.

When reading poetry, take your time. Slow down. Read it out loud. Though we may be used to skimming, coming to poetry we must change our pace. Poetry should not be skimmable. The best poems ask for slow reading, for reading aloud, for savoring with the mouth and the ear.

You don't need to know anything to feel rhythm; from infancy we've responded to it:

> Round and round the mulberry bush,
> The monkey chased the weasel.
> Round and round the mulberry bush,
> Pop! goes the weasel.

A small child hearing this sung doesn't need to know what a mulberry bush, weasel, or monkey is (or that they make a rare trio!), yet because the rhythm sets up an expectation, the child will laugh when she hears the surprise of "Pop!" You won't get the same response if you try to sing this version:

> Innumerable times
> The representative of the weasel family was
> Pursued by an
> Insistent simian around the morus rubra
> In circles.
> What a surprise when the weasel suddenly confronted his pursuer!

The meter of the original nursery rhyme is strong because its stressed and unstressed syllables occur in a regular pattern emphasized by the structure of the phrases and how they are placed in the lines. We might sketch out the rhythm of the verse by using waves, marking stressed syllables with the peaks of waves and unstressed syllables with troughs:

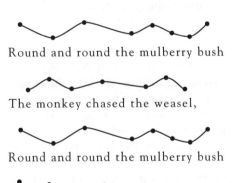

Round and round the mulberry bush

The monkey chased the weasel,

Round and round the mulberry bush

Pop! goes the weasel.

The wave pattern shows us what our ears register: a relatively consistent rising and falling pattern supported by syntax and lineation. Normally, when singing this verse to a child, we make a dramatic stop after "Pop!" that substitutes for an unstressed syllable and a pause; the meter then resumes with "goes." The strength of the meter tells us to take the same amount of time to sing "Round and round the mulberry bush" as "Pop! goes the weasel." After we say "Pop!"

> *Most arts attain their effects by using a fixed element and a variable.*
>
> —Ezra Pound

we automatically wait a count. Try singing it without the stop, running it all together, and you'll notice how awkward it sounds.

Alternating between stressed and unstressed syllables in English sounds natural and rhythmic. When unstressed and stressed syllables don't seem to alternate, when many stressed or many unstressed syllables pile up in a row, we begin to hear dissonance, for example: "Innumerable times the representative of the weasel family...." Decorating a sentence with modifiers and polysyllabic latinate words often hobbles its sound and makes for clunky diction. The rule of strong writing tells us not to use a lot of words when a few will do; this rule makes for rhythmic writing too.

Like "Round and Round the Mulberry Bush," most verse written in English (that is, most songs and most vernacular poetry, like cowboy poetry, chants, jeers, cheers, and the poems you wrote in grade school) is composed with four strong stresses per line with one or two unstressed syllables between the stressed ones. This pattern of alternating stressed and unstressed syllables creates a powerful, predictable beat. You might know this one:

> Oh! Who lives in a pineapple under the sea?
> SpongeBob SquarePants!
> Absorbent and yellow and porous is he!
> SpongeBob SquarePants!

The meter is so strong that even when the phrases are not lineated we enact it, reading (or singing) quickly the first and third lines and slowly the refrain in the second and fourth lines. If you listen to the verse on YouTube, you'll hear that "SpongeBob SquarePants" takes about as long to sing as "Absorbent and yellow and porous is he." The words "absorbent and" are run together so much that only "sor," the stressed syllable in "absorbent," is clear. When you're in doubt about where the stress falls in a word or phrase, it helps to sing it. Through the emphasis of song, native speakers of English will automatically put the stress where it belongs.

"Round and Round the Mulberry Bush" and the SpongeBob lyrics follow the most powerful meter in English, what Derek Attridge calls the Four by Four Formation, or the 4 × 4 formation, for its tendency to work in four line units of four stressed syllables. This is the measure of country-western songs like "Friends in Low Places," church hymns, Lewis Carroll's "Jabberwocky" (p. 159), ancient ballads, and Dickinson's "I Heard a Fly Buzz" (p. 121). Even in free verse poems, like Naomi Nye's "Famous" (p. 18) and Matthew's "Men at My Father's Funeral" (p. 98), we can feel this meter undergirdding the lines. The poets' careful orchestration of enjambment and syntax keeps the poems from becoming sing-song.

Often in a 4 × 4 stanza, the fourth stressed syllable in the second and fourth syllables is dropped, but a beat still occurs; we pause and count. Read again aloud (or sing!) "Mulberry Bush" or "SpongeBob" and notice that you naturally wait a couple of counts after you finish the second and fourth lines. Listen to how you naturally draw out the word "weasel" before repeating "Round and round...."

Try saying aloud this stanza from Samuel Taylor Coleridge's "Rime of the Ancient Mariner":

And now there came both mist and snow,
And it grew wondrous cold:
And ice, mast-high, came floating by
As green as emerald.

Although we might normally pronounce "emerald" with two syllables, in feeling the meter here we would probably pronounce it as three, not dramatically so, but we do give it a little extra energy. Look again at Coleridge's stanza. Say it outloud a few more times, getting the feel for it, then draw the wave pattern above the lines. You might get something like this:

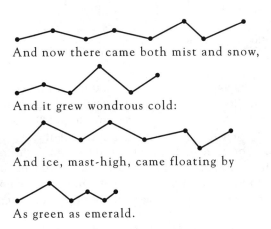

Coleridge's handling of the meter helps to evoke the strangeness of the ancient mariner's tale. The rhythm of the first line sets up a baseline of rising and falling. As the stanza progresses, the stressed syllables become more packed. The density of the third line helps to convey the sense of the ice-bound ship; the lightness of the fourth line suggests the sparkle in the ice.

Something wonderful happens when the words of a poem progress through a metrical pattern. We hear a human voice at a heightened moment, speaking a rhythm that is never precisely regular or mechanical. The

> *Formal poetry should continually remain in contact with the speech and the life around it....*
> —Louise Bogan

usual stresses of words, their varying importance or placement in lines, their sounds, as well as the pauses and syntactic links among them, all work to give each line an individual movement and flavor, a distinct rhythm.

Poetic rhythm comes from blending the fixed (meter) and the flexible (speech). It's neither precisely the *te TUM te TUM* of meter nor a reproduction of casual speech. A poem is read as something between the two. We may show the relationship this way:

$$\frac{\text{speech}}{\text{meter (line)}} = \text{poetic rhythm}$$

The flow of speech slows, becoming more distinct, as we listen for the binary values of stressed and unstressed syllables that flow into the meter. Subtleties we may be unaware of in the hurry of speech become magnified in poetry. Consider a simple sentence (which is part of the first line of Richard Wilbur's "Juggler"): "A ball will bounce, but less and less." It would be robotic to read the line mechanically, emphasizing each stressed syllable with equal emphasis ("a BALL will BOUNCE, but LESS and LESS"); it would also be faulty to read it as we might normally speak it ("a ball will BOUNCE, but less and less"). Because this sentence appears in a poem, we read it neither in rigid rhythm nor in the usual dash of speech. *Speech overlaying meter produces rhythm.*

Wilbur's regular *te TUM te TUM te TUM te TUM* within the sentence creates its own deliciously distinctive rhythm. Within regularity or, rather, because of it, small differences in stress give the effect of less and less force and so seem to imitate the way a ball slows to a stop in smaller and smaller arcs. The difference in stress from "A" to "ball" is relatively great, that from "will" to "bounce" somewhat less great, and so on through the line. The *difference* between each unstressed syllable and the following stressed syllable diminishes in succession. If we draw the difference of stress in each **foot,** a unit of measure, it might look something like this:

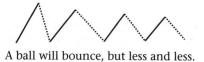

A ball will bounce, but less and less.

Using the conventions of scansion, we would mark it:

Ă báll | wĭll bóunce | bŭt léss | ănd léss.

The first depiction shows the flexibility of the rhythm; the second shows its steadiness. Notice the unstressed and stressed meter in each foot (indicated by |), which creates a pattern throughout the line. The meter is regular, yet fluid as motion, and is technically called iambic tetrameter. More information about the various types of stress patterns and feet appears in Appendix II.

Stress

Some linguists claim they can hear seven levels of stress, but for metrical purposes poets count only two: A syllable is either relatively stressed or relatively unstressed. The stress is *relative* to the context in which we hear the syllable, which is why reading poetry aloud is so important. When writing is organized in lines and phrases in such a way that the syllables alternate between stressed and unstressed ones, the poet creates a context for us to hear a rhythm.

Read these lines *out loud* a few times, considering which syllables seem stressed and which don't:

> The broad-backed hippopotamus
> Rests on his belly in the mud;
> Although he seems so firm to us
> He is merely flesh and blood.
>   from T. S. Eliot's "The Hippopotamus"

> I should have been a pair of ragged claws
> Scuttling across the floors of silent seas.
>   from Eliot's "The Love-Song of J. Alfred Prufrock"

In general, stress falls on the most significant syllables, on "content" words, those that offer the most meaning or information: nouns, verbs, adverbs, and adjectives. We easily hear these syllables stressed: "rests," "flesh," "blood," "pair," "rag" in "ragged," "claws," and "scut" in "scuttling." Unstressed syllables are normally function words—those that depend on other words for meaning or information; these are articles ("a," "the"), prepositions ("in," "of," "to"), conjunctions ("and," "when"), pronouns ("I," "his," "it"), auxiliary verbs ("have"), demonstratives ("these"), and adverbs that accompany adjectives and adverbs ("so," "more").

But stress is often a matter of degree and context. A syllable that is not stressed in one context might naturally be stressed in another. Because Eliot has organized his sentences in lines with a regular rhythm, we place stress on syllables that in another context we might not. In Eliot's phrase "so firm to us," we put stress on the pronoun "us" because it follows the word "to" which gets comparatively less stress. However, in the phrase "give us money," we'd hear "us" as unstressed. The word "should" receives stress in Eliot's "I should have been a pair," but in another context, it wouldn't receive stress: "If I should die before I wake." To native English speakers, rhythmic phrasing sounds better than nonrhythmic, and when we speak, we organize what we say so that one or two unstressed syllables come between the stressed syllables. When three syllables that normally are not stressed come in a row, it sounds best to us, if possible, to give the middle one a little bit more attention or to rearrange what we have to say to make alternating stresses possible. In Eliot's phrase "belly in the mud," we give a little more weight to the prepostion "in" than we do to "ly" in "belly" or to "the." Certainly, we don't pronounce "in" as strongly as "mud"; we just give it more power than the syllables on each side of it.

Similarly, when many stressed syllables appear together, we'll try to give less stress to a syllable that might be stressed in another context. In Eliot's phrase "the broad-backed hippopotamus," we give a little less emphasis to "backed" than we would in most contexts. For compounds in English, the first syllable gets the **primary stress** (´) and the next syllable gets a **secondary stress** (ˋ). We say bédroòm, tówn hàll, Whíte Hoùse. "She lives in a gréen hoùse" and "she lives in a gréenhoùse" mean very different things because of the way we stress the words, not how we spell them.

Polysyllabic words take stress on at least one syllable. In the line "Scuttling across the floors," the syllable "-cross" becomes stressed because just before and after it, we have syllables we hear as unstressed. The primary stress of a polysyllabic word usually falls on its root syllable, as in *móvable, imprácticAl, hómelessness.*

If you look up the five syllable "hippopotamus" in the dictionary you'll find an entry like this: hi-pə-'pä-tə-məs, indicating that the third syllable receives the primary stress, the first a secondary stress, and that the second, fourth, and last are unstressed. But when we say Eliot's line out loud, we pronounce the final syllable with a little more weight than the second and fourth; the syllable's position at the end following an unstressed syllable makes this possible.

Speech, Rhythm, and the Line

To paraphrase Robert Frost, there are two kinds of lines, strict and loose.[1] English poetry constantly goes through changes in style. Eighteenth-century poets faulted Shakespeare on his loose meter; they valued strict meter and exact rhyme more than naturalness of expression. These lines from Mary Wortley Montagu are typical of the style:

Think not this paper comes with vain pretense
To move your pity, or to mourn th' offense.

---

[1] "[W]ith meters—particularly in our language…there are virtually but two, strict iambic and loose iambic."

Too well I know that hard obdurate heart;
No softening mercy there will take my part....

from "Epistle from Mrs. Yonge to Her Husband"

At the end of the century, the style began to shift, and Wordsworth proclaimed that poets should speak "the real language of men in a state of vivid sensation,"[2] meaning that the language of a good poem should sound like well-written prose (an argument Ezra Pound made again in the early twentieth century). While the eighteenth century found perfectly acceptable the **elision,** or omission, of an unstressed syllable when followed by another unstressed syllable (poeticisms like "o'er," "e'er," or "th" offense), later generations found such techniques quaint and overblown. The syntactic inversion Montagu uses in clauses like "Think not this paper" or "Too well I know" was thought elegant in her time; to modern ears such inversion sounds silly or sarcastic. Montagu carefully sets her syntax within the metrical line so that phrase and line coincide (a technique still popular in many of today's songs), creating a sense of control, clarity, and balance; later generations cut across syntax with enjambment (a technique Milton deployed earlier), creating drama, tension, ambiguity, and nuance.

Let's look at some lines of poetry written as prose. Read over the following passage, considering how it sounds:

The boy's first outcry was a rueful laugh, as he swung toward them holding up the hand, half in appeal, but half as if to keep the life from spilling. Then the boy saw all—since he was old enough to know, big boy doing a man's work, though a child at heart—he saw all spoiled.

Take a pencil to these two sentences, and draw a slash mark (/) at those places where you feel a line should break. Or copy out the sentences and lineate them. When you've finished, go back over the passage, and redo the exercise, making another set of line breaks in other places. Compare the two versions. In each case, what considerations did you make as you constructed the lines? How does the emphasis change as the lines change?

Now read the following poem by Robert Frost. If you can't read it aloud, at least read it slowly, paying attention to how your facial muscles would move if you said it out loud. The title appears in quotation marks because it is an **allusion** (a historical, mythic, or literary reference) to Macbeth's soliloquy: "Out, out, brief candle." As you read, try to notice where the rhythm seems strict or loose, and where it seems to speed up or slow down.

---

[2]Preface to *Lyrical Ballads* (1802).

"Out, Out—"

The buzz saw snarled and rattled in the yard
And made dust and dropped stove-length sticks of wood,
Sweet-scented stuff when the breeze drew across it.
And from there those that lifted eyes could count
Five mountain ranges one behind the other   5
Under the sunset far into Vermont.
And the saw snarled and rattled, snarled and rattled,
As it ran light, or had to bear a load.
And nothing happened: day was all but done.
Call it a day, I wish they might have said   10
To please the boy by giving him the half hour
That a boy counts so much when saved from work.
His sister stood beside them in her apron
To tell them "Supper." At the word, the saw,
As if to prove saws knew what supper meant,   15
Leaped out at the boy's hand, or seemed to leap—
He must have given the hand. However it was,
Neither refused the meeting. But the hand!
The boy's first outcry was a rueful laugh,
As he swung toward them holding up the hand,   20
Half in appeal, but half as if to keep
The life from spilling. Then the boy saw all—
Since he was old enough to know, big boy
Doing a man's work, though a child at heart—
He saw all spoiled. "Don't let him cut my hand off—   25
The doctor, when he comes. Don't let him, sister!"
So. But the hand was gone already.
The doctor put him in the dark of ether.
He lay and puffed his lips out with his breath.
And then—the watcher at his pulse took fright.   30
No one believed. They listened at his heart.
Little—less—nothing!— and that ended it.
No more to build on there. And they, since they
Were not the one dead, turned to their affairs.

Although it is written in the same meter as Montagu's poem (**iambic pentameter,** roughly a ten-syllable line, alternating between unstressed and stressed syllables), Frost's poem sounds to us more like someone speaking or telling a story. Its lack of rhyme, of course, contributes to its more casual sound, but Frost also deliberately varies the syntax, enjambs lines, ends sentences within lines, and works in a looser rhythm, all of which support the poem's content.

The harsh image of the buzz saw at work dominates the opening: humans are present only by implication and seem almost to have become extensions of the machines. Stressed syllables crowd the first few lines to emphasize the machines at work, but when the speaker turns to the mountain vista, the rhythm relaxes and opens. Meter works with content; in the rhythm itself we can feel the relief of the speaker as he looks out on the mountains. If we mark out the primary and secondary stresses, we can compare lines 1 and 2 with lines 5 and 6:

The búzz sàw snárled and ráttled ín the yárd

And máde dúst and drópped stóve-lèngth stícks of wóod

Five móuntain ránges óne behínd the óther

Únder the súnsèt fár intó Vermónt.

Both sets of lines move rhythmically, with rising and falling energy, but the second set displays more regularly spaced waves. Remember, hearing stress is all about context. In the first line, though "saw" is more powerful than "in," we hear it in context with "buzz" and "snarled," which receive relatively more stress. At first reading, the phrase "the buzz saw snarled" forces us to back track and readjust as we realize that "saw" isn't a verb but part of the compound "buzz saw." As we accommodate ourselves to the poem's rhythm, we give "in" a bit of stress because it follows "rattled" and precedes "buzz."

When the speaker turns his attention back to the saw, the rhythm again feels troubled:

Ănd thĕ sáw snárled ănd ráttlĕd, snárled ănd ráttlĕd,

Ăs ĭt rán líght, ŏr hád tŏ béar ă lóad.

Both lines begin quickly with two unstressed syllables, then jam up with stressed syllables. Speaking the lines, we have to slow way down for "saw snarled" and somewhat for "ran light." Notice that snarling and rattling describe two rhythms of the buzz saw in operation. It *snarls* as wood is pressed into the whirling teeth of the blade, producing sharp noise. Then as it idles, the saw *rattles* as engine, belt, and blade run slack. The repetition—"snarled and rattled, snarled and rattled"—expresses the repetitiousness of the job of cutting wood. The blade spins freely, slows as it bites into the wood, then speeds up as the wood is cut.

Frost organizes the lines to produce a steady rhythm, which he can then vary to create tension and drama. Without the steadiness, we wouldn't hear the variation. In the passage you broke into lines earlier, you likely ended up with lines different from Frost's. Your version isn't wrong; it's useful. It demonstrates the effects of Frost's own lineation. Again, say the lines aloud:

> The boy's first outcry was a rueful laugh,
> As he swung toward them holding up the hand,
> Half in appeal, but half as if to keep
> The life from spilling. Then the boy saw all—
> Since he was old enough to know, big boy
> Doing a man's work, though a child at heart—
> He saw all spoiled.

To test how tuned in you are to the rhythm, ask yourself if you pronounced "toward" as one syllable instead of two in the phrase "as he swung toward them." By giving it one syllable, you're allowing for the easy alternation of stressed and unstressed syllables. Frost's lineation subtly suggests the mangling of the boy's hand and the cutting short of his life. "Half in appeal" begins a series of lines that use enjambment and caesura, which carry clauses over the lines and end them inside the lines. The position of the caesura shifts around in the lines, from the left in line 3 (after "appeal"), to the center in line 4, to the far right in line 5, to the center in line 6. The quickness and enjambment of "as if to keep / The life from spilling" helps to suggest the hopelessness of the boy's situation as his blood—and life—drain away.

Our hearts beat steadily. We breathe steadily. Shock, hilarity, terror, bursts of joy—intense emotions spike our hearts and make us gasp for breath. The rhythm of Frost's lines allows him to ripple emotional undercurrents beneath the cool tone of the speaker. The boy pleads with his sister not to let the doctor take his hand ("'The doctor, when he comes. Don't let him, sister,'"), and Frost continues:

> So. But the hand was gone already.
> The doctor put him in the dark of ether.

The rhythm becomes disturbed here, then returns to steadiness. The line "So. But the hand..." contains nine syllables. The lines in the rest of the poem contain ten or eleven syllables—those immediately before and after contain eleven. Frost forces us to stop after "So." We take a breath, then resume with "But the hand was gone already." In a sense, the syllable missing after "So" registers the missing hand.

The ragged breath and dying pulse of the boy are enacted in the rhythm of the poem's closing lines. Double lines (‖) below indicate the caesuras:

> Líttlĕ—‖ léss—‖ nóthĭng!—‖ ănd thăt éndĕd ít.
>
> Nŏ móre tŏ búild ŏn thére. ‖ Ănd théy, sĭnce théy
>
> Wĕre nót thĕ óne déad, ‖ túrned tŏ thĕir ăffáirs.

Design and invention are the father and mother of all the arts.

—Giorgio Vasari

Frost builds many stops and silences into the rhythm, helping him to evoke an unnerving emptiness. In less than a line, the boy's life is over. The pronouns "it," "they" (emphasized through repetition and enjambment), "the one," and "their" further dehumanize the scene. The detachment of the diction in "their affairs" makes the tone all the more chilling and implies the workers have witnessed this kind of loss before. Rhythmically, the final lines capture how the survivors quickly go back to their lives. The caesura in the final line creates balance, five syllables on each side, with a peak in the middle. The boy's death is a disruption they quickly overcome.

Line Length

As you lineated the Frost passage, you might have contemplated how rhythm is affected by long and short lines. If Frost's poem were lineated in any other way, its rhythm would be affected. Breaking the lines into neat phrases lessens the impact of events that deserve attention:

> Little—less—nothing!
> And that ended it.
> No more to build on there.
> And they, since they were not the one dead,
> turned to their affairs.

Longer lines seem slack and muddy the rhythm:

> Little—less—nothing!—and that ended it. No more to build on there.
> And they, since they were not the one dead, turned to their affairs.

We might play with indentation, and create lines of five syllables each. This looks tidy, but the drama is defused:

> Little—less—nothing!
>   And that ended it.
> No more to build on
>   there. And they since they
> were not the one dead,
>   turned to their affairs.

Line breaks might literally break against the phrase and suggest fracture and disjunction:

> Little— less—
> nothing!
>   And that

ended
it. No more to
    build on there.   And they
        since
they were not the
    one dead, turned
                to their
affairs.

The length of a poetic line carries with it associations from the long history of poetry. Most sonnets have been written in iambic pentameter. Most *poetry* in English has been written in lines that vary between six and eleven syllables; this is the default length, but a poet can form a line of any length, short or long, to create particular effects. There isn't any one right or wrong way to make lines in poetry; it all depends on the poem and figuring out what affect feels right. Some kinds of lines create greater rhythmic control than others. Some emphasize the visual over the oral. Some are weighty, some thin and nervous. As you work on your own poems, play around with the lines, change them up, and listen to the rhythm they create. At times, a poem that feels stuck will unspool itself when you readjust its lines so that you can hear it another way.

QUESTIONS AND SUGGESTIONS

1. Stuart Murdock, front man and song writer for Belle and Sebastian, has said, "In a sense, pop music is bad poetry, with a sweetener," or with a melody attached. But those rhythms can be a good place to start. Use song lyrics to write an imitation poem, that is, a poem that follows the syntax and line breaks of the song as closely as possible. You might start by rewriting the song lyrics by hand and replacing nouns, then verbs, and so on with your own language. Remember to keep your language and imagery fresh and beware of abstractions.

2. Experiment with writing a poem based on an allusion, such as Robert Frost's "Out, Out—" (p. 49) or D. A. Powell's [writing for a young man on the redline train: "to his boy mistress"] (p. 153). Research a play by Shakespeare, such as *Romeo and Juliet*, or choose a character from Greek mythology, such as Hera or Apollo. Then invent a narrative in which Hera visits the earth, or use first person and write a poem from Juliet's perspective. Books, visual depictions, and the Internet can help get you started.

3. The practice of scanning stresses in poetry will help you train your ear. Scan the following poems and consider how rhythmic variations support

the content. Remember to read out loud as you scan. Then compare your scanned poem with a classmate's version.

Sonnet 116

WILLIAM SHAKESPEARE (1564–1616)

> Let me not to the marriage of true minds
> Admit impediments. Love is not love
> Which alters when it alteration finds,
> Or bends with the remover to remove:
> Oh, no! It is an ever-fixéd mark   5
> That looks on tempests and is never shaken;
> It is the star to every wand'ring bark,
> Whose worth's unknown although his height be taken.
> Love's not Time's fool, though rosy lips and cheeks
> Within his bending sickle's compass come;   10
> Love alters not with his brief hours and weeks,
> But bears it out even to the edge of doom.
> If this be error, and upon me proved,
> I never writ, nor no man ever loved.

Delight in Disorder

ROBERT HERRICK (1591–1674)

> A sweet disorder in the dress
> Kindles in clothes a wantonness;
> A lawn about the shoulders thrown
> Into a fine distraction,
> An erring lace, which here and there,   5
> Enthralls the crimson stomacher,
> A cuff neglectful, and thereby
> Ribbands to flow confusedly;
> A winning wave, deserving note,
> In the tempestuous petticoat,   10
> A careless shoe-string, in whose tie
> I see a wild civility,
> Do more bewitch me than when art
> Is too precise in every part.

#328 [A Bird came down the Walk—]

EMILY DICKINSON (1830–1886)

> A Bird came down the Walk—
> He did not know I saw—
> He bit an Angleworm in halves
> And ate the fellow, raw,

And then he drank a Dew   5
From a convenient Grass—
And then hopped sidewise to the Wall
To let a Beetle pass—

He glanced with rapid eyes
That hurried all around—   10
They looked like frightened Beads, I thought—
He stirred his Velvet Head

Like one in danger, Cautious,
I offered him a Crumb
And he unrolled his feathers   15
And rowed him softer home—

Than Oars divide the Ocean,
Too silver for a seam—
Or Butterflies, off Banks of Noon,
Leap, plashless as they swim.   20

4. Try scanning one of your own poems and count how many stresses are in
   each line. What happens when you maintain a relatively equal number of
   stresses per line? What effect does that have on your line breaks and the
   overall poem? Are there one or two lines or moments that would benefit
   from having fewer or more stresses?

5. Write a sonnet using rhyme words you start with, or those suggested
   here. The following scheme corresponds to the pattern for the English
   (or Shakesperean) sonnet; the letters to the left represent rhymes:

a	stain
b	lift
a	plane
b	shift
c	stack
d	seat
c	hack
d	fleet
e	white
f	ranger
e	might
f	anger
g	entice
g	ice

   Let the starting words be guide ropes, but by no means feel bound to
   them. If something really appealing shows up, go for it.

POEMS TO CONSIDER

 Signs   1985

GJERTRUD SCHNACKENBERG (B. 1953)

> Threading the palm, a web of little lines
> Spells out the lost money, the heart, the head,
> The wagging tongues, the sudden deaths, in signs
> We would smooth out, like imprints on a bed,
>
> In signs that can't be helped, geese heading south,   5
> In signs read anxiously, like breath that clouds
> A mirror held to a barely open mouth,
> Like telegrams, the gathering of crowds—
>
> The plane's X in the sky, spelling disaster:
> Before the whistle and hit, a tracer flare;   10
> Before rubble, a hairline crack in plaster
> And a housefly's panicked scribbling on the air.

Ghost Images   2008

DEBORAH BOGEN (B. 1950)

1.

> The mind's a mad cupboard, blackened silver, cups and thimbles.
> The mind's a jerky focusing machine still stuck on the girl
> who hung by her knees.
>
> And within the camera [opening : closing]—fireworks.
>   I mean, within the empty box the light's frantic,   5
> grappling with: *the monk, the match, the gasoline.*
>
> The mind is likewise occupied, its light piteously stark, distorted
> —but which of us can ever look away?

2.

> Into the angular cranium levers lift cold light, but
>   how dark and small the box.   10
> And hands must hold the camera still, so stop your breath
>
>   [so stop your breath]
>
> That's how you coax something into the box, something bloody or blood-lit,
> a headless rooster or snipe—your attention split.
>
> Seeing the two worlds.   15

Eva Braun° at Berchtesgaden

VICTORIA CHANG (B. 1970)

2005

The lightning tucked
behind cypress trees.

Even the crickets gone
away. The phonograph

with its straw voice of   5
static and skips. Her silk

robe swelled through
corridors, tangles

of foam curlers, lipstick.
Then military boots,   10

chandelier covered by webs
of cigar smoke. All evening,

snow growing on the cypress,
knives on china, scent of

roast beef, plucks of muscle.   15
Then the key sliding into her

bedroom lock, loosened
ribbons on her nightgown,

his cold tongue,
like sponge and beef.   20

Title: Eva Braun was Adolph Hitler's lover and, for a short time, his wife.

Her Web

ERIN BELIEU (B. 1965)

2000

Spirit of the ratio
one above and one below,
she takes figures in a script
that haunts the cryptic willow.

Spoken in the dialect   5
known to every architect,
her cathedrals made of string
hold the stirring circumspect.

The web, a clock stitched from will,
chronologs which hours to kill;   10
when she rests, it's just a clause
in her gauzy codicil.

And when readying her bed,
she feels a pulse down the thread
current through the living weave,   15
she pins her sleeve to the dead.

 ## One Art   1976
ELIZABETH BISHOP (1911–1979)

The art of losing isn't hard to master;
so many things seem filled with the intent
to be lost that their loss is no disaster.

Lose something every day. Accept the fluster
of lost door keys, the hour badly spent.   5
The art of losing isn't hard to master.

Then practice losing farther, losing faster:
places, and names, and where it was you meant
to travel. None of these will bring disaster.

I lost my mother's watch. And look! my last, or   10
next-to-last, of three loved houses went.
The art of losing isn't hard to master.

I lost two cities, lovely ones. And, vaster,
some realms I owned, two rivers, a continent.
I miss them, but it wasn't a disaster.   15

—Even losing you (the joking voice, a gesture
I love) I shan't have lied. It's evident
the art of losing's not too hard to master
though it may look like (*Write* it!) like disaster.

4

MAKING THE LINE (II)

Although it takes many forms, nonmetrical verse falls under the catchall term **free verse.** Borrowed from the French *vers libre*, the term is attractive because everyone likes freedom; but it doesn't tell us much—only what such verse is *not* (metrical) and nothing at all about what it is.

No verse is free, T. S. Eliot says, "for the poet who wants to do a good job." Another great American innovator in free verse, William Carlos Williams, was quite certain that "there is no such thing as free verse. It's a contradiction in terms. The verse is measured. No measure can be free." The nature of verse itself means that we pay attention to and control the way lines cut across phrases and sentences of speech. However, scant practical descriptions of free verse exist. Poets writing free verse successfully have done so mostly by intuition—often adapting traditional forms and techniques to free verse. A well-tuned ear—a delicate sensitivity to idiom—finds the unique form and rhythm, which in Ezra Pound's words "corresponds exactly to the emotion or shade of emotion to be expressed." Denise Levertov puts it this way: "There is a form in all things (and in our experience) which the poet can discover and reveal." Much free verse falls short, she notes, because "the attention of the writer has been switched off too soon, before the intrinsic form of the experience has been revealed." The riskiest temptation for the poet writing in free verse may be to settle for the easy spontaneity the term seems to promise. In poetry, no gesture or word is an accident. Free verse, like all poetry, requires conscious deliberation of language and form.

Until we have an adequate theory of nonmetrical verse, rough distinctions will help. As poems such as "Those Winter Sundays" (p. 6) and "Traveling through the Dark" (p. 39) remind us, many free verse poems look and move like metrical verse. Although the composition of their lines is nonmetrical, those lines can interact with other poetic elements to create tensions much like those in traditional verse. As a result, a free verse poem can be as powerful a construction as any more formal creation.

Many principles developed through formal verse apply to free verse. For instance, whether the poem's stresses are regular or not, many stressed syllables bunched together create a feeling of density, slowness, or weight (e.g., "in the blueblack cold," in "Those Winter Sundays," p. 6). Conversely, a series of lightly stressed syllables evokes lightness, swiftness, or precariousness (e.g., "Reflected on the world for a mirror" in "People and a Heron," p. 63). Poets working in the free verse tradition break lines for various reasons, such as to emphasize or undercut rhyme and sound; to end-stop, enjamb, and vary line breaks; to emphasize a word; to isolate an action; to control pacing; to maintain consistent line length throughout a poem; to break syntax or phrases against the line; and to correspond to the breath.

Although most free verse grew out of metrical verse, some types of free verse stand out as distinctive. These are poems written in *very long* lines (like Whitman's), in *very short* lines (like William Carlos Williams's), or in lines of *greatly varying* or uneven lengths. Each type creates different ways of organizing and using the unit of the line. Each offers a unique resonance and opportunity for merging content and form.

These three subtypes of nonmetrical verse developed, logically enough, to expand the possibilities of poetry beyond the strictly metrical. At the center of the traditional poetic spectrum are poems in lines of about eight to ten syllables (corresponding to tetrameters and pentameters); less frequent, but common, are poems of around six syllables or twelve syllables (corresponding to trimeters and hexameters; see Appendix II for more information on types of meter and feet). Lines shorter or longer than these seldom show up in metrical verse. Moreover, poems in meter often keep to one line length throughout, or vary only a little. Poets, however, continue to find ways to create new forms of the nonmetrical poetic line.

In this chapter, we will discuss these three fairly open-ended types, as well as syllabics and the prose poem.

Longer Lines

Walt Whitman is the great originator of the poem of long lines in modern English, although he had antecedents in the "verse" of Psalms and Ecclesiastes in the King James Bible (1611) and poems by Christopher Smart, William Blake, and others. Whitman's "A Noiseless Patient Spider" (p. 30) exemplifies free verse in longer lines. Lines as long as Whitman's are usually end-stopped, breaking at natural syntactic or grammatical pauses or intervals. Structured by these pauses, the rhythm may then be modulated by caesural pauses—internal breaks within the lines. The cadence of such verse derives from the tension between the caesura and end-stopped line. The rolling rhythm we hear in long-lined verse dwindles with shorter lines. In the extreme—where every syntactic unit is given a line—the tension disappears and all that remains is chopped-up prose. Suppose lines of "A Noiseless Patient Spider" were rearranged:

> Surrounded,
> detached,
> in measureless oceans of space,
> ceaselessly musing,
> venturing,
> throwing,
> seeking the spheres to connect them...

N*ature has no outline. Imagination has.*

—William Blake

The lineation now merely repeats the phrasal pauses of prose and the tension evaporates; the poem becomes labored and trite. Beginning writers of free verse sometimes divide lines this way into tidy phrases and miss the opportunity to create texture. When the lines of a poem cut across the flow of sentences, they can create new rhythms and a sense of surprise and suspense that pulls the reader through the poem. In any case, the content of the poem should justify the choice of line lengths.

Let's look at another example of nonmetrical verse in longer lines, also by Whitman:

 ## When I Heard the Learn'd Astronomer

> When I heard the learn'd astronomer,
> When the proofs, the figures, were ranged in columns before me,
> When I was shown the charts and diagrams, to add, divide, and
>   measure them,
> When I sitting heard the astronomer where he lectured with much
>   applause in the lecture-room,
> How soon unaccountable I became tired and sick,   5
> Till rising and gliding out I wander'd off by myself,
> In the mystical moist night-air, and from time to time,
> Look'd up in perfect silence at the stars.

All one sentence, the poem gets its rhythmic force through Whitman's handling of syntax. Lines 1 to 4, describing the lecture, lack a main clause, and so seem indecisive, repetitious, and bogged down in details, like a boring lecture. Whitman uses a device called **anaphora,** organizing lines or sentences by repeating a word or phrase at the start, as with "When" in the first four lines. Though anaphora can be used for a variety of effects, here it underscores the tediousness of the lecture. Moreover, the verbs in lines 2 and 3 are passive ("were ranged," "was shown"), and "[w]hen I sitting heard" in line 4 repeats the structure of line 1. We almost feel, in the pointedly awkward syntax, the speaker's fidgeting on a hard seat and his boredom in the redundant thump of "*lectured* . . . in the *lecture*-room." The rhythm enacts his discomfort, as it does again in line 5. The adverb "unaccount*ably*" would make sense, but we get instead the displaced adjective "unaccount*able* I." The speaker finally leaves the lecture, suggesting neither he nor the stars can be counted in figures and neatly packaged or contained.

Free verse poetry and even prose can be scanned. As if by magic, the natural rhythms of language are ever present and can be manipulated for desired effect by those writers especially attuned to sound. Let's look at a stresses-per-phrase scansion of Whitman's poem:

When I Heard the Learn'd Astronomer

When I héard the léarn'd astrónomer,   3

When the próofs, ‖ the fígures, ‖ were ránged in cólumns before mé,   1/1/3

When Í was shówn the chárts and díagráms, ‖ to ádd, ‖ divíde, ‖ and

    méasure thém,   5/1/1/2

When Í sítting héard the astrónomer ‖ where he léctured with múch

    appláuse in the lécture-róom,   4/5

How sóon unaccóuntable Í becáme tíred and síck,   6

Till rísing and glíding óut ‖ I wánder'd óff by mysélf,   3/3

In the mýstical móist níght-aír, ‖ and from tíme to tíme,   4/2

Lóok'd úp in pérfect sílence át the stárs.   6

Whitman's use of repetition and modification in lines 2 to 4 creates a dense and dull lecture. The syntax of line 2 (short clauses followed by a long one) is reversed in line 3 (a long clause followed by short ones); *two* long clauses in line 4 make plain the lecturer's tediousness. Even though Whitman is not writing metrical verse, he still uses rhythm and syntax to support the poem's content.

After the complex opening lines, both syntax and rhythm begin to clarify, simplify, and open up—even in line 5 where, despite the awkward construction, the single clause shows the speaker recognizing the cause of his distress. The shorter final line expresses unity and awe. The adjectives "rising" and "gliding" are familiar terms for heavenly motion; "wander'd" recalls the literal meaning ("wanderer") of the Greek root of the English word *planet*. The balancing rhythm in line 6 parallels the speaker's growing awareness of himself as part of the universal whole. The poem's sentence culminates in the phrasal unity of line 8—which also happens to be iambic pentameter (a line with five alternating stresses):

Look'd up in perfect silence at the stars.

The line's familiar music evokes the natural experience of standing beneath the stars and effectively resolves the poem. Even when writing free verse, paying attention to the arrangement of stresses within lines can add another resonant layer to your poems.

Lines of Mixed Length

The category of nonmetrical verse of mixed-length lines falls between that of verse in longer lines and that of verse in shorter lines. We can look at it here by considering this poem by Robinson Jeffers (1887–1962):

People and a Heron

A desert of weed and water-darkened stone under my western windows
The ebb lasted all afternoon,
And many pieces of humanity, men, women, and children, gathering shellfish,
Swarmed with voices of gulls the sea-breach.
At twilight they went off together, the verge was left vacant, an evening heron   5
Bent broad wings over the black ebb,
And left me wondering why a lone bird was dearer to me than many people.
Well: rare is dear: but also I suppose
Well reconciled with the world but not with our own natures we grudge to see them
Reflected on the world for a mirror.   10

Looking down on a rocky beach as the tide ebbs, the speaker wonders why he prefers the lone heron to the families "gathering shellfish." He presents the people indifferently, as "pieces of humanity" that "[s]warmed" like insects, hinting at his misanthropy. He offers two explanations for this response. The first—"rare is dear"—suggests a rationale he doesn't seem to feel, so he considers a second reason. We may be "[w]ell reconciled with"—at peace with—the physical world, but not "our own natures," he says, though he doesn't explain that deep dissatisfaction.

The choice of a jagged form underscores the many disconnects between the speaker and other people, the speaker and the natural world, and people and their own natures. Scanning the poem also reveals a disconnection created through the *regular alternation* of longer and shorter lines. This alternation of line lengths and stresses reflects the poem's crucial oppositions: tidal flow and ebb, many and one, nature and human nature, self and mirror. The poem is about two states of mind, the solitary and the communal—*and* is of two minds about them. Lines 5 and 6 demonstrate this:

At twilight they went off together, ‖ the verge was left vacant, ‖

   an evening heron   5/3/2

Bent broad wings over the black ebb,   6

Through its expressive enjambment and phrasal unity, line 6 characterizes the lone heron as it sails down to replace people on the beach. The alliteration (*v*'s in line 5 and *b*'s in line 6) create a unity of sound which helps suggest the aptness of the lone bird's arrival. Except for line 8, the shorter lines have phrasal unity. By contrast, the longer lines, through the stopping and starting of caesuras, suggest multiplicity and encroaching industry.

Because iambic lines generally sound natural in English, poets often use them in free verse to create a sense of fulfillment or orderliness. Thom Gunn notes in an interview, "If you look at most of my contemporaries and most new poems, they write something that's not quite free verse and not quite meter." We can discover iambs even in longer lines like Whitman's:

When í | wăs shówn | thĕ chárts | ănd dí|ăgráms, | tŏ ádd, | dĭvíde, | ănd

   méas|ŭre thém

The poet writing free verse understands that metrical cadences are one of poetry's resources.

Shorter Lines

We can think of verse in shorter lines as being, loosely, of two kinds. The simpler may be called *phrasal verse*, because the poet divides lines at phrase or clause boundaries. Most of what was thought of as "free verse" early in the twentieth century was of this kind—following almost literally Pound's injunction "to compose in the sequence of the musical phrase, not in sequence of a metronome." This poem by William Carlos Williams shows the potential of phrasal verse:

Pastoral

When I was younger
it was plain to me
I must make something of myself.
Older now
I walk back streets   5
admiring the houses
of the very poor:
roof out of line with sides
the yards cluttered
with old chicken wire, ashes,   10
furniture gone wrong;
the fences and outhouses
built of barrel-staves
and parts of boxes, all,
if I am fortunate,   15
smeared a bluish green
that properly weathered
pleases me best
of all colors.
              No one
will believe this   20
of vast import to the nation.

In a few places the lines might have been broken somewhat differently: "admiring / the houses of the very poor," for instance, or "admiring / the houses / of the
very poor." But poets writing strictly phrasal verse have limited options; because
caesuras will inevitably be rare, the poet has few opportunities for creating tension within the line.

   In the scansion of the poem that follows, caesuras appear only in lines 10, 14, and
19. Williams, however, gains a declarative public voice that resounds at the poem's
end as the speaker defiantly claims the beauty of weathered houses to the nation.
Notice the change in the phrasal line breaks and the poem's shape as the speaker ac-
cepts his grand rhetorical statement might not succeed in changing the nation's mind.

   To look closely at what Williams's short free verse lines achieve, we turn now
to another informal kind of notation for *drag, advance,* and *balance.* **Drag** identifies a line whose weight lies primarily at its beginning (stressed syllables running
to unstressed syllables), and we mark it with an arrow pointing left (←); **advance**
identifies a line whose weight lies primarily at the end (unstressed syllables running
to stressed syllables), and we mark it with an arrow pointing right (→); **balance**
identifies a line whose stressed syllables are distributed fairly symmetrically, and we
mark it with an arrow that points both ways (↔). In a dragged line, then, stressed

syllables predominate in the first half of the line; in an advanced line they predominate in the second half; in a balanced line they are about equal. With this notation tool, let's turn back to Williams's "Pastoral."

The norm in the poem is two to three stresses per line; there are nine lines of each. Three lines have four stresses (lines 8, 10, and 19). In general, nothing fancy—in keeping with Williams's belief in "the American idiom." We also note drag, balance, and advance.

Whĕn Í wăs yóungĕr   ↔

ĭt wăs pláin tŏ mé   →

Ĭ mŭst máke sómethĭng ŏf mȳsélf.   →

Óldĕr nów   ↔

Ĭ wálk báck stréets   →

ădmírĭng thĕ hóusĕs   ↔

ŏf thĕ vérȳ póor: →

róof óut ŏf líne wĭth sídes   ←

thĕ yárds clúttĕred   ↔

wĭth óld chíckĕn wíre, ‖ áshĕs,   ↔

fúrnĭtŭre góne wróng;   →

thĕ féncĕs ănd óuthóusĕs   →

búilt ŏf bárrĕl-stáves   ↔

ănd párts ŏf bóxĕs, ‖ áll,   →

ĭf Í ăm fórtŭnăte,   ←

sméared ă blúish gréen   ↔

thăt próperlȳ wéathĕred   ↔

pléasĕs mĕ bést   ↔

o̮f a̓ll co̓lo̮rs.‖

       No̓ o̓ne

wi̮ll be̮li̓eve thi̓s

o̮f va̓st i̓mpo̮rt to̓ the̮ na̓tio̮n.

In the first third and last third of the poem, Williams uses mostly two-stress lines, but uses only one in lines 8 to 14, where the rhythm is appropriately denser when presenting the clut-

One writes for oneself and strangers....
—Gertrude Stein

tered landscape. Nine lines showing advance and ten showing balance are spread fairly evenly throughout the poem. The poem's end shows balance, registering the speaker's notion that others will not recognize the importance of this urban scene, which despite its poverty kindles in him admiration (line 6) and aesthetic pleasure (line 18). These values oppose the more typically American ambition, recalled in line 3, "to make something" of himself. Also, though the speaker does not argue his preference, the title "Pastoral" suggests the idyllic world of the pastoral poetry tradition. We may find meaning and beauty now, Williams implies, not among happy shepherds, but in such gritty everyday scenes the poem shows us—thereby cunningly undercutting the reader's expectations of a pastoral poem.

The other kind of nonmetrical verse in shorter lines may be called *radically enjambed*. The poet breaks some or many of the lines at radical or dramatic points *within* phrases—between adjective and noun, for example, or even between preposition and article, article and noun, and so on. We may feel a slight *speeding up* as the momentum of the interrupted phrase and sentence reasserts itself and seems to pull the voice around the corner into the next line. Enjambment, especially radical enjambment, releases a lot of energy, but when overused, the device can quickly lose impact.

Robert Hass suggests that training readers to re-see was one of Williams's goals in his poems:

A lot of William Carlos Williams's individual perceptions are a form of iambic music, but he has arranged them so that the eye breaks the iambic habit. The phrase—"a dust of snow in the wheeltracks"—becomes

    a dust of
    snow in
    the wheeltracks

and people must have felt: "Yes, that is what it is like; not one-TWO, one-TWO. A dust of / snow in / the wheeltracks. That is how perception is. It is that light and quick."

Presumably Williams is aware of and counts on his readers hearing the iambs that are muted by enjambment.

Especially when enjambment impels a sentence forward, shorter lines often produce abrupt rhythms (as in Sylvia Plath's "Balloons," p. 73). But this isn't always the case. The cat in Williams's "Poem," in spite of radical enjambments, moves in slow motion, due in part to the handling of stresses in each line:

 Poem

As the cat
climbed over
the top of

the jamcloset
first the right   5
forefoot

carefully
then the hind
stepped down

into the pit of   10
the empty
flowerpot

One notable detail: The poem is unpunctuated. This omission of commas and periods opens the sentence to the white space of the page. End-stops become softened, as in line 4, where we would expect a comma, or in the last line, where the almost seamless motion seems poised to continue. Williams can omit punctuation because he deftly manages line break and form. The lack of punctuation also helps to embody the lithe movement of the cat.

Scansion shows a norm of one or two stresses per line:

Ăs thĕ cát   →

clímbed óvĕr   ←

thĕ tóp ŏf   ↔

thĕ jámclŏsĕt   ↔

fírst thĕ ríght   ↔

fórefóot   ↔

cárefúllў   ←

then thĕ hĭnd   ↔

stépped dówn   ↔

íntŏ thĕ pít ŏf   ↔

thĕ émptў   ↔

flówĕrpót   ↔

The drag-advance notation reveals that only line 1 shows advance. Lines 2 and 7 show drag, and the rest—*nine* of the poem's twelve lines—show balance. This preponderance of lines in balance, these symmetrical rhythms, produces a feeling of stasis that even the momentum of radical enjambments can scarcely overcome. This overarching balance of stresses reinforces the cat's assured steps. It moves freely with poise and purpose (even though it humorously ends up in a flower pot).

Poems, of course, aren't written through calculation or complicated analysis. No doubt Williams, a doctor, wrote "Poem" rapidly, perhaps on the back of a prescription pad. But he had trained himself to listen for the rhythm he needed among the words that were suggesting themselves. And you, too, can train your ears to the nuance of rhythm and sound.

Syllabics

Syllabics, a form which counts the number of syllables in each line, is often a variant of radically enjambed verse. As developed with great success by Marianne Moore (1887–1972), syllable counts link lines of often visually complex stanzas. Consider this example by Moore.

 To a Steam Roller

The illustration
is nothing to you without the application.
    You lack half wit. You crush all the particles down
        into close conformity, and then walk back and forth on them.

Sparkling chips of rock   5
are crushed down to the level of the parent block.
    Were not "impersonal judgment in aesthetic
        matters, a metaphysical impossibility," you

might fairly achieve
it. As for butterflies, I can hardly conceive   10
    of one's attending upon you, but no question
        the congruence of the complement is vain, if it exists.

This poem is an example of **quantitative** syllabics: The number of syllables per line varies, and each stanza repeats the syllabic pattern of the first. In Moore's poem, each first line has five syllables; each second line, twelve; each third line, twelve; and each fourth line, fifteen. Especially in stanzas 1 and 3, the longer last lines mimic visually and rhythmically the effect of something rolled and flattened by a steamroller. And the rhyme in each stanza's lines 1 and 2 is followed by no rhyme in lines 3 and 4, as if the last two rhymes had been squashed down. Even the chopped-off "achieve / it" seems an effect of steamrolling. Another example of Moore's delightful syllabics, "The Fish," appears in Chapter 11 (p. 207).

Another kind of syllabics is **normative,** in which each line throughout a poem has the same number of syllables. Sometimes a significant line of the poem becomes the baseline around which the poet builds the poem. Or a poet may choose a particularly significant number and write the poem's syllabics around that number. Donald Hall wrote a series of poems about baseball that had nine syllables per line, nine lines to a stanza, and nine stanzas. Later he wrote a series of three "Extra Innings" with—you guessed it—the syllabics organized around ten, eleven, and twelve. Whatever shape syllabics take, poets find them attractive not because they offer a particular rhythm, but because they offer a discipline—though a relatively casual one—around which the poet can create the poem.

Prose Poems

Stretching from margin to margin, prose poetry looks like prose but uses all the resources of poetry—except line breaks. The rhythms of a prose poem originate in its syntax, and the intensity of poetic elements (such as metaphor, imagery, and sound) carry the weight of the poem. Prose poetry developed in the 1850s as a radical new form (some argue, a distinct genre). Prose poetry can be loosely categorized into two types: a surrealistic, dreamlike narrative or a work of associative imagery and ruptured syntax that questions the very nature of poetry and the ability of language to represent meaning. Often these two categories overlap.

When poets leave out punctuation in lineated poems, line break and form need to guide readers to make sense of the syntax. When poets leave out line breaks, as in prose poetry, other poetic elements need to compensate for the tension and surprise line breaks can offer. Here is an example by Stefi Weisburd (B. 1957):

 ### Behind My Ear Is a Little Palace in Broad Daylight

Naturally I think of Him when she taps the needle into the top of my foot. So this is the oft-spoken-of willingness to be pricked on a deity's meridian, blood beading up waxy like a bindi. Under my skin, I picture migraine demons grown frantic as steel pokes through a pore; Godzilla over Tokyo.

Dr. Li posts a lightning rod on the top of my head as if she were a pilgrim to the North Pole. This is where pain pools after commuting from my neck in tiny axiomatic taxies. Listen. Behind my knee, the universe hums in its velvet bag. Through my wrists, a pulse shimmers with electric eels. I imagine leaking out through the needles, diffusing into the little room papered with Chinese music. Imagine sleep gently tacked to the table like a beetle specimen. How dream minions shriek and scatter when Dr. Li returns, bursting into the dark. I have not yet been resurrected I want to proclaim but she is already extracting that desire. Seven times she carries the needles, like offerings, to the red box. Traffic outside is relentless. She says go home little godling. Put on your socks.

In subject, tone, and imagery, "Behind My Ear Is a Little Palace in Broad Daylight" differs considerably from what we expect in a short story, essay, or medical text. Weisburd begins at the **triggering moment,** that is a moment of urgency that launches the poem into existence. Here, Western ideas of spirituality and medicine confront Chinese medicine as the speaker seeks alternative methods to treat migraines. The poem is loosely narrative, and follows the speaker's acupuncture treatment from start to finish, though beginning with thoughts of God and ending with socks certainly creates a sense of narrative surprise. Weisburd also delivers imagery of great intensity: "migraine demons grown frantic as steel pokes through a pore," "pain pools," "the universe hums in its velvet bag," and the treatment room is "papered with Chinese music." Syntax is varied and used in striking ways, as in the one-word imperative: "Listen." Notice the syntax throughout the poem and the effect of varying short and long sentences, such as the blunt "I have not yet been resurrected" or "Put on your socks," both of which allow the reader to register a tone of disappointment. The speaker isn't ready to leave, and, as readers, neither are we.

QUESTIONS AND SUGGESTIONS

1. Write a poem in syllabics. Try either repeating a stanza pattern of different line lengths or establishing one length and developing the poem around that.

2. Choose a favorite object—a ring, an iPod, or a leaf, for example—and explore it through your senses. Experiment with writing three lines for each of your senses: What does it look like, feel like, or smell like? What might it taste like? Use your strongest lines to create a poem.

3. Similar to Weisburd's poem "Behind My Ear Is a Little Palace in Broad Daylight" (p. 70), write a prose poem about an experience visiting a doctor or other health care practioner. What elements of setting (both temporal and spatial), sound, rhythm, syntax, and imagery can you use to help your readers be in the office with you? What specialized diction might you include? Remember: Though prose poetry is written in prose lines, it still practices the same economy of language found in verse poems.

4. To test the integrity and possible effects of lines, try out different free verse versions of the following prose sentence (though any prose sentence will do): "The rain dribbled down the window pane and pooled on the window sill." You might emphasize the phrases, use indentation and white space, or use syllabics (try two syllables per line) to organize the lines and create the visual effect of a rivulet. Come up with as many possibilities as you can.

5. Look closely at the selections in the "Poems to Consider" section that follows, and consider how the poets' use of line, stanza, and form help carry the poems' subjects, tones, and imagery. How does Richard Siken justify his staggered lines in "Meanwhile" (p. 72)? How does Sylvia Plath's "Balloons" (p. 73) earn its short lines and its few longer lines? Take one of the poems that particularly appeals to you and type it up on a computer. Then recast the lines, making them longer, then shorter, then of mixed lengths. Compare your version with the original. See if you can determine why the poet chose to break the lines and how different lineation strategies affect the poem.

POEMS TO CONSIDER

Meanwhile   2005
RICHARD SIKEN (B. 1969)

Driving, dogs barking, how you get used to it, how you make
                     the new streets yours.
Trees outside the window and a big band sound that makes you feel like
              everything's okay,
       a feeling that lasts for one song maybe,   5
                   the parentheses all clicking shut behind you.
        The way we move through time and space, or only time.
The way it's night for many miles, and then suddenly
                            it's not, it's breakfast

and you're standing in the shower for over an hour,   10
                 holding the bar of soap up to the light.
I will keep watch. I will water the yard.
      Knot the tie and go to work. Unknot the tie and go to sleep.
                    I sleep. I dream. I make up things
that I would never say. I say them very quietly.   15
              The trees in wind, the streetlights on,
      the click and flash of cigarettes
being smoked on the lawn, and just a little kiss before we say goodnight.
      It spins like a wheel inside you: green yellow, green blue,
                    green beautiful green.   20
It's simple: it isn't over, it's just begun. It's green. It's still green.

Balloons   1963
SYLVIA PLATH (1932–1963)

Since Christmas they have lived with us,
Guileless and clear,
Oval soul-animals,
Taking up half the space,
Moving and rubbing on the silk   5

Invisible air drifts,
Giving a shriek and pop
When attacked, then scooting to rest, barely trembling.
Yellow cathead, blue fish—
Such queer moons we live with   10

Instead of dead furniture!
Straw mats, white walls
And these traveling
Globes of thin air, red, green,
Delighting   15

The heart like wishes or free
Peacocks blessing
Old ground with a feather
Beaten in starry metals.
Your small   20

Brother is making
His balloon squeak like a cat.
Seeming to see
A funny pink world he might eat on the other side of it,
He bites,   25

Then sits
Back, fat jug
Contemplating a world clear as water.
A red
Shred in his little fist.   30

Don't Look Back   2000

KAY RYAN (B. 1945)

This is not
a problem
for the neckless.
Fish cannot
recklessly   5
swivel their heads
to check
on their fry;
no one expects
this. They are   10
torpedoes of
disinterest,
compact capsules
that rely
on the odds   15
for survival,
unfollowed by
the exact and modest
number of goslings
the S-necked   20
goose is—
who if she
looks back
acknowledges losses
and if she does not   25
also loses.

The Guides   2006

RIGOBERTO GONZÁLEZ (B. 1970)

A birthmark creeping up your face.
If we had mouths we'd kiss it, but the gods who made us
gave us windows through which everything escapes.
The last man who loved us flew out like a sink

and he took the entire kitchen with him.   5
Let us fondle your mole like a wet papaya seed
and we'll build something bigger, beautiful and black—
an avocado with a bubble of gold instead of a testicle.
In autumn we grow fingertips and the tulips change back
to the poor white roots who growl like scars.   10
And the spidering commences: leaf crawling after leaf.
We will remember you each time a cricket
because its chirp is another small thing we can't hold.
And though the gods who made us gave us legs
we are like chairs to be weighed down into place.   15
We travel nonetheless. When you sleep we move
into darkness; when you dream we hide among objects.
When you die we walk you through the funnels
of final song. Let us know when you finish
making pumice from the beehive of your heart   20
and we'll teach you how to burn the bed from the inside out:
from the wood a casket, from the sheets a shroud,
from the flesh a million cherries on the ends of cigarettes.

1. the fever (starring kristy b)   2010
from "Orange Girl Cast"
SIMONE MUENCH (B. 1970)

Sweet Kristy of the culvert, the ankle turn, the verb imperfect, and sailors'
notebooks. In this metropolis of binoculars and chicken bones, in this
city black with chicken-wire alchemists and bloody gutters, she feigns
a fever in her red brassiere, her lavender dress lilting across headlights
of chrome sedans: skin livid-exquisite with light bulbs and batteries beneath sinister-shouldered men, zombie drunk from fermented peaches
and her silk stocking smell. Sweet Kristy of the corset, born of Anne
Boleyn and a bird collector, born of alum and blindfolds, born to unzip
men's breath, their clamorous wrists with an alphabet on her breast, a
switchblade pinned to her taffeta thigh. Where are you leading with your
eyelets and hooks, catching men with clothespins and rain in the perfect
sphere of your dance hall mouth.

Gruss   2008
DEAN YOUNG (B. 1955)

Whenever I'm not drunk enough
is a waste of time.
I carry within me a hypnagogic dawn,

maybe the insulation gnawed by rats,
maybe I'll never be back.   5
Ha ha to the mating swans.
Ha ha to the sepulchral golden slime
that shines and shines and shines.
This party started long before I arrived
with the last of wacko youthful chatter,   10
a curious crew, prone to slam-dance depression.
What's the matter? Don't know, maybe so
much hilarity is a strain on us or at least
we like to boast in loopy communiqués
to those who've seen through us   15
and love us for what they see,
maybe some trees, a packing factory,
some secretive birdie hopping about
with a grasshopper in its mouth.
I don't know what I'd do without you   20
although that's how I spend most of my time.
It'd be unbearable otherwise,
like a vacation without sleeping pills,
without some creaking rain
abating the granite's breakdown.   25
Such a paltry gesture, my surrender.

5

THE SOUND
(AND LOOK) OF SENSE

Before printing was developed in the fifteenth century, poetry was primarily an oral art. Instead of seeing it on the page, the audience heard it in songs, ballads, epics, and tales. Formal meters, with countable stresses, helped the poet compose and remember the poem and allowed a poem's form to be followed by its hearers; rhyme signaled line ends like a typewriter bell. Since the sixteenth century, and especially after the rise of general literacy in the nineteenth century, poetry has increasingly emphasized the visual. Today we are more accustomed to seeing a poem than to hearing it, and we must remind ourselves to read poems aloud lest we miss their essential music.

In this famous passage from "An Essay on Criticism," Alexander Pope (1688–1744) shows some of the tricks verse can perform while he calls to task poets who plod along by writing only by the "numbers," by meter and rhyme alone.

> But most by numbers judge a poet's song;
> And smooth or rough, with them, is right or wrong:
> In the bright muse though thousand charms conspire,
> Her voice is all these tuneful fools admire;
> Who haunt Parnassus° but to please their ear,   5
> Not mend their minds; as some to church repair,
> Not for the doctrine, but the music there.
> These equal syllables alone require,
> Though oft the ear the open vowels tire;
> While expletives their feeble aid do join;   10
> And ten low words oft creep in one dull line:
> While they ring round the same unvaried chimes,

With sure returns of still expected rhymes;
Where'er you find "the cooling western breeze,"
In the next line, it "whispers through the trees":   15
If crystal streams "with pleasing murmurs creep,"
The reader's threatened (not in vain) with "sleep":
Then, at the last and only couplet fraught
With some unmeaning thing they call a thought,
A needless Alexandrine ends the song,   20
That, like a wounded snake, drags its slow length along.

5 Parnassus: Greek mountain, sacred to the Muses.

The passage constitutes a library of poetic effects. In mentioning the tediousness of too many open vowels, he provides a line of them: "though oft the
ear the open vowels tire" (line 9). He illustrates how filler words such as "do"
can result in awkward lines: "[w]hile expletives their feeble aid do join," and
how monotonously monosyllables can move: "And ten low words oft creep in
one dull line." He makes an illustrative hexameter (the "Alexandrine") sinu-
ously sluggish with the line, "That, like a wounded snake, drags its slow length
along." Further on in his "Essay," Pope demonstrates how sound should echo
sense:

True ease in writing comes from art, not chance,
As those move easiest who have learned to dance.
'Tis not enough no harshness gives offense,
The sound must seem an echo to the sense:
Soft is the strain when Zephyr° gently blows,   30
And the smooth stream in smoother numbers flows;
But when loud surges lash the sounding shore,
The hoarse, rough verse should like the torrent roar:
When Ajax strives some rock's vast weight to throw,
The line too labors, and the words move slow;   35
Not so, when swift Camilla scours the plain,
Flies o'er th' unbending corn, and skims along the main.

30 Zephyr: the west wind.

Pope's lines show the difference between a "smooth stream" and "loud surges," between the heaving of strongman Ajax and the graceful stride of Camilla, who was
said to be able to run so fast that the stalks of grain wouldn't move under her feet.

In this chapter we will examine the effects produced by a poem's visible
shape and by its sounds: *visible form, repetition, alliteration, assonance, onomatopoeia,* and *rhyme.*

Visible Form

As poets in the past century turned more and more to nonmetrical verse, they relied heavily on the visual dimension of poetry. On the page every poem has a visible form, a shape that conveys a message and supports the poem's content. Is the poem slender, bony, quick? Solid, heavy, full? Are the lines even, orderly, smooth? Or raggedy, jumpy, anxious, mixing long and short lines? Or perhaps lines get gradually longer or shorter? Are some lines indented irregularly or in a pattern? Does the poem use stanzas of the same or of a varying number of lines? Are the stanzas in narrow couplets, long tercets, or do they have a distinctive shape, like those of Moore's "To a Steam Roller" (p. 69)?

In short, visible form can give readers an accurate first impression of the poem. Like a good title, appearance can be informative, as well as enticing. How does the visible impact of form help readers respond to the poem?

Stanzas, for instance, can express—often create—a poem's organization. They may be "closed," ending with a completed sentence, or "open," continuing a sentence across the stanza break. (The word *stanza* is Italian for "room"; each room must be self-contained yet somehow lead into the other rooms of the poem.) Like paragraphs in prose, stanzas may correspond to segments of an idea or argument, as in Whitman's "A Noiseless Patient Spider" (p. 30), where they present the comparison of venturing spider and venturing soul, or stanzas can delineate a series of directives, as in Frank Bidart's "Song" (p. 84). Open stanzas help Williams express the cat's poise and hesitancy in "Poem" (p. 68) and help Moore express the fluid undersea world of "The Fish" (p. 207). When writing, the careful poet seizes the opportunities visible form offers.

Fixed stanzas of a certain number of lines can often help form a trellis over which the poem can grow. In general, **couplets** (two-line stanzas) have a stark focusing power and lend themselves to poems about contrasts, contradictions, and couples (love, romance, break ups, etc.); **tercets** (three-line stanzas) can convey a sense of unevenness and tension; and **quatrains** (four-line stanzas), due to their longer length, are helpful for narrative poems and poems exploring balance. In Thom Gunn's "The Beautician" (p. 116), the five-line stanzas of rhymed iambic pentameter create a stable unit through which the story of the beautician and her dead friend unfold; the patient craft of each stanza mirrors that of the beautician herself. Thus, there is an essential equanimity between form and content.

In this poem, Liz Rosenberg (B. 1955) uses increasingly shorter stanzas to suggest the silencing of women:

 ## The Silence of Women

Old men, as time goes on, grow softer, sweeter,
  while their wives get angrier.
You see them hauling the men across the mall

or pushing them down on chairs,
"Sit there! and don't you move!"   5
A lifetime of *yes* has left them
hissing bent as snakes.
It seems even their bones will turn
against them, once the fruitful years are gone.
Something snaps off the houselights,   10
and the cells go dim;
the chicken hatching back into the egg.

Oh lifetime of silence!
words scattered like a sybil's leaves.
Voice thrown into a baritone storm—   15
whose shrilling is a soulful wind
blown through an instrument
that cannot beat time

but must make music
any way it can.   20

In this poem, women have words, but they have been scattered; they have a voice, but it has been drowned out by men's "baritone storm" and turned into "a soulful wind" that "must make music / any way it can." The poem realizes this suppression visually in the dwindling of stanzas from twelve to six to two lines, as well as in the shortening of the lines. The poem's shape acts as an emblem of its meaning.

> *Guiding the intellect and senses, form presents the detailed textures of the world and the language with renewed attentiveness.*
>
> —Peter Campion, from "Grasshoppers: A Notebook"

Dropped-line is another formal visual element, which probably originated in verse plays. In printing Shakespeare's plays, for instance, when a single pentameter line is divided between two speakers, the second part of the line is shown as "dropped":

Hamlet: Did you not speak to it?
Horatio: My lord, I did,
            But answer made it none. Yet once methought....

Dropped-line produces rhythmical variation and visual emphasis. In Charles Wright's "January II" (p. 92), dropped lines suggest alternative paths, asides, and modifications the mind makes as it considers and responds to a winter scene. In the following poem, Nancy Eimers (B. 1954) uses dropped-line and indentation to indicate rhythmic subordination, guiding both eye and voice:

A Night Without Stars

And the lake was a dark spot
           on a lung.
Some part of its peace was dead; the rest was temporary. Sleeping ducks
       and geese,
goose shit underfoot   5
       and wet gray blades of grass.
The fingerlings like sleeping bullets
           hung deep in the troughs of the hatchery
and cold traveled each one end to end,
such cold,   10
      such distances.

We lay down in the grass on our backs—
beyond the hatchery the streetlights were mired in fog and so
there were no stars,
           or stars would say there was no earth.   15

Just a single homesick firefly lit on a grass blade.
Just our fingers
       curled and clutching grass,
this dark our outmost hide, and under it
            true skin.   20

The speaker and a companion go to a fish hatchery where the eerie fog seems like a lung, and the lake is an ominous spot. The tiny fish are "like sleeping bullets" and the speaker interprets the lone firefly as "homesick." The outing is a failure; they can't lie happily on the grass and watch the stars. Notice how the visual form suggests the current of the lake, as well as the lone firefly and the fingers clutching the grass.

In a general way, the device of dropped-line registers disjunction between expectation and event. We read, for instance,

    such cold,
       such distances

somewhat differently than we would if the second phrase appeared either on the same line with the first or as a completely separate line flush left. The device suggests a remoteness, a dropping of the voice. Each of the eight dropped lines or indentations has its own singular tone or effect. The combined length of lines 7 and 8, for instance, suggests the long rectangular pools or troughs in which the young fish are raised, and the dropping of line 8 implies the depth fingerlings lie beneath the surface of the water. Facing the current that runs through the troughs, the fish seem in touch with distances as well as the chill, fresh water. The brevity of the dropped-line—"true skin"—helps register the vulnerability the speaker feels beneath the foggy darkness that closes over "our outmost hide."

In some poems, the visual or spatial element dominates and becomes explicitly pictorial. "Easter Wings" by George Herbert (1593–1633), written in meter, is an early example of this tradition:

Easter Wings

Lord, who createdst man in wealth and store,
   Though foolishly he lost the same,
      Decaying more and more
         Till he became
           Most poore;   5
         With thee
       O let me rise
     As larks, harmoniously,
   And sing this day thy victories;
Then shall the fall further the flight in me.   10

My tender age in sorrow did beginne;
   And still with sicknesses and shame
      Thou didst so punish sinne,
         That I became
           Most thinne.   15
         With thee
       Let me combine,
     And feel this day thy victorie;
   For if I imp° my wing on thine,
Affliction shall advance the flight in me.   20

19 imp: to graft. Alludes to a term in falconry.

The lines of each stanza decrease and then increase by one foot, to make the poem look like two pairs of angels' wings (turn the book on its side to see them). This rhythmic visual shape embodies the theme of how grace gives the speaker spiritual flight. Poets have used the shapes of a Coke bottle, key, fireplug, umbrella, lightbulb, New York State, and even a swan and its reflection to construct visual poems. Most poets writing today handle such playful visual impulses with subtlety. You want to surprise your readers, not bore them by being obvious.

Often the shape of a poem offers a subtle undercurrent, like this famous William Carlos Williams poem:

The Red Wheelbarrow

so much depends
upon

a red wheel
barrow

glazed with rain   5
water

beside the white
chickens

One could view each stanza as a miniature wheelbarrow in side view, with the longer first line suggesting the handle. Visual and rhythmic forms combine. This tiny still life catches energy in stasis, a vital moment at rest, where each line balances upon the next. Without punctuation,

> *In* ception! We must
> go deeper!
>
> *Every poem is a poem within a poem: the poem of the idea within the poem of the words.*
> —Wallace Stevens, from "Adagia"

the poet must rely on line breaks and stanza breaks to help the reader make sense of the syntax. Notice how Williams does not simply use phrasal line breaks but instead uses the form to visually and even sensually isolate each element, and pull the reader in.

Repetition

Repetition lies at the heart of all the arts. Consider, for instance, how necessary both repetition and variation are to making music. In poetry we find repetition in the small echo sounded in rhyme, in the larger rhyme schemes of a poem, in patterns of form, and in the concept of *verse* itself, which turns and returns on the line. Repeating elements—whether a rhyme scheme, a chorus, or a catalogue of heroes—helped oral poets compose by ear. Repeating shapes—or even avoiding repeating them—helps poets today form the poem on the page.

In poems written in fixed forms, a particular kind of repetition often defines the form. The **villanelle** (Elizabeth Bishop's "One Art," p. 58) is based on repeating the poem's first and third lines in alternating stanzas. The first stanza of a **sestina** (Weldon Kees's "After the Trial," p. 93) establishes end words that are repeated in a different order in subsequent stanzas. The **ghazal** repeats an end word established in its first couplet. In the **pantoum,** the second and fourth lines of a quatrain recur as the first and third lines of subsequent stanzas. A fuller discussion of these and other forms appears in Appendix II.

In nonfixed forms, repetition often serves as a structural device in a variety of ways, as in Robin Becker's "When Someone Dies Young" (p. 148). More formally, repetition becomes the **refrain** often found in songs. The refrain is the line or lines regularly repeated from stanza to stanza, usually at the end. Often we remember only the refrain of a song. In "Recuerdo" (Spanish for *recollection* or *memory*), Edna St. Vincent Millay (1892–1950) organizes the poem by beginning the stanzas with a refrain:

Recuerdo

We were very tired, we were very merry—
We had gone back and forth all night on the ferry.

It was bare and bright, and smelled like a stable—
But we looked into a fire, we leaned across a table,
We lay on a hill-top underneath the moon;   5
And the whistles kept blowing, and the dawn came soon.

We were very tired, we were very merry—
We had gone back and forth all night on the ferry;
And you ate an apple, and I ate a pear,
From a dozen of each we had bought somewhere;   10
And the sky went wan, and the wind came cold,
And the sun rose dripping, a bucketful of gold.

We were very tired, we were very merry,
We had gone back and forth all night on the ferry.
We hailed, "Good morrow, mother!" to a shawl-covered head,   15
And bought a morning paper, which neither of us read;
And she wept, "God bless you!" for the apples and pears,
And we gave her all our money but our subway fares.

Of course, as her poem suggests, memory is itself a form of repetition. The refrain mimics how we return to a powerful memory and draw from it lingering images. Simply repeating a word or phrase, perhaps with variations, can lend a tune to a passage, as in Robert Hayden's "Those Winter Sundays" (p. 6); we hear emotion in the doubled phrase: "What did I know, what did I know / of love's austere and lonely offices?" Judicious, meaningful repetition can enrich a poem's emotional currency; careless repetition, however, can dull the impact of a phrase or image.

Repetition in this poem helps Frank Bidart (B. 1939) convey a loaded invitation to the reader:

 ## Song

You know that it is there, lair
where the bear ceases
for a time even to exist.

Crawl in. You have at last killed
enough and eaten enough to be fat   5
enough to cease for a time to exist.

Crawl in. It takes talent to live at night, and scorning
others you had that talent, but now you sniff
the season where you must cease to exist.

Crawl in. Whatever for good or ill   10
grows within you needs
you for a time to cease to exist.

It is not raining inside
tonight. You know that it is there. Crawl in.

"Crawl in" is repeated four times in stanzas 2, 3, 4, and 5 and invites the reader into the poem and into the metaphoric cave. Bidart uses this directive to lure us in, even though the cave is a scary space in which we may "cease to exist," another phrase repeated in the first four stanzas. In effect, the two refrains act as bookends, which trap the reader and suspend us in the poem's world, as in a haunted place. Bidart uses syntactic variety, line breaks, placement in the line, and imagery to make each repetition daunting and fresh.

Alliteration and Assonance

Alliteration is the repetition of consonant sounds in several words in a passage; **assonance** is the repetition of vowel sounds. Alliteration that begins a word or phrase usually jumps out at us and when overused can become dull. In Pope's line, "But when loud surges lash the sounding shore," the *l*'s of "*l*oud" and "*l*ash" and the *s*'s of "*s*urges" and "*s*ounding" are balanced with meaning. More subtle is the alliteration of "la*sh*" and "*sh*ore," because the first word of the pair doesn't start with the syllable's sound. Assonance may also be subtle, as in "l*ou*d" and "s*ou*nd-ing," where it links the noise of surf and breakers striking the shore—echoing, too, in the *d*'s following the vowel sounds.

Consider another line in Pope's passage:

Thĕ líne | tŏo lá|bŏrs, ̆and | thĕ wórds | móve slów.

Long vowels and alliterating *l*'s in "*l*ine," "too," "*l*abors," "*m*ove," and "*sl*ow" in-crease the dragging effect of the line, though the assonance in "t*oo*" and "m*o*ve" also slows the sentence's progress.

With the same devices Howard Nemerov (1920–1991) creates a very different music in these lines from "The Fourth of July":

> It is, indeed, splendid:
> Showers of roses in the sky, fountains
> Of emeralds, and those profusely scattered zircons
> Falling, and falling, flowering as they fall
> And followed distantly by a noise of thunder.
> My eyes are half-afloat in happy tears.

The flowing alliteration of *f*'s and *l*'s centers on the repetitions in "Falling, and falling, flowering as they fall." The assonance in "Sh*ow*ers" and "f*ou*ntains," which frames the first full line, shows up two lines below as internal rhyme in "fl*ow*ering"—which also picks up the *er* sound in "em*er*alds," "scatt*er*ed," "zir-cons," and then in "thund*er*." Assonance and internal rhyme also link "roses," "those," and "profusely," and both alliteration and assonance link "*half*-" and "*happy*" in the last line.

Alliteration, assonance, repetition, and other sound techniques form a map over the poem, allowing for nonlinear connections across a poem's surface. Alliteration, assonance, and rhyme may serve both as a musical and as an organizing device. Howard Nemerov gets the last word in this short poem:

 Power to the People

Why are the stamps adorned with kings and presidents?
That we may lick their hinder parts and thump their heads.

Alliteration strategically links "*h*inder parts" and "*h*eads"; the assonance in "presi-d*e*nts" and "h*e*ads" helps make the couplet formally complete, nearly rhyming, and funny.

Rhyme

By definition, **rhyme** repeats stressed vowel sounds and the consonants that fol-low. Examples of **exact rhymes** include J*ane*–re*strain*, gr*oan*–b*one*, ensn*are*–h*air*, appl*ause*–g*auze*, and pr*iest*–y*east*. Rhymes usually fall on stressed syllables. Unlike the mellifluous Romance languages, English is difficult to rhyme. Many common words have no natural rhymes, such as "circle" or "month." For some words, there is only one natural rhyme; str*ength*–l*ength* and f*ountain*–m*ountain* are examples. *Gloves* and *doves* have often reared up in love poems only because of rhyme. Also, because many rhymes in English have become cliché, poets find it hard to make fresh exact rhymes and consequently turn to **blank verse** (unrhymed iambic pentameter) and to **slant rhyme** (inexact rhyme). Often poets use a combination of exact and slant rhymes.

Slant rhymes can be inventive, created through alliteration, for instance, as in l*ove*–m*ove*, br*ain*–g*one*, or ch*ill*–f*ull*; or through **consonance** (the same or similar consonants with different main vowels), as in s*ad*–s*od*, b*ell*–b*ull*, or p*illow*–p*alor*. Assonance can also create a vocalic echo as in b*ean*–sw*eet* or h*ow*–cl*oud*. Another slant rhyme technique involves rhyming stressed with unstressed syllables, as in s*ee*–pret*ty*, f*ull*–e*agle*, and und*er*–st*ir*.

Whereas exact rhyme can give us an impression of rightness, precision, or fulfillment, off-rhyme can give us a sense of something amiss, as in the rhyme of "wished–vanished" that closes Christian Wiman's "Poštolka" (p. 37), the rhymes "skill–beautiful–all" in the final stanza of Thom Gunn's "The Beautician" (p. 116), or in the following World War I poem by Wilfred Owen. The poem's persistent refusal to rhyme gives it an off-key sound that fits its ironic theme.

Arms and the Boy

Let the boy try along this bayonet-blade
How cold steel is, and keen with hunger of blood;
Blue with all malice, like a madman's flash;
And thinly drawn with famishing for flesh.

Lend him to stroke these blind, blunt bullet-leads   5
Which long to nuzzle in the hearts of lads,
Or give him cartridges of fine zinc teeth,
Sharp with the sharpness of grief and death.

For his teeth seem for laughing round an apple.
There lurk no claws behind his fingers supple;   10
And God will grow no talons at his heels,
Nor antlers through the thickness of his curls.

Owen's linking together of "flash" and "flesh," "leads" and "lads," and other rhyme pairs help make his argument against war. Rhymes also can occur irregularly to emphasize certain key words or moments in a poem. Here, Robert Frost varies line length and rhyme pattern in "After Apple-Picking":

 ## After Apple-Picking

My long two-pointed ladder's sticking through a tree
Toward heaven still,
And there's a barrel that I didn't fill
Beside it, and there may be two or three
Apples I didn't pick upon some bough.   5
But I am done with apple-picking now.
Essence of winter sleep is on the night,
The scent of apples: I am drowsing off.
I cannot rub the strangeness from my sight
I got from looking through a pane of glass   10
I skimmed this morning from the drinking trough
And held against the world of hoary grass.
It melted, and I let it fall and break.
But I was well
Upon my way to sleep before it fell,   15
And I could tell
What form my dreaming was about to take.
Magnified apples appear and disappear,
Stem end and blossom end.
And every fleck of russet showing clear.   20
My instep arch not only keeps the ache,

It keeps the pressure of a ladder-round.
I feel the ladder sway as the boughs bend.
And I keep hearing from the cellar bin
The rumbling sound   25
Of load on load of apples coming in.
For I have had too much
Of apple-picking: I am overtired
Of the great harvest I myself desired.
There were ten thousand thousand fruit to touch,   30
Cherish in hand, lift down, and not let fall.
For all
That struck the earth,
No matter if not bruised or spiked with stubble,
Went surely to the cider-apple heap   35
As of no worth.
One can see what will trouble
This sleep of mine, whatever sleep it is.
Were he not gone,
The woodchuck could say whether it's like his   40
Long sleep, as I describe its coming on,
Or just some human sleep.

Ars celare artem ("The art is to hide the art")
—Horace

Although they occur sometimes in adjacent lines, the rhymes may be separated by as many as three other lines, as are "break–take" in lines 13 and 17 and "end–bend" in lines 19 and 23. The triple-rhyme "well–fell–tell" in the quickly turning lines 14, 15, and 16 helps to convey the indefinable transition from waking to dreaming.

Near the end of the poem, "heap" in line 35 doesn't find its closing end-rhyme until "sleep" in line 42, although the word teasingly occurs three times *within* intervening lines, as does the assonant "see." This irregular rhyme scheme suggests the tired gathering of apples and the speaker's exhaustion. Unlike end-rhyme, **internal rhyme** may occur anywhere within lines for expressive effects, as in the "*um*" sounds that rumble through these lines:

And I keep hearing *from* the cellar bin
The r*um*bling sound
Of load on load of apples c*om*ing in.

Internal rhyme may be overt and corny as in the old song's "the l*azy*, h*azy*, cr*azy* d*ays* of summer" or subtle as in these lines of Richard Wilbur's "Year's End":

> I've known the wind by water banks to shake
> The late leaves down, which frozen where they fell
> And held in ice as dancers in a spell
> Fluttered all winter long into a lake...

The whirling sound at the end of line two results mainly from the internal rhyme of "held," which links the end-rhyme "fell" and spins the voice toward the end-rhyme "spell." Although hardly noticeable, the rhyme, or repetition, of two *in*'s— "*in* ice as dancers *in* a spell"—also produces the feeling of whirling, as does the assonance in "A*nd*" and "d*a*ncers."

The best rhymes uncover subliminal connections between emotions and ideas in a poem. Renaissance poets quickly seized the implications that rhymes such as *womb–tomb* and *birth–earth* made, but such rhymes became too expected for later generations to use. The advantage of working in rhyme is that it can help you think beyond the logical and obvious, leading you to a word or sound that wouldn't otherwise come to mind. But when the poet writes only for the rhyme, the poem will likely thud and can even sound silly. Robert Frost tested for rhymes by seeing if he could detect which had occurred to the poet first. Both words had to seem equally natural, equally called for by what was being said. If one or the other seemed dragged in more for rhyme than sense, he considered the rhyming a failure. Besides creating sound patterns and connections across the poem, rhyme, whenever used, should support a poem's content.

Onomatopoeia

Words can have sound effects built in: *clunk, snarl, buzz, hiss, crunch, whirr, murmur, roar, boing.* Such words, called onomatopoetic (noun: **onomatopoeia**), imitate their meaning. They will often imitate sounds, like those just listed, but also express size, motion, touch, and other qualities. Notice *skimpy, skinny, spindly,* or *fat, rotund, humongous, pudge-pot.* Notice how lightly *delicate* hits its syllables, how heavily *ponderous* does. Feel how your mouth says *pinched, shut, open, round, hard, soft, smooth.* A familiar example of onomatopoeia follows by Tennyson:

> The moan of doves in immemorial elms
> And murmuring of innumerable bees

Overdoing it is the fun of this poem by Bob Hicok (B. 1960):

See Side

> Mind as wave: whoosh. As wet. As yet
> thinking needs a dress to wear, what better look
> than sea green or sea foam, within
> never gets out without without, how cool

is that, that the sealed self's   5
not an option, hence the object of my affection's
conception. As in, I notice you
on your boogie board, therefore I exist
to see you're bad at balance, a savant
of oops. The fall's all we've perfected,   10
reaching for the apple with the words of our hands,
the yums, the Henny Pennys at our disposal.
I com one-ly, you two. Boo-hoo. Group hug, the all
of us, this wave charging hard, foaming
at the mouth, as if to slather with embrace.   15

The density of diction and sound effects here—alliteration, assonance, onomatopoeia, rhyme, and rhythm—capture the effect of the sea. Notice the allusions to the Bible (the fall and the apple) and to children's stories (Henny Penny) to create a poem bursting with lush sounds and ambiguity. The "sealed self's / not an option" nods to seals and the metaphor of the sea as well as to the blurring of individual identity and human nature. Hicok's dense diction and syntax strain against language itself ("the words of our hands" that are also strangely "Henny Pennys'"), as the poem takes on themes of loneliness and encounter, singularity and multiplicity. Though too many sound effects can be risky, all the poetic elements work together in Hicok's poem. Readers are immersed in the sound of the sea and the poem's playfulness.

QUESTIONS AND SUGGESTIONS

1. Read aloud the poems in the "Poems to Consider" section in order not to miss the sound effects of repetition, rhyme, alliteration, and assonance. Jean Toomer's "Reapers" (p. 92) offers several striking sound techniques. Notice the alliteration of "*Black*," "*bleeds*," "*blade*," and "*Blood*," which adds rich, sensory resonance to this short poem. Experiment with writing a short poem in which each line interconnects with other lines through the use of sound devices discussed in this chapter.

2. Similar to Cate Marvin's "Dear Petrarch" (p. 91), write an **epistolary poem** (that is, a poem in the form of a letter) to another poet from this anthology. What sound devices, imagery, or diction can you adapt to your response poem? If you borrow any lines, be sure to italicize them and give credit to the original author.

3. Recalling Herbert's "Easter Wings" (p. 82), use shape to form a visual poem of your own. Try a car, a mouse, a shoe, or a state with a recognizable shape.

What can writing visual poems teach you about form and line breaks in general?

4. Experiment with writing a love poem that uses harsh-sounding words (e.g., *screech, sludge, wretched, frump*). Let the sounds guide the poem. What challenges and delights did you encounter? How do diction and sound affect the overall mood of the poem?

5. Similar to Charles Wright's poem "January II" in the "Poems to Consider" section that follows, write a poem in homage of a particular month that similarly uses the technique of dropped lines. Experiment with ending your poem on a strong image, as Wright does with "panting, lolling its black tongue."

POEMS TO CONSIDER

Dear Petrarch   2001
CATE MARVIN (B.1969)

> *The sweet singing of virtuous and beautiful ladies...*
> More like dogs barking, more like a warning now.
> When our mouths open the hole looks black,
> and the hole of it holds a shadow. Some keep
>
> saying there's nothing left to tell, nothing to tell.   5
> If that's the truth I'll open my door to any
> stranger who rattles the lock. When my mouth
> opens it will scream, simply because the hole
>
> of it holds that sound. As for your great ideas,
> literature, and the smell of old books cracked—   10
> the stacks are a dark area, and anyone could find
> herself trapped, legs forced, spine cracked.
>
> It's a fact. Everyone knows it. If I lived in your
> time, the scrolls of my gown would have curled
> into knots. It's about being dragged by the hair—   15
> the saint, the harlot both have bald patches. Girls
>
> today walking down the street may look sweet,
> chewing wads of pink gum. And the woman at the bar
> may never read. Lots of ladies sing along to the radio
> now. But the hole of our mouths holds a howl.   20

Do Not Disturb   2003
MARY RUEFLE (B. 1952)

In a milk-white mist in the middle of the wood
there are two dead vowels.

The vowels in the wood are cared for by birds
who cover them in strawberry leaves

and in the winter when the bodies are mounded   5
with snow, owls keep a vigil
from a nearby branch
by the light of the moon.

Poor vowels in the wood!
Poor vowels in the wood!   10

They can't remember the vows in the wood
when they did woo.

How before they were dead
they lay on their backs
and looked at the clouds,   15
speaking softly to one another for hours.

Reapers   1923
JEAN TOOMER (1894–1967)

Black reapers with the sound of steel on stones
Are sharpening scythes. I see them place the hones
In their hip-pocket as a thing that's done,
And start their silent swinging, one by one.
Black horses drive a mower through the weeds,   5
And there, a field rat, startled, squealing bleeds,
His belly close to ground. I see the blade,
Blood-stained, continue cutting weeds and shade.

January II   2002
CHARLES WRIGHT (B. 1935)

A cold draft blows steadily from a crack in the window jamb.
It's good for the soul.
For some reason, I think of monuments in the high desert,
                              and what dissembles them.

We're all born with a one-way ticket, of course,   5
Thus do we take our deaths up on our shoulders and walk and walk,
Trying to get back.

We'd like to move as the water moves.
We'd like to cover the earth
                         the way the wind covers the earth.   10
We'd like to burn our way there, like fire.

It's not in the cards.
Uncertainty harbors us like winter mist—
                         the further we go, the deeper it gets.
Sundown now, and wind from the northwest.   15

The month is abandoned.
                     Volvos go wandering to and fro
Like lost polar bears. The landscape is simple and brown.
The future's behind us, panting, lolling its black tongue.

After the Trial   1941
WELDON KEES (1914–1955)

    Hearing the judges' well-considered sentence,
    The prisoner saw long plateaus of guilt,
    And thought of all the dismal furnished rooms
    The past assembled, the eyes of parents
    Staring through walls as though forever   5
    To condemn and wound his innocence.

    And if I raise my voice, protest my innocence,
    The judges won't revoke their sentence.
    I could stand screaming in this box forever,
    Leaving them deaf to everything but guilt;   10
    All the machinery of law devised by parents
    Could not be stopped though fire swept the rooms.

    Whenever my thoughts move to all those rooms
    I sat alone in, capable of innocence,
    I know now I was not alone, that parents   15
    Always were there to speak the hideous sentence:
    "You are our son; be good; we know your guilt;
    We stare through walls and see your thoughts forever."

    Sometimes I wished to go away forever;
    I dreamt of strangers and of stranger rooms
    Where every corner held the light of guilt.   20
    Why do the judges stare? I saw no innocence
    In them when they pronounced the sentence;
    I heard instead the believing voice of parents.

I can remember evenings when my parents,   25
Settling my future happily forever,
Would frown before they spoke the sentence:
"Someday the time will come to leave these rooms
Where, under our watchful eyes, you have been innocent;
Remember us before you seize the world of guilt."   30

Their eyes burn. How can I deny my guilt
When I am guilty in the sight of parents?
I cannot think that even they were innocent.
At least I shall not have to wait forever
To be escorted to the silent rooms   35
Where darkness promises a final sentence.

We walk forever to the doors of guilt,
Pursued by our own sentences and eyes of parents,
Never to enter innocent and quiet rooms.

PART

II

CONTENT

6

SUBJECT MATTER

Though no subject today is off-limits to the poet, several misconceptions can blind the beginning poet to the freedom of subject matter. Sometimes students assume that poems should be about traditional or momentous subjects such as the seasons, love (especially a lost love), and "the meaning of life." Similarly, some beginning poets suppose the ordinary, everyday things that we experience—things close to the nose, as William Carlos Williams says—aren't proper subjects. Writing under such assumptions, the poet misses scores of opportunities. As filmmaker and writer Jean Cocteau said, "Take a commonplace, clean and polish it, light it so that it produces the same effect of youth and freshness and spontaneity as it did originally, and you have done a poet's job."

Pay attention to the everyday world we usually ignore, and you will find ripe subjects for poems. The common sparrows in the backyard, a construction site at night, a reclusive neighbor, or a cat stepping carefully into and out of a pot can offer you as much raw material as any elaborate subject.

Also blinding for the beginning poet is the assumption that poetry is mainly direct self-expression: what happened to *me*, what *I feel*. Poets risk psychobabble—merely reporting their own feelings and experiences without considering the reader. Looking only inward can keep poets from looking outward. If they notice the construction site, the aging neighbor, or the cat, they only write about how such things affect them personally, rather than reveal through evocative images something a reader might be interested in and want to experience. The object of poetry, says Hugo Williams, "is to find out something you didn't know by collaborating with the language...poetry is research not self-expression." The poet determined to talk just about him or herself isn't likely to notice how fast a tree's shadow moves in an hour or a vapor trail unraveling in the sky.

We're all tempted to write poems that spill out our feelings and proclaim our thoughts. And poets, of course, do express themselves, though rarely as directly as it may seem. Telling your reader to feel sad won't likely work. However, using sensory information and showing a sad scene allows the reader to experience sadness. In the following poem, notice how William Matthews (1942–1997) begins by deflecting attention away from the speaker, thereby taking in the scene's deeper significance:

Men at My Father's Funeral

The ones his age who shook my hand
on their way out sent fear along
my arm like heroin. These weren't
men mute about their feelings,
or what's a body language for?   5

and I, the glib one, who'd stood
with my back to my father's body
and praised the heart that attacked him?
I'd made my stab at elegy,
the flesh made word: the very spit   10

in my mouth was sour with ruth
and eloquence. What could be worse?
Silence, the anthem of my father's
new country. And thus this babble,
like a dial tone, from our bodies.   15

By decentering the son's grief (which nevertheless lies at the heart of this poem), Matthews foregrounds the small gestures that reveal the mourners' hidden feelings: a mixture of generosity and selfishness. The older men lament the loss of their friend and at the same time fear for their own lives. The men don't admit they have such feelings, but the poet makes these feelings palpable in the awkward handshake between the men and the son, which jolts his arm "like heroin"—powerful, dangerous, and forbidden.

Another poet might simply say he stood before his father's coffin to eulogize him, but Matthews has his speaker stand with his *back* to his father's body, suggesting he, too, wanted to avoid confronting death. The son, "the glib one," speaks the appropriate words of praise for his father, though they turn sour in his mouth for all that remains unsaid. All this noise—body language and spoken language, gestures meaningless as a "dial tone"—speaks of the survivors' desire to drown out the silence they feel hovering around them. Matthews's poem shows how small commonplace actions speak more powerfully than grand pronouncements and demonstrates how effective understatement is as a tool for writing about crises. Of course, a funeral is sad, and the poet who uses inflated language and abstractions won't convince us to feel any sadder. Understatement and concrete details, however, invite the reader to feel as much or as little is necessary.

Subjects and Objects

New poets sometimes despair that everything has already been written. Love, loss, death, birth—the great universal themes of humanity have been written many times over. But the poets of each generation must explore them from their unique perspective in their own idiom and voice. The world is much the same place it has always been. We have cruelty and heroism, wars and famine, peace and bounty; we are selfish and narrow, generous and wise. We love, we work, we try to make sense of life. But we experience these things differently from other ages. Our relationship with the natural world and technology has changed, as have relationships between men and women, children and parents, and citizens and governments. We live with adult day care centers, surveillance cameras, GPSs, and gated communities.

Find what is close to your nose. Venture into the parts of your neighborhood you have always passed up. Step into the bingo hall, bait shop, or paint store. Talk to the butcher at the supermarket or your cable repair person. Hang out in a coffee shop and listen to the banter, or start up a conversation at a yard sale.

Explore what makes you and your world unique—your point of view, your particular upbringing, your heritage. Family stories may open out into vivid land-scapes as they did for Rita Dove (B. 1952) in her Pulitzer-Prize-winning sequence about her grandparents, *Thomas and Beulah* (1986). Dove began with a story her grandmother told about her grandfather "when he was young, coming up on a riverboat to Akron, Ohio, my hometown." And her curiosity led, poem by poem, to a re-creation of the African American experience in the industrial Midwest. "Because I ran out of real fact, in order to keep going, I made up facts...." Poems have their own sense of truth, their own demands that, like historical fiction, use imagination to make an experience real for the reader. Like an old photograph coming to life, Dove's poem that follows shows how to deeply explore a subject. Notice how the Depression of the 1930s provides a resonant background:

 A Hill of Beans

One spring the circus gave
free passes and there was music,
the screens unlatched
to let in starlight. At the well,
a monkey tipped her his fine red hat   5
and drank from a china cup.
By mid-morning her cobblers
were cooling on the sill.
Then the tents folded and the grass

grew back with a path   10
torn waist-high to the railroad
where the hoboes jumped the slow curve
just outside Union Station.
She fed them while they talked,
easy in their rags. *Any two points*   15
make a line, they'd say,
and we're gonna ride them all.

Cat hairs
came up with the dipper;
Thomas tossed on his pillow   20
as if at sea. When money failed
for peaches, she pulled
rhubarb at the edge of the field.
Then another man showed up
in her kitchen and she smelled   25
fear in his grimy overalls,
the pale eyes bright as salt.

There wasn't even pork
for the navy beans. But he ate
straight down to the blue   30
bottom of the pot and rested
there a moment, hardly breathing.
That night she made Thomas
board up the well.
Beyond the tracks, the city blazed   35
as if looks were everything.

The specific objects in the poem—the screen door, the monkey with the red cap, the waist-high grass, the cat hairs, overalls, and navy beans—make it feel authentic. Dove doesn't tell us times were hard; she shows us, and that way we enter the scene and experience it for ourselves. When the couple can't afford peaches for cobblers, the wife gathers rhubarb. They enjoy the brief wonder of the circus, then return to their routines of eking out a living and helping out those worse off. Unlike the usual hoboes Beulah feeds—who at least enjoy their freedom—the man in the grimy overalls reeks of fear, suggesting he's on the run; from what or whom, Dove doesn't reveal. Instead, she allows the tension his secret creates to percolate through the lives of her characters.

> *If what has happened in...one person were communicated directly to the other, all art would collapse, all the effects of art would disappear.*
>
> —Paul Valéry

Anything can become a fertile subject if you dig deep. As William Matthews says in his essay "Dull Subjects," "It is not, of course, the subject that is or isn't dull, but the quality of attention that we do or do not pay to it. . . . Dull subjects are those we have failed." Cathy Song (B. 1955) puts a spotlight on young mothers taking their babies out in strollers and makes the familiar seem wonderfully strange:

 Primary Colors

They come out in warm weather
like termites
crawling out of the woodwork.
The young mothers chauffeuring
these bright bundles in toy carriages.   5
Bundles shaped like pumpkin seeds.

All last winter,
the world was grown up,
gray figures hurrying along
as lean as umbrellas;   10
empty of infants,
though I heard them at night
whimpering through a succession
of rooms and walls;
felt the tired, awakened hand   15
grope out from the dark
to clamp over the cries.

For a while, even the animals vanished,
the cats stayed close to the kitchens.
Their pincushion paws left padded tracks   20
around the perimeters of houses
locked in heat.
Yet, there were hints of children
hiding somewhere,
threatening to break loose.   25
Displaced tricycles and pubescent dolls
with flaxen hair and limbs askew
were abandoned dangerously on sidewalks.
The difficult walk of pregnant mothers.
Basketfuls of plastic eggs   30
nestled in cellophane grass
appeared one day at the grocer's
above the lettuce and the carrot bins.

When the first crocuses
pushed their purple tongues   35
through the skin of the earth,
it was the striking of a match
The grass lit up, quickly,
spreading the fire.
The flowers yelled out   40
yellow, red, and green.

All the clanging colors of crayolas
lined like candles in a box.
Then the babies stormed the streets,
sailing by in their runaway carriages,   45
having yanked the wind
out from under their mothers.
Diapers drooped on laundry lines.
The petals of their tiny lungs
burgeoning with reinvented air.   50

Song puts a new spin on a commonplace subject and makes it compelling. Images normally suggestive of fruitfulness become menacing. The speaker connects babies, young mothers, spring flowers, and grass to termites, clanging crayons, and fire, suggesting that behind the most familiar world lurks something threatening. The poem's scene seems alien to the speaker and so she renders it as foreign and sinister, including the "plastic eggs / nestled in cellophane grass" that "appeared...one day at the grocer's," as if she had never seen Easter decorations before. The hidden children of stanza 3 are *"threatening to break loose"*; in stanza 4 the "flowers *yelled out* / yellow, red, and green," and "the babies *stormed* the streets." Such observations and well-chosen verbs create an insidious undercurrent that suggests the speaker feels a mixture of disgust and delight in children and spring.

Uncovering a productive subject may be partly luck, but luck comes to poets who are alert and open to sensory possibilities. The photographer Brassai affirms: "If reality fails to fill us with wonder, it is because we have fallen into the habit of seeing it as ordinary." Pay attention. Look at things. Examine the tiny furrows in your T-shirt. Move beyond clichés about the shirt on your back and how cotton was king. Look at the shirt, the threads, the fine filaments. What stories does it have to tell?

Focusing only on what everybody else sees is easy. The result is cliché—not only clichés of language, but clichés of observation, thought, and feeling. We all can fall victim to them, and the result is a dead poem. In retelling the story of Romeo and Juliet or September 11th, the poem that merely reports what we already know won't interest a reader. The poem must see the subject from a unique perspective. What about Juliet's mother at a niece's wedding? What about a hot dog vendor who watched the planes fly into the Twin Towers?

Trying to see something fresh stands at the center of making good poems. Insights don't have to be large. In fact, the most original ones are often small. In "Primary Colors," Cathy Song describes the bundled babies as "shaped like pumpkin seeds." Rita Dove gives us "pale eyes bright as salt." Matthews calls the "babble" of mourners a "dial tone." Such careful attention to detail makes the world of the poem vivid and real for the reader.

Poems compete with everything else for our attention. As E. E. Cummings says, "It is with roses and locomotives (not to mention acrobats Spring electricity Coney Island the 4th of July the eyes of mice and Niagara Falls) that my 'poems' are competing. They are also competing with each other, with elephants, and with El Greco." Today, poems compete with even more things—cell phones, reality TV, and a culture that wants things *now*. If you have special knowledge of a subject (rock climbing, I-10 through Louisiana, how to make soap, your messy car, spider web building), exploit it and fascinate a reader. Charles Harper Webb (B. 1952) draws on his lifelong experience of living with his own name, all three parts of it, to give us a poem no one else could write:

 ## Charles Harper Webb

"Manly," my mother said my first name meant.
I enjoyed sharing it with kings, but had nightmares
about black-hooded axmen lifting bloody heads.

I loved the concept of Charlemagne, and inked
it on my baseball glove and basketball.   5
I learned that females pronounce "Charles" easily;

males rebel. Their faces twitch, turn red as stutterers.
Finally they spit out Charlie or Chuck.
Charles is a butler's name, or a hairdresser's, they explain.

(I'll bet Charles Manson would straighten   10
those guys' tails. I'll bet he'd fix their hair just right.)
My name contains its own plural, its own possessive.

Unlike Bob or Bill or Jim, it won't just rhyme with anything.
I told Miss Pratt, my eighth-grade French teacher,
"Charles sounds like a wimp." I switched to German to be Karl.   15

Of all possible speech, I hear "Charles" best.
I pluck it from a sea of noise the way an osprey plucks a fish.
In print, it leaps out before even sex-words do.

My ears twitch, eager as a dog's. What sweet terror
in the sound: Is Charles there? Oh, Charles.   20
Oh, Charles. Oh, Charles. Charles, see me after class.

Get in this house, Charles Harper Webb!
Harper—nag, angel, medieval musician.
Webb, from Middle English webbe, weaver (as in the web

of my least favorite crawling thing), my pale ancestors   25
stoop-shouldered, with sneezing allergies,
stupefied by the loom's endless clack clack clack,

squatting in dirt-floored cottages year after year,
poking out every decade or so to see brawny men in armor gallop past,
followed by the purple passage of a king.   30

By following the particular leads that his names offer, Webb deftly organizes the
poem. The opening references to manliness, kings, and Charlemagne return in the
poem's closing, giving us a satisfying sense of closure as the squatting ancestors
poke their heads out of their hovels to watch the king and his armored entourage
gallop by.

Memory

Although poems are neither immediate as diaries nor factual as news reports, they
can draw from the vast ocean of personal memory. But the poet doesn't just pull
up the bucket, pour out the memory, and Eureka! the poem. Memory doesn't work
that way. Although the metaphor of photography is popular, even the most vivid
memories aren't snapshots, aren't complete, self-contained units. Memories are
fluid, mysterious, and tied up with everything else we remember, everything else we
are. For a memory to feed a poem, it must be investigated and shaped. Discovering
how to approach a memory and exploring its significance often urges the poet to
write the poem in the first place. Consider this poem by Mark Jarman (B. 1952):

 Ground Swell

Is nothing real but when I was fifteen,
Going on sixteen, like a corny song?
I see myself so clearly then, and painfully—
Knees bleeding through my usher's uniform
Behind the candy counter in the theater   5
After a morning's surfing; paddling frantically
To top the brisk outsiders coming to wreck me,
Trundle me clumsily along the beach floor's
Gravel and sand; my knees ached with salt.
Is that all that I have to write about?   10

You write about the life that's vividest,
And if that is your own, that is your subject,
And if the years before and after sixteen
Are colorless as salt and taste like sand—
Return to those remembered chilly mornings,   15
The light spreading like a great skin on the water,
And the blue water scalloped with wind-ridges,
And—what was it exactly?—that slow waiting
When, to invigorate yourself you peed
Inside your bathing suit and felt the warmth   20
Crawl all around your hips and thighs,
And the first set rolled in and the water level
Rose in expectancy, and the sun struck
The water surface like a brassy palm,
Flat and gonglike, and the wave face formed.   25
Yes. But that was a summer so removed
In time, so specially peculiar to my life,
Why would I want to write about it again?
There was a day or two when, paddling out,
An older boy who had just graduated   30
And grown a great blond moustache, like a walrus,
Skimmed past me like a smooth machine on the water,
And said my name. I was so much younger,
To be identified by one like him—
The easy deference of a kind of god   35
Who also went to church where I did—made me
Reconsider my worth. I had been noticed.
He soon was a small figure crossing waves,
The shawling crest surrounding him with spray,
Whiter than gull feathers. He had said my name   40
Without scorn, just with a bit of surprise
To notice me among those trying the big waves
Of the morning break. His name is carved now
On the black wall in Washington, the frozen wave
That grievers cross to find a name or names.   45
I knew him as I say I knew him, then,
Which wasn't very well. My father preached
His funeral. He came home in a bag
That may have mixed in pieces of his squad.
Yes, I can write about a lot of things   50
Besides the summer that I turned sixteen.
But that's my ground swell. I must start
Where things began to happen and I knew it.

About this poem, Jarman says:

> The poem "Ground Swell" is a record of its own composition. Finding myself writing again about Santa Monica Bay, where I grew up, I wondered to myself if I had nothing else to write about, since the landscape of the beach and the waves continued to be one memory that could always move me to write and since I continued returning to it as a subject, often nostalgically. As I asked myself this question, the boy I describe in the poem came skimming into my mind, paddling past me during the summer of 1968, out into the morning surf, headed toward the larger swells. Everything I say about him in the poem is true, that is, he was a couple of years older than I, had just graduated from high school, attended my church, was about to go into the army, and had grown a moustache. But for the purposes of composition, his appearance in my memory was crucial. I realized that his death in the Vietnam War, just about a year later, had an enormous effect on my church, my family, and my father. And the memory of him, bringing along with it such historical significance, answered my question. I return to Santa Monica Bay as a subject, again and again, because that is where I first discovered I was connected to history and a larger world.

The poem's authenticity in part stems from how its memories have been allowed to steep; time has distilled the memory of one summer so that the poet can investigate its greater significance. Memory poems often work best when they strive not just to record what happened, but to use the poem to explore memory's depths, even the nature of memory. Jarman uses many poetic elements to render this poem, not merely memory. As such, his poem works on many layers, from symbol to setting to form.

Imagery

Emotions, in themselves, are not subject matter. Being in love, scared, lonely, or happy because it's the weekend are all common experiences. Poems that merely state these emotions won't be interesting to readers. We respect such statements but aren't moved by them. To present a poem's complex emotional world, poets rely on **imagery,** or sensory information. While we often think of imagery as visual, imagery can register any sense; it can be aural (sound), tactile (touch), gustatory (taste), olfactory (smell), and kinesthetic (movement). Poems that excite many of our senses draw us in and convince us. We can live inside them. In this poem, Theodore Roethke (1908–1963) brings many kinds of images into play to create an intense memory poem.

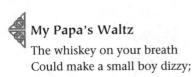

My Papa's Waltz

The whiskey on your breath
Could make a small boy dizzy;

But I hung on like death:
Such waltzing was not easy.

We romped until the pans   5
Slid from the kitchen shelf;
My mother's countenance
Could not unfrown itself.

The hand that held my wrist
Was battered on one knuckle;   10
At every step you missed
My right ear scraped a buckle.

You beat time on my head
With a palm caked hard by dirt,
Then waltzed me off to bed   15
Still clinging to your shirt.

We see the pans slide from the shelves and hear them bang on the floor. We feel the rollicking dance of the father, hear and feel him beating time. We can even smell the whiskey. The speaker doesn't state his feelings about his father in "My Papa's Waltz"; he doesn't need to. The poet lets us feel for ourselves by presenting us with the particular scene out of which the feelings came.

> *Go in fear of abstractions. Don't retell in mediocre verse what has already been done in good prose.*
>
> —Ezra Pound

While emotions in themselves aren't subject matter, the *circumstances* of particular emotions, the scenes or events out of which they come, are fruitful subject matter. Don't tell the emotion; show the context. When a poem presents a scene through imagery, it convinces the reader of its authenticity and emotion. The writer Stephen Dobyns explains, "the reader has to be able to make the emotion his or her own. It is not enough for the reader to understand, to be a witness to somebody else's experience. So it can be said that the poem is not about the writer but the reader, and that without this link to the reader the poem is only a jumble of words."

In Jarman's "Ground Swell," the speaker doesn't say he admired the older surfer, he shows his admiration by comparing the older boy to "a smooth machine" and to "a kind of god." In "A Hill of Beans," Dove doesn't tell us the circus felt magical; she shows us "the screens unlatched / to let in starlight," so that we are able through our imaginations to witness the startlight, too.

Showing the scene will often be the only adequate way of making your point or presenting the emotion. What word or list of words that describes the emotions of love, fear, pain, mischief, panic, delight, and helplessness could begin to sum up what the boy and the grown man feel in "My Papa's Waltz"?

The key is *showing*, not telling. To enact, not summarize. Put in the poem how "the sun struck / The water surface like a brassy palm." Put the god-like older surfer with a "great blond moustache, like a walrus" into the poem. Put the circus monkey *into* the poem. Put the handshake between mourners *into* the poem.

And present the subject sharply. Accurate information, concrete details, and appropriate diction make a poem convincing. As a good liar knows, if you're going to say you were late because you had a flat tire, you'd better give a vivid description of struggling with the jack, traffic whizzing by, and have a plausible explanation for your clean hands. Whether writing about genetics, antique rifles, Asian elephants, surfing, Finland, or the physics of hurricanes, the poet should know enough, or find out enough, to be reasonably authoritative. Whales aren't fish. Rivers flow downhill. Hurricane Katrina happened in 2004 (though its impact is still being felt). Common knowledge, careful observation, and a keen memory are useful, though good reference books, the Internet, and other resources can help, too. Jarman knows how dead soldiers were shipped during the Vietnam War. Though Song sees the spring day from an odd angle, she is still accurate about when termites come out and crocuses bloom and what Easter displays look like. Sometimes poets come upon a subject that sends them to the library and requires their becoming something of a specialist.

Resonant Detail

In presenting subject matter, *particulars* offer overtones of thought and emotion to a poem, giving it depth and substance. We don't need (or want) *every* detail, only those that are significant and resonant. A poem will bore us with inconsequence if it crams in random information. The right detail in the right place moves us. Here, Ruth Stone (B. 1915) deftly handles details to create an atmosphere of loss:

A Pair

The black and white cat
means to get off
the screened-in porch.
Castrated but suave,
he lives with this older woman   5
whose husband, dead thirty years,
secretly puts his cheek to hers
in a dime store photograph.
The children no longer visit.
The cat holds all the threads   10
of her detonated psyche.
He is the master key without
a lock. She picks him up.
The porch screen has been mended.
He thinks there are the old openings.   15

Birds, insects leap
out of the flecked light.
Inside the screen, her hands
stroke his electric body.

The careful selection of details—the black and white cat, dime-store photograph, and mended porch screen—bring this vivid and strange scene of grief to life. The castrated cat serves as poor replacement for the widow's

> *Poetry is not the record of an event: it is an event.*
> —Robert Lowell

husband and her children; however, both cat and woman receive a strained pleasure as she strokes "his electric body." Consider the details and the difference between "dime-store photograph" in line 8 and the generic "framed portrait," between "flecked light" in line 17 and the flat "porch light." These details illuminate the scene and provide context.

In Roethke's "My Papa's Waltz," the detail about the "pans" sliding from the "kitchen shelf" does more than indicate the rowdiness of the drunken father's dancing. It tells us something about the working-class family—a kitchen neither large nor elegant. More importantly, it sets the scene in the kitchen. The father (affectionately "Papa" in the title) who works with his hands ("a palm caked hard by dirt") has come home late from work, after a bit of whiskey. He has come through the back door into the kitchen. Dinner is over and the pans are back on the shelf, but the boy and his mother are still in the kitchen. They have not waited for the father to come home to have dinner, indicating the mother's stored-up anger, as does the word "countenance." In terms of diction choices, she is the more formal "mother," not the warmer "mama." The incongruity of the father's merriment is made stronger because the waltzing begins in the kitchen in front of the mother and clearly leaves her out.

As the novelist Elizabeth Bowen observed, "Nothing can happen nowhere. The *locale* of the happening always colors the happening, and often, to a degree, shapes it." As you work your way into a poem—through imagination, memory, or both—anchor it somewhere in space. Be somewhere in your poems. Particulars, such as setting, can give a poem a striking singularity and place the reader within the world of the poem. They may also, implicitly, provide a sort of running commentary on the subject or action—and on the speaker's attitude. Consider the selection of detail in this poem by Elizabeth Bishop (1911–1979):

First Death in Nova Scotia

In the cold, cold parlor
my mother laid out Arthur
beneath the chromographs:
Edward, Prince of Wales,

with Princess Alexandra,   5
and King George with Queen Mary.
Below them on the table
stood a stuffed loon
shot and stuffed by Uncle
Arthur, Arthur's father.   10

Since Uncle Arthur fired
a bullet into him,
he hadn't said a word.
He kept his own counsel
on his white, frozen lake,   15
the marble-topped table.
His breast was deep and white,
cold and caressable;
his eyes were red glass,
much to be desired.   20

"Come," said my mother,
"Come and say good-bye
to your little cousin Arthur."
I was lifted up and given
one lily of the valley   25
to put in Arthur's hand.
Arthur's coffin was
a little frosted cake,
and the red-eyed loon eyed it
from his white, frozen lake.   30

Arthur was very small.
He was all white, like a doll
that hadn't been painted yet.
Jack Frost had started to paint him
the way he always painted   35
the Maple Leaf (Forever).
He had just begun on his hair,
a few red strokes, and then
Jack Frost had dropped the brush
and left him white, forever.   40

The gracious royal couples
were warm in red and ermine;
their feet were well wrapped up
in the ladies' ermine trains.
They invited Arthur to be   45

the smallest page at court.
But how could Arthur go,
clutching his tiny lily,
with his eyes shut up so tight
and the roads deep in snow?   50

Her first experience with death so absorbs the speaker that she mentions almost
nothing outside the "cold, cold parlor"; the details radiate around Arthur in his
coffin, the color lithographs of the royal family, and the stuffed loon on its marble-
topped table. No other furnishings appear in the poem, and yet from these we can
draw the impression of a rather formal room, and a household that values patrio-
tism, family loyalty, and propriety.

The pattern of Bishop's imagery links the poem's details. Like Arthur himself
and his coffin ("a little frosted cake"), the loon and the chromographs of the royal
family are studies in white and red. The loon's breast and the "frozen lake" of the
marble-topped table are white; his glass eyes red. Similarly the "gracious royal
couples" look "warm in red and ermine." Arthur is "white, forever," except for the
"few red strokes" of his hair. The red and white of the loon (killed by her uncle)
and of the chromographs (in which the royal family keeps warm wearing other
dead animals) seem to connect in the girl's mind with her dead cousin. Such associative connections create the poem's icy, layered unity: red and white; warm
(royal family) and cold (loon).

The nature of the girl's associations reveal her childlike innocence; the coffin reminds her of a "little frosted cake," and the loon is not dead so much as
silenced: "Since Uncle Arthur fired / a bullet into him, / he hadn't said a word."
Like the girl, the loon is cautious; he "kept his own counsel" and only "eyed"
little Arthur's coffin. Struggling to find comfort in the scene, the girl shifts her
attention from Arthur's corpse to the loon and chromographs. The girl's fantasy
that the royal family had "invited Arthur to be / the smallest page at court" shows
her translating her cousin's death into something familiar and comforting. "Jack
Frost" suggests the storybook dimensions of that experience.

Although the girl doesn't understand, she senses that the confusion between
life (red) and death (white) will resolve itself ominously: "But how could Arthur
go, / clutching his tiny lily, / with his eyes shut up so tight / and the roads deep
in snow?" This question implies the fragility of her defense against the grim truth.
The final lines shift from the close-up view of Arthur, eyes shut ("clutching his tiny
lily"), to the wide-angle shot ("roads deep in snow"). The distance sets the small boy
against a forbidding landscape; both children are up against great, strange forces.

Thinking of visual detail as *cinematography* can remind you of your options as
you explore a scene; think of camera angle or location, a close-up or distant shot,
fade-in or fade-out, panning, montage, and so on. Bishop describes the loon's
"white, frozen lake, / the marble-topped table," and the transformation from
lake to table happens so fast we scarcely notice. The poet has picked an exact

angle, a vantage point, so that the girl's mother must lift her up to view Arthur, reinforcing the girl's youth. In "My Papa's Waltz" we never glimpse the father's face, though we see his hand twice: close-ups of the hand on the boy's wrist, the battered knuckle, and of the "palm caked hard by dirt." We see close-ups of the buckle and the shirt. The camera is at the boy's eye level. Note that he says "My right ear scraped a buckle," not the expected reverse: "His buckle scraped my right ear." How perfectly we see that he cannot blame his father for anything! Good description means not only choosing effective details but also visualizing them effectively, from the right angle and the right distance.

Details—like the props on the stage and the characters' costumes—bring a scene to life, not just for the reader but also for the poet struggling to discover the poem. Details like Stone's mended porch screen, Roethke's sliding kitchen pans, and Bishop's dead loon carry with them a psychological or dramatic undercurrent. Notice, however, that none, if any, of the poems we have been discussing is wholly or mainly descriptive. Purely descriptive poems are likely to be tedious, like a video of someone's Hawaiian vacation. Description needs some dramatic or thematic thrust to carry it. In trying to render a scene's emotional authenticity, poets often go wrong by overdecorating. It's best to choose the most evocative details, as Bishop does with the minimal furnishings that suggest the entire psychological realm of the young speaker.

While the right detail can convince, careless abstraction can undermine the reader's confidence in the poet. In the work of many beginning poets, words like *love, truth, war, poverty, innocence,* and *evil* ring hollow and pretentious. Trust William Carlos Williams's famous dictum, "No ideas but in things." He does not mean *no* ideas, but rather ideas arrived at through particulars. In a general sense, the subjects of "Ground Swell" are memory, growing up, surfing, war, identity, and lost innocence, but such inert abstractions can't touch us as the poem's details do.

The difference between statement and implication is crucial. Abstractions state a meaning, whereas particulars convey it. Abstractions fail when they draw conclusions unsupported by imagery. Trust your imagery to do the work of abstractions, to help you show versus tell, and to share the world of your poems with your readers.

QUESTIONS AND SUGGESTIONS

1. This exercise was adapted from poet Bernadette Meyer, who would walk a block in Manhattan and write a line of poetry (incidentally, she would bump into other poets doing the same thing). Experiment with this technique. Take a walk, and use all of your senses to create a vivid picture of

what you experience on each block—or similar stretch of ground—and remember to capture the luminous details.

2. Consider Charles Harper Webb's poem (p. 103), and write a poem about your own name. Research the history and significance of your first, last, and middle name. Interview your family members. Do you have specific stories related to your name you can weave in to the poem?

3. Examine Claude McKay's poem "Tropics in New York" (p. 115), and write a poem about a city you have visited. Make the setting as three-dimensional as possible. What sights, sounds, and flavors come to mind? How do you feel about this city now? How can you use imagery to show how you feel?

4. Take another look at "First Death in Nova Scotia" (p. 109). What details does Bishop use that work simultaneously as symbols and metaphors? Write a poem about a person in which you select objects that operate as details *and* symbols to bring this character to life.

5. Recalling the "authority list" you created in Chapter 1, create a "research list," that is, a list of things you are familiar with, but would like to learn more about. Topics might include various languages or cultures, what a typical day was like for Nefertiti, the life of Miles Davis, and beyond. Watch movies, surf the net, and read books and articles on your topic. Then use your research to inspire your own poetry.

POEMS TO CONSIDER

Bitch   1984
CAROLYN KIZER (B. 1925)

Now, when he and I meet, after all these years,
I say to the bitch inside me, don't start growling.
He isn't a trespasser anymore,
Just an old acquaintance tipping his hat.
My voice says, "Nice to see you,"   5
As the bitch starts to bark hysterically.
He isn't an enemy now,
Where are your manners, I say, as I say,
"How are the children? They must be growing up?"
At a kind word from him, a look like the old days,   10
The bitch changes her tone: she begins to whimper,

She want to snuggle up to him, to cringe.
Down, girl! Keep your distance
Or I'll give you a taste of the choke-chain.
"Fine, I'm just fine," I tell him.   15
She slobbers and grovels.
After all, I am her mistress. She is basically loyal.
It's just that she remembers how she came running
Each evening, when she heard his step;
How she lay at his feet and looked up adoringly   20
Though he was absorbed in his paper;
Or, bored with her devotion, ordered her to the kitchen
Until he was ready to play.
But the small careless kindnesses
When he'd had a good day, or a couple of drinks,   25
Come back to her now, seem more important
Than the casual cruelties, the ultimate dismissal.
"It's nice to know you are doing so well," I say.
He couldn't have taken you with him;
You were too demonstrative, too clumsy,   30
Not like the well-groomed pets of his new friends.
"Give my regards to your wife," I say. You gag
As I drag you off by the scruff,
Saying, "Good-bye! Good-bye! Nice to have seen you again."

 ## The Man. His Bowl. His Raspberries.   1994
CLAUDIA RANKINE (B. 1963)

The bowl he starts with
is too large. It will never be filled.

Nonetheless, in the cool dawn,
reaching underneath the leaf, he frees
each raspberry from its stem   5
and white nipples remain suspended.

He is being gentle, so does not think
I must be gentle as he doubles back
through the plants
seeking what he might have missed.   10

At breakfast she will be pleased
to eat the raspberries and put her pleasure
to his lips.

Placing his fingers beneath a leaf
for one he had not seen, he does not idle.   15
He feels for the raspberry. Securing, pulling
gently, taking, he gets what he needs.

The Tropics in New York   1920
CLAUDE McKAY (1890–1948)

Bananas ripe and green, and ginger-root,
  Cocoa in pods and alligator pears,
And tangerines and mangoes and grape fruit,
  Fit for the highest prize at parish fairs,

Set in the window, bringing memories   5
  Of fruit-trees laden by low-singing rills,
And dewy dawns, and mystical blue skies
  In benediction over nun-like hills.

My eyes grew dim, and I could no more gaze;
  A wave of longing through my body swept,   10
And, hungry for the old, familiar ways,
  I turned aside and bowed my head and wept.

Chrysanthemums   2004
SPENCER REECE (B. 1963)

When I am in the hospital there is this boy.
He is seventeen and has survived a circus fire.

His eye sockets are gouges.
The eyes themselves are like slugs

inching. His fingers are missing,   5
the stumps are black.

When the nurse undoes his gauze bandages,
his mouth collapses.

The shower room is soundproofed
so we cannot hear the screams   10

when they debride him.
The hours pass: quick, then slow.

Outside my window—
the chrysanthemums,

their petals yellow and scalloped as woodcuts.   15

 The Beautician   1992
THOM GUNN (1929–2004)

She, a beautician, came to see her friend
Inside the morgue, when she had had her cry.
She found the body dumped there all awry,
Not as she thought right for a person's end,
Left sideways like that on one arm and thigh.   5

In their familiarity with the dead
It was as if the men had not been kind
With her old friend, whose hair she was assigned
To fix and shape. She did not speak; instead
She gave her task a concentrated mind.   10

She did find in it some thin satisfaction
That she could use her tenderness as skill
To make her poor dead friend's hair beautiful
—As if she shaped an epitaph by her action,
She thought—being a beautician after all.   15

7

METAPHOR

"The greatest thing by far," Aristotle declared, "is to be a master of metaphor. It is the one thing that cannot be learned from others; and it is also a sign of genius, since a good metaphor implies an intuitive perception of the similarity in dissimilars." Perhaps more than any vehicle open to the poet, metaphor carries the greatest potential for creating a poem's psychological density; through its metaphors a poem reveals how the speaker's mind works. Inextricably entwined with the ways we think and the nature of language itself, metaphor in theory seems a knot of complexity. Luckily, just as we can use a cellphone without understanding the electronics involved, we can make metaphors without understanding linguistic theory.

Robert Frost's definition suffices: "saying one thing in terms of another." **Metaphor** means (literally, from the Greek) *transference:* We transfer the qualities from one thing to something else, as in "The sky was a sea of stars." In an instant, qualities of a vast, blue, shimmering fluid transfer to the Milky Way. We call the subject, the thing that undergoes transference, the **tenor** (stars) and the source of transferred qualities the **vehicle** (sea). A metaphor that is syntactically announced by *like* or *as* is called a **simile.** Simile denotes *similarity* between tenor and vehicle as in "The moon floats above us like an eye."

From the initial simile in the poem below, "It's rather like snow," B. H. Fairchild (B. 1945) builds up a winter scene transformed by snowfall, then melts it down to create the sense of loss we feel when a place we love disappears:

 ### The Death of a Small Town

It's rather like snow: in the beginning,
immaculate, brilliant, the trees shocked
into a crystalline awareness of something

remarkable, like them, but not of them,
perfectly formed and yet formless.   5
You want to walk up and down in it,

this bleak, maizeless field of innocence
with its black twigs and blue leaves.
You want to feel the silence crunching

beneath your houseshoes, but soon everyone   10
is wallowing in it, the trees no longer
bear sunlight, the sky has dragged down

its gray dream, and now it's no longer snow
but something else, not water or even
its dumb cousin, mud, but something used,   15

ordinary, dull. Then one morning at 4 a.m.
you go out seeking that one feeble remnant,
you are so lonely, and of course you find

its absence. An odd thing, to come upon
an absence, to come upon a death, to come upon   20
what is left when everything is gone.

One reason people read poetry is to experience a transformation or a change of some sort. Just by looking at snow, the primary metaphor in this poem, we can see change unfolding: the snow is "immaculate, brilliant," then "dragged down" and "dull," and then the poet surprises us by moving beyond melted snow to its palpable absence. Well-made metaphors, like the one in Fairchild's poem, work literally as well as metaphorically. They surprise us by pairing two things not normally associated with one another. Through the use of metaphor, we are able to see both the snow and the small town in a new light.

> *If a metaphor works well, the two images appear simultaneously in the mind, suspended in a field of parallel resonance.*
> —Tony Hoagland

When the comparison does not use *like* or *as*, it is called **metaphor.** A metaphor so compresses its elements that we *identify* the tenor with the vehicle; the connection happens in a flash, as in "The gun barked" or "The sun is a bauble hung in the trees." As you work on your poems, strive for the intensity of metaphoric compression so that "Filled with elation, I quickly left the house" might become "I tangoed out the door." When metaphors flash before us, we can suddenly see new connections.

Metaphor often eludes exact translation; through its dense evocativeness, it not only compresses and compacts but also expresses the inexpressible. Metaphor is italicized in this example from Elizabeth Bishop's "First Death in Nova Scotia"

(p. 109): "Arthur's coffin was / *a little frosted cake.*" Bishop uses metaphor to subtly suggest Arthur will not have any more birthdays, or birthday cakes. Emily Dickinson in "My Life had stood—a Loaded Gun" writes: "My Life *had stood—a Loaded Gun— / In Corners*—till a Day." Notice the quick image of dammed-up power, of the desire to explode like a loaded gun, but being muffled, even hidden in a corner.

The metaphors of this poem help carry the freight of its ambivalent attitudes:

The White Dress
LYNN EMANUEL (B. 1949)

What does it feel like to be this shroud
on a hanger, this storm cloud hanging
in the closet? We itch to feel it, it itches
to be felt, it feels like an itch—

encrusted with beading, it's an eczema   5
of sequins, rough, gullied, riven,
puckered with stitchery, a frosted window
against which we long to put our tongues,

a vase for holding the long-stemmed
bouquet of a woman's body.   10
Or it's armor and it fits like a glove.
The buttons run like rivets down the front.

When we're in it we're machinery,
a cutter nosing the ocean of a town.
Right now it's lonely locked up   15
in the closet; while we're busy

fussing at our vanity, it hangs there
in the drooping waterfall of itself,
a road with no one on it, bathed
in moonlight, rehearsing its lines.   20

Emanuel undercuts the somewhat pretty metaphors (*frosted window, vase, waterfall, bathed / in moonlight*) with unpleasant associations (*shroud, eczema, road with no one on it*). By playing the metaphors off each other and pairing unlike things, she goes beyond our perceived notions of tradition and of "whiteness" and depicts the wedding dress as a gorgeous trap.

In writing a poem, knowing the differences between simile and metaphor matters far less than recognizing their similarities. Because the way they link tenor and vehicle is explicit, similes may seem simpler and closer to the straightforward, logical uses of language. And metaphors, because their linkage is often buried, may seem more surprising. But the evocative quality of any metaphor or simile depends on context. The popular notion that metaphor is stronger or more evocative than a simile doesn't really hold up.

Consider these two lines from Emanuel's poem: "Or it's armor and it fits like a glove. / The buttons run like rivets down the front." The metaphor of armor and the simile of a glove draw equally on our expectations of clothes; the armor doesn't do more or less work for the poem than the glove. The image of the buttons in the next line might easily be recast as metaphor: "The buttons are rivets running down the front." Inserting static "to be" verbs for the more dynamic "run" dulls the line's energy. Varying simile and metaphor within your poems, as Emanuel does, can help keep the language fresh.

Figuratively Speaking

Metaphors and similes fall into a larger group called *figures of speech* or *tropes*. Under this larger heading fall literary devices such as *irony, hyperbole,* and *understatement,* which we mention in other chapters. Another device is **personification,** in which an inanimate object behaves like a person, as does Emanuel's white dress that "itches / to be felt" and feels "lonely locked up."

A figure of speech similar to personification is **animism,** assigning animal characteristics to humans, as in "They galloped down the hall," or "She snaked her arms around him." Consider the rollicking invective conjured up by the figures of speech in this poem by Pamela Alexander (B. 1948):

Look Here

Next time you walk by my place
in your bearcoat and mooseboots,
your hair all sticks and leaves
like an osprey's nest on a piling,
next time you walk across my shadow   5
with those swamp-stumping galoshes
below that grizzly coat and your own whiskers
that look rumpled as if something's
been in them already this morning
mussing and growling and kissing—   10
next time you pole the raft of you downriver
down River Street past my place
you could say hello, you canoe-footed fur-faced
musk ox, pockets full of cheese and acorns
and live fish and four-headed winds and sky, hello   15
is what human beings say when they meet each other
—if you can't say hello like a human don't
come down this street again and when you do don't

bring that she-bear, and if you do I'll know
even if I'm not on the steps putting my shadow   20
down like a welcome mat, I'll know.

On an immediate level, this poem presents a speaker who has been rejected by a
man for another woman (a "she-bear"). The speaker delivers a tirade against the
man, calling him inhuman for his behavior. On a more fundamental level, the
poem takes us on a ride where one delightful metaphor follows the next. The victim of this string of insults has hair "like an osprey's nest" and stinks like a "musk
ox" with "pockets full of cheese" and "live fish." These inventive metaphors,
centered on animals, suggest the speaker's control over her anger. Though the
speaker may be incensed by this man, she hasn't lost her spirit.

Two other figures of speech that involve associations and comparisons are
metonymy and *synecdoche*. In **metonymy,** one thing is substituted by something
associated with it. Metonyms can distill a notion down to its essentials, as in *"The
White House* was in a panic." In his poem "Out, Out—" (p. 49), Robert Frost deftly
expresses the boy's desperate attempt to save his hand by holding up his arm, "to
keep the *life* from spilling"; by substituting "life" for "blood," Frost foreshadows
the boy's death. In **synecdoche,** we substitute a part for the whole or a whole for
the part. Very like metonyms, synedoches can capture the essence of an image as
in *"The hired hand* dug the potatoes"; "She bought herself a new *set of wheels*"; or
"There wasn't *a dry eye* at the funeral." Often metonymy and synecdoche overlap.

Through synecdoche and metonymy, Emily Dickinson (1831–1886) depicts a
family gathered around the bed of a dying person in "I heard a Fly buzz—when
I died—":

I heard a Fly buzz—when I died—
The Stillness in the Room
Was like the Stillness in the Air—
Between the Heaves of Storm—

The Eyes around—had wrung them dry   5
And Breaths were gathering firm
For that last Onset—when the King
Be witnessed—in the Room—

I willed my Keepsakes—Signed away
What portion of me be   10
Assignable—and then it was
There interposed a Fly—

With Blue—uncertain stumbling Buzz—
Between the light—and me—
And then the Windows failed—and then   15
I could not see to see—

Dickinson sketches the gathered relatives (lines 5–6) as "Eyes around" (synecdoche) and "Breaths" (metonymy), highlighting how grief possesses them. The family and speaker anticipate the moment of death, a moment of revelation, "when the King / Be witnessed—in the Room." Whether the "King" is God or death personified, they all expect an apotheosis, but only a fly, associated with decay, "interposed."

A third figure of speech appears in the final stanza. The speaker fuses the visual with the aural as the fly knocks around the room "With Blue—uncertain stumbling Buzz." This device is called **synesthesia:** the perception, or description, of one sense mode in terms of another, as when we describe language as "salty" or musical notes as "bright."

Dickinson's poem uses "light" literally and figuratively; it evokes the actual light coming from the windows, the hope and sadness of the family members, the light of understanding, as well as the light of spirituality. The final lines record the speaker's consciousness before she dies: "I could not see to see—." The dash suggests her consciousness shuts down at the moment of the expected king's arrival, but whatever she finally experiences, she can't tell us.

Because Dickinson has framed a clear picture, the questions the poem asks about death, nature, and the spirit hit us hard. Further enriched by associative images, the light imagery helps construct a poem both direct and dense, able to provoke fundamental issues of epistemology and metaphysics even as the poem depicts a simple deathbed scene, and Dickinson does it all in sixteen lines.

Poems that operate only on a literal level risk seeming thin. Conversely, poems that operate wholly on a symbolic level often seem overblown. A poem that makes passionate declarations with tired formulas ("I hungered for your touch as the sands of time sifted through my heart") will more likely make us bored than draw us in. As with metaphor and simile, and metonymy and synecdoche, balancing the literal and the metaphorical is key.

Even in highly symbolic poems like "I heard a Fly buzz—when I died—," images let us respond to something real; we can *see* and *hear* a buzzing fly. Physical elements of Dickinson's poem—*light, fly, windows*—operate as **symbols** (they represent something else), but these symbols are grounded in the scene. The common housefly might represent death, but its presence is perfectly normal and subtle. How obvious the appearance of other death symbols would be: a turkey vulture perching on the windowsill or the branches outside the window forming a skull. The one figure not grounded in the scene, "King," sticks out, emphasizing the speaker's and mourners' high-flown expectations.

Though it must be apt, a symbol can be generalized and still be powerful, as the masks are in this poem by Paul Laurence Dunbar (1872–1906):

 ## We Wear the Mask

We wear the mask that grins and lies,
It hides our cheeks and shades our eyes,

This debt we pay to human guile;
With torn and bleeding hearts we smile,
And mouth with myriad subtleties.   5

Why should the world be overwise,
In counting all our tears and sighs?
Nay, let them only see us, while
    We wear the mask.

We smile, but, O great Christ, our cries   10
To thee from tortured souls arise.
We sing, but oh the clay is vile
Beneath our feet, and long the mile;
But let the world dream otherwise,
    We wear the mask!   15

The mask deceives onlooker and wearer; it hides the true self and hinders the wearer's abilities—it "shades our eyes." On the other hand, the mask may afford the speaker a kind of shield with which he protects his inner self from onlookers. Knowing that Dunbar, the son of slaves, lived during a time of lynchings and the intensification of Jim Crow laws, we may infer that the poem describes the African American experience. The "mask that grins and lies" may refer to minstrelsy and to the burden of a racially stereotyped identity. However, the symbol of a suffering group masking pain is also universal. Here, it reveals a defiance and resistance to being cast down, while the "hidden" speaker reasserts his power.

Poets needn't strain to find symbols. The images at hand make the most compelling figures—like Dickinson's light and fly, the snow and ice in "First Death in Nova Scotia" (p. 109), and the wedding gown in "The White Dress" (p. 119). Notice in Emanuel's poem that she doesn't bring up notions of virginity and purity, which the wedding dress conventionally symbolizes—she knows we'll bring those associations to the poem. Instead, the poem's metaphors invest the heavily symbolic wedding gown with strangeness and loneliness: the dress is "a road with no one on it, bathed / in moonlight, rehearsing its lines." The dress suggests the burden of becoming the symbolic bride. Recast with original metaphors, the cliché wedding dresss becomes fraught with psychological tension.

Although you can make just about any image serve as a symbol, don't get carried away. To paraphrase Freud, it's better sometimes to let a cigar be a cigar.

A Name for Everything

Without us, the world remains wordless. The story of Adam's naming the animals of Eden stands as archetype for one of humanity's greatest concerns: naming things so we can recognize and talk about them. Whenever we invent something new, we find a new term or adapt an old one to express it—thus, the Inter*net,* the World Wide *Web,* and *surfing.*

The classical Roman orator Quintillian praised metaphor for performing the supremely difficult task of "providing a name for everything." The more complex the issue, the more we need something else to explain it, as the double helix helps us understand DNA and the Möbius strip, relativity. Metaphors work in an amazing variety of ways. They illustrate, explain, emphasize, heighten, communicate information and ideas, and carry a poem's tone.

The roots of language lie in metaphor. We speak of *the eye* of a needle, *the spine* of a book, the *head* and *mouth* of a river (which are oddly at opposite ends), a flower *bed, bouncing* a check, or *going haywire,* without thinking of the buried metaphors— of faces, bodies, sleeping, jumping, or the tangly wire used for baling hay.

When a subject is abstract, such as the emotion in Emily Dickinson's "After great pain, a formal feeling comes—" (p. 186), metaphor allows the poet to express in particular terms what would otherwise remain vague and generalized. Dickinson ends that poem with exacting metaphors to evoke a *particular* feeling:

This is the Hour of Lead—
Remembered, if outlived,
As Freezing persons, recollect the Snow—
First—Chill—then Stupor—then the letting go—

As Marianne Moore wittily says, "Feeling at its deepest—as we all have reason to know—tends to be inarticulate." The more powerful the emotion, the more it requires metaphor to affect a reader; through metaphor Dickinson expresses the experience of deadness that follows "great pain."

Generic words for emotions—*love, hate, envy, awe, respect, rage*—don't express *particular* feelings, and it is precisely their particularity that makes emotional content in a poem matter to us. For centuries, lovers have struggled to describe their particular feelings, grumbling that *words can't begin to express* their love, how their *love is beyond words,* and how *no one has ever felt* as they do.

As we attempt to articulate what we feel, we turn to metaphor, borrowing the vocabulary of other things—in Dickinson's case, freezing to death—to say what no exact words can say. Often, finding the link between some abstract feeling and a physical sensation allows us to explore complex emotions. For instance, in "A Noiseless Patient Spider" (p. 30), Whitman takes the spider's throwing out its filaments to show his soul's "musing, venturing, throwing, seeking."

In this poem, Molly Peacock (B. 1947) navigates an abstract sea of emotion on the sturdy craft of metaphor:

 Putting a Burden Down

Putting a burden down feels so empty
you almost want to hoist it up again,
for to carry nothing means there is no "me"

almost. Then freedom, like air, creeps in
as into a nearly airtight house, estranging   5
you and your burden, making a breach to leap in,

changing an airless place into a landscape,
an outdoors so full of air it leaves you breathless,
there's so much to breathe. Now you escape

what you didn't even know had held you.   10
It's so big, the outside! How will you ever carry it?
No, no, no, you are only meant to live in it.

This wide plain infused with a sunset? Here?
With distant mountains and a glittering sea?
With distant burdens and a glittering "me," here.   15

Peacock takes the metaphors that the phrase "putting a burden down" suggests
and uses them to open a complex of emotions and ideas. The "airless place,"
which heavy responsibility and anxiety pro-
duce, gives way when "freedom, like air, creeps
in" to a "landscape, / an outdoors so full of air
it leaves you breathless." Peacock salvages the
familiar imagery of mountain and sea in the
penultimate line by mocking it and tweaking

> *If you respect the reality of the world, you know that you can only approach that reality by indirect means.*
> —Richard Wilbur

the phrasing in the final line. As such, she captures the startling sense of release
one feels after being unburdened. The metaphors unlock the emotion.

Pattern and Motif

The distance between the two parts of a metaphor—between tenor and vehicle—
gives metaphor its resonance. In the best metaphors, the meeting of tenor and
vehicle acts like a small chemical reaction and creates a flash of recognition. Tenor
and vehicle too closely related (the sun *is a star*) won't spark; metaphors too unrelated (the sun is *a tow truck*) may shimmer with strangeness, only to leave a reader
in the dark. A metaphor must do more than flash and dazzle. It should establish a
commitment that what follows the metaphor somehow will be connected with it.

When you recognize and follow the possibilities of metaphor, using it as a system
through which to build your poems, you can create great intensity. Metaphors help
poets think and write. Consider this poem by Hart Crane (1899–1932):

My Grandmother's Love Letters

There are no stars tonight
But those of memory.
Yet how much room for memory there is
In the loose girdle of soft rain.

There is even room enough   5
For the letters of my mother's mother,
Elizabeth,
That have been pressed so long
Into a corner of the roof
That they are brown and soft,   10
And liable to melt as snow.

Over the greatness of such space
Steps must be gentle.
It is all hung by an invisible white hair.
It trembles as birch limbs webbing the air.   15

And I ask myself:

"Are your fingers long enough to play
Old keys that are but echoes:
Is the silence strong enough
To carry back the music to its source   20
And back to you again
As though to her?"

Yet I would lead my grandmother by the hand
Through much of what she would not understand;
And so I stumble. And the rain continues on the roof   25
With such a sound of gently pitying laughter.

On a rainy night in an attic the speaker finds his grandmother's love letters. Notice how many ways—through similes, metaphors, images, and connotations—Crane unveils the many delicate and tenuous layers of memory and of love. The speaker's tone—his doubt about how he can cross the distance between his grandmother's intimate life and his own life—registers this delicacy.

The opening stanza builds a parallel between the stars that exist only in memory (for it is a rainy night) and the grandmother, who lives on in the speaker's memory and in the love letters. Stars, even on a clear night, are themselves echoes, light that has traveled millions of light-years from its source; we see only what has reached us across great time and space. Stanza 2 shifts the focus from the more general ruminations about memory to the care and caution that engaging with the past requires. The closing phrase, "liable to melt as snow" (line 11), makes the letters so frail that even touching them could destroy them. "Frail," "delicate," "flimsy," "friable"—none of these adjectives satisfies as much as the simile comparing the letters to snow. Notice how much we lose if the line were to rely on metaphor alone: "and liable to melt." We can touch snow; it is visceral and activates our senses.

The "room for memory" and "loose girdle of soft rain" of stanza 1 and the fragile letters of stanza 2 lead us to the realization in stanza 3: "Over the greatness

of such space / Steps must be gentle." These resonant "steps" offer multiple possi-
bilites, suggesting the stairs to the attic; the speaker's actual and metaphoric footsteps (setting up his stumbling in the last stanza); the stages of memory; and the
piano's elusive music of stanza 5, which, in turn, suggests *keys* that might unlock
the grandmother's intimate life.

Images of whiteness underlie the poem, tying together its multiple strains: The
white piano keys connect with the white starlight, and the soft letters are likened
to snow. The "invisible white hair" that "trembles as birch limbs webbing the air"
(lines 14–15) associates the delicacy of memory and the letters with the attic's
hair-like cobwebs, with the birch branches, with the previously undisturbed attic
and its secrets, and with the color of the grandmother's hair.

Through pattern and motif, Crane connects past and present, strength and
delicacy, time and space, love and loss, and distance and intimacy in a poem that
itself subtly examines the nature of interconnections. Crane celebrates the fragile
but persistent connection between himself and another generation now gone.
The metaphors work together to create a system in which the pieces fit. Thinking
of a poem as a system, in which certain elements work and others don't, can be
especially helpful as you construct metaphors and revise your poems.

Metaphor says more in an instant than do pages of explication. Instantly the
reader apprehends the pertinent elements. Consider the associations prompted by
the last stanza of Sylvia Plath's famous "Lady Lazarus": "Out of the ash / I rise with
my red hair / And I eat men like air." We understand the speaker's bold claim of
rising like a phoenix and destroying men, but what goes into our understanding?
Metaphors ask us to slow down and unpack these associations. Eating something
suggests we have power over it, and perhaps we have killed it (or will when we eat it).
Eating something "like air" further reduces it, making it inconsequential, common,
negligible. Air, as Plath uses it, takes on a different tone than "air" as Dickinson uses
it in this stanza of "After great pain, a formal feeling comes—" (p. 186):

> The Feet, mechanical, go round—
> Of Ground, or Air, or Ought—
> A Wooden way
> Regardless grown,
> A Quartz contentment, like a stone—

The speaker's indecisiveness or indifference in settling on one metaphor—"Ground,
or Air, or Ought—/ A Wooden way"—dramatizes how stone-like or numb intense
pain makes its victim. Plath's speaker exudes boundless energy; Dickinson's
is down for the count—her feet are earth, air, wood, or nothing ("ought" is
a variation of "aught")—she doesn't seem to know or care. Crane's phrase
"webbing the air" can allude to music because he has woven musical metaphors
into the poem's texture. In each occurrence of "air," we screen out qualities that
might undermine the metaphor. We don't consider how eating air might make

Lady Lazarus hiccup, or that Dickinson's "mechanical" feet might be musical. Nevertheless, these metaphors create layered associations that make the poems unique, complex, and satisfying.

Conceits

When metaphors dominate or organize a passage or even a whole poem, we call them extended metaphors or **conceits.** Secondary metaphors and images spring from the controlling metaphor, as we can see in the metaphors of an airless house and an open landscape in Peacock's "Putting a Burden Down" (p. 124). To talk about the give and take of marriage, its pleasures and challenges, Jeffrey Harrison takes us "Rowing" (p. 134).

The extended metaphor in the following poem by Mary Oliver (B. 1935) identifies music with a brother "Who has arrived from a long journey," a brother whose presence seems to tame the world's danger, the "maelstrom" outside the house.

 Music at Night

Especially at night
It is the best kind of company—
A brother whose dark happiness fills the room,
Who has arrived from a long journey,
Who stands with his back to the windows   5
Beyond which the branches full of leaves
Are not trees only, but the maelstrom
Lashing, attentive and held in thrall
By the brawn in the rippling octaves,
And the teeth in the smile of the strings.   10

Oliver so densely weaves the conceit into the poem that we can't precisely state whether the trees outside the windows are part of the metaphorical description of the brother or part of the literal scene. The real and the imagined combine in one scene, as music is embodied in the arrival of the brother, the lashing maelstrom, and the animated instruments.

In this poem, Kevin Young (B. 1970) uses nature as a metaphor for desire and longing. Because a madrigal is a kind of song for multiple voices, Young underscores the isolation of the speaker through his title and claims both song and trees as metaphors.

 Madrigal

Who can stand
spring? The weeping

willows drooping
The azaleas bright

The bow-legged beauties   5

who walk me into frenzy
All this returning

My eyes burning

Road windstrewn with limbs
severed like Roman statues   10

I am not brave
like the dogwood shade

Pray, soon autumn
will come, undress the trees

Young builds the metaphor of trees stanza by stanza. Whether "weeping" or "bow-legged," these personified trees act on the speaker's imagination and fill him with longing ("eyes burning" suggests both allergies and tears); however, lines 9 and 10 surprise with their violence and tonal complexity. If the trees are metaphors for potential lovers, then both the trees and lovers have severed limbs. Here, the metaphor asks us to register the pain of unrequited desire and the violence of longing. "Pray" in the final couplet nods both to the song as metaphor suggested by the title as well as to the speaker's emotional plea for physical and spiritual intimacy.

A **mixed metaphor** occurs when a poet fails to control, focus, or consider nuances of a metaphor. Mixed metaphor combines unrelated or contradictory elements, as in this sentence's mixing of military, baseball, and artistic metaphors: "If we're to marshal our forces, we'd better swing at every pitch and try to etch our cause into their consciousness." Mixed metaphors often occur when the poet ignores a metaphor's literal for its figurative meaning. Metaphors usually work literally *and* figuratively. Otherwise, they risk losing their power and sense.

Metaphoric Implication

The simplest metaphors may work with an almost inexhaustible subtlety and work harder than either poet or reader may be aware. Even metaphors that are essentially nonimages—muted echoes, shadowy partial shots, or momentary flashes to a different scene—can work on our imaginations. Consider Shakespeare's Sonnet 30:

When to the sessions of sweet silent thought
I summon up remembrance of things past,
I sigh the lack of many a thing I sought,
And with old woes new wail my dear time's waste:

Then can I drown an eye, unused to flow,   5
For precious friends hid in death's dateless night,
And weep afresh love's long since cancelled woe,
And moan the expense of many a vanished sight:
Then can I grieve at grievances foregone,
And heavily from woe to woe tell o'er   10
The sad account of fore-bemoaned moan,
Which I new pay as if not paid before.
But if the while I think on thee, dear friend,
All losses are restored and sorrows end.

Shakespeare draws much of the poem's diction from the legal and quasilegal realms: "sessions," "summon," "dateless," "cancelled," "expense," "grievances," "account," "pay," "losses," and "restored." Together these images suggest a court proceeding over some financial matter (in Shakespeare's time, debts were jailable offenses). The implicit metaphors make for a complex tone: a certain judicial solemnity, an irrecoverable loss, some technical injustice, which the miraculous appearance of the "dear friend" overturns. We see no definite courtroom and yet we feel the speaker's sense of relief—as though he'd been sprung from jail—when he thinks about his "dear friend." The metaphoric implication is well-constructed. The legal diction conveys literal *and* metaphoric imprisonment, as well as genuine gratitude to the friend who intervenes.

Metaphoric implication can allow the poet to explore another person's complex inner life, without making that person seem overly self-involved or self-conscious. Through metaphors the speaker in the following poem suggests—rather than reports—the depth of her feelings and scope of her insight:

The House Slave
RITA DOVE (B. 1952)

The first horn lifts its arm over the dew-lit grass
and in the slave quarters there is a rustling—
children are bundled into aprons, cornbread

and water gourds grabbed, a salt pork breakfast taken.
I watch them driven into the vague before-dawn   5
while their mistress sleeps like an ivory toothpick

and Massa dreams of asses, rum and slave-funk.
I cannot fall asleep again. At the second horn,
the whip curls across the backs of the laggards—

sometimes my sister's voice, unmistaken, among them.   10
"Oh! pray," she cries. "Oh! pray!" Those days
I lie on my cot, shivering in the early heat,

and as the fields unfold to whiteness,
and they spill like bees among the fat flowers,
I weep. It is not yet daylight.   15

The metaphors depict the disparity between the powerful and the powerless while folding in the implication that those in control have forfeited their humanity. The opening metonym—"The first horn lifts its arm"—reverses the normal order; the horn controls the arm rather than vice versa, suggesting that the bugler who calls the slaves to work has submerged his identity in his job. Similarly, at the second horn, "the whip curls across the backs of the laggards—": the whip seems to have a life independent of its wielder. This disembodied quality adds another horrific layer to the poem.

While she presents the masters as destructive and static, Dove presents the slaves as dynamic and productive. The lively images associated with the slaves ("dew-lit grass," "children...bundled into aprons," "cornbread," "water gourds," "salt pork") contrast with the parasitic nature of the masters. The slaves rush about their cabins, gathering their babies and provisions for the day "while their mistress sleeps like an ivory toothpick" and "Massa dreams of asses, rum and slave-funk."

Dove's metaphors more convincingly testify against the slave system than pages of preaching can. Look how much the toothpick simile implies. The mistress appears frail, brittle, and allied with death, for though ivory is precious and white, it is also the product of slaughter and the exploitation of Africa. Also, by likening the mistress to the negligible luxury of an ivory toothpick, Dove equates the mistress with an ornament; her role in the household pales against the active and vital slaves who "spill like bees among the fat flowers."

The poet's choice of metaphor helps articulate the speaker's sadness, isolation, and helplessness. Though the speaker's position in the house seems to cushion her from the toil in the fields and suffering from the whip, it also shuts her off from human contact and shuts her in a house associated with death and the master's sexual appetites. Trapped, the speaker cannot assuage her sister's or the others' pain. She can only lie on her cot, "shivering in the early heat" and listening to their cries. Dove closes the poem with the speaker's quiet desperation, "I weep. It is not yet daylight." The lonely day is still to come.

> *One needs the specific image to unlock the deeper sensations....*
> —Francis Bacon

QUESTIONS AND SUGGESTIONS

1. Keeping in mind Mary Oliver's "Music at Night" (p. 128), use a specific type of music as your primary metaphor to write a poem. What music type is most appropriate? Classic rock? Opera? Hip hop? Techno? Country?

Make a list of specific words associated with that type of music and weave them into your poem.

2. Similar to Reginald Shepherd's "Blue" (p. 135), write a poem in which you assign colors to different ideas or emotions. You can also use this activity to help you revise and emphasize imagery and setting. What ideas do you associate with red? What feelings with yellow or blue?

3. Write an imitation poem (a poem that follows syntax and form as closely as possible) of a poem from this book. To begin, rewrite the original poem and then replace nouns and verbs with your own choices. As the poem takes shape, feel free to add and cut lines, and change the syntax and form as needed. As you revise, consider ways you can develop your poem as a system in which all the elements fit.

4. Make a list of ten emotions and a list of ten metaphors. Use the metaphors in one list to describe the emotions in the other without actually stating the emotion. Develop the best into a poem.

5. *For a group*: Each person in the group should list a concrete noun on a small piece of paper and an active, present-tense verb on another piece of paper; for example: *blade, crank, plug, flag, bark, sleet, curdle, jar, gravy, brace, towel, clover*. (Notice how many words can be either nouns or verbs.) Now, collect the nouns in one pile and the verbs in another. Randomly pick a piece of paper from each pile and write a poem in which you connect them, so that "the towels flag on the clothesline," or "the gravy showers down like sleet." Use associations with your original nouns and verbs to build the poem stanza by stanza. ("Sleet" may lead you to "snow" or "Vermont"; "Crank" may lead you to "broken" or "flat.")

POEMS TO CONSIDER

 The Empire in the Air   2005
KEVIN PRUFER (B. 1969)

It was a fragile empire
with knobs and wires, like a bomb.
It lived in a blue suitcase in the airplane's belly.
It had a little screen that flashed the time
and the moments we had left, ticked them gently away.   5
We laughed and sipped our drinks

while the empire, wrapped in its inevitable wires,
imagined the airplane splitting like a milkweed pod,
the clothing that would burst from our broken suitcases
into the air.   10

My Arms   2007
PAUL GUEST (B. 1983)

My arms are mostly cosmetic. When I say this
to a stranger, often he'll wince
like he wants to hide inside his eyes.
Vanish from the day. I shouldn't laugh,
should be tired twenty-one years   5
into the telling of a poor joke,
made of pain, nerves snuffed like wicks. Back
then, I was a boy. No secret
that I fell through that
summer like a star. And here I am   10
wanting spring and birdsong
after tedious winter. Once I prayed
my arms might serve me
again, roll toothpaste from the tube,
dump rice into boiling water,   15
swat dead the mosquito
drilling its derrick face
through my skin. That symmetry,
left and right, one and one—
it's not a math I know,   20
not anymore. There are days I want
to lament broken glass
or put my fist through the door
or throttle the blue sky's silent
throat. There are nights   25
full of ache, full of nothing nimble.
No music but smashed guitars
would be enough. How many clasps
and how many buttons
did I try with my teeth   30
until her hands did for me what I could not?
Untrue to say I lost count
of what I never hoped to keep.
A lie to say that when

she held my hands to her hips   35
and her body above mine,
I loved such need, I did not hate us both.

Rowing   2001
JEFFREY HARRISON (B. 1957)

How many years have we been doing this together,
me in the bow rowing, you in the stern
lying back, dragging your hands in the water—
or, as now, the other way around, your body
moving toward me and away, your dark hair swinging   5
forward and back, your face flushed and lovely
against the green hills, the blues of lake and sky.

Soon nothing else matters but this pleasure,
your green eyes looking past me, far away,
then at me, then away, your lips I want to kiss   10
each time they come near me, your arms that reach
toward me gripping the handles as the blades
swing back dripping, two arcs of droplets
pearling on the surface before disappearing.

Sometimes I think we could do this forever,   15
like part of the vow we share, the rhythm
we find, the pull of each stroke on the muscles
of your arched back, your neck gorged and pulsing
with the work of it, your body rocking
more urgently now, your face straining with something   20
like pain you can hardly stand—then letting go,

the two of us gliding out over the water.

The Way Things Work   1980
JORIE GRAHAM (B. 1951)

is by admitting
or opening away.
This is the simplest form
of current: Blue
moving through blue;   5
blue through purple;
the objects of desire
opening upon themselves
without us;

the objects of faith.   10
The way things work
is by solution,
resistance lessened or
increased and taken
advantage of.   15
The way things work
is that we finally believe
they are there,
common and able
to illustrate themselves.   20
Wheel, kinetic flow,
rising and falling water,
ingots, levers and keys,
I believe in you,
cylinder lock, pully,   25
lifting tackle and
Crane lift your small head—
I believe in you—
your head is the horizon to
my hand. I believe   30
forever in the hooks.
The way things work
is that eventually
something catches.

Blue   1995
REGINALD SHEPHERD (1963–2008)

See my colors come apart? Green
to yellow with just one shade gone,
the changing tints of your sun-struck eyes,
if there were sun. Today the prism held to mine's

a prison, locking in the light. In one of those mirrors   5
the colors are true. In one of these pictures the pigment's
my own. The sound there is aquarelle and indigo,
and dripping distant water, the day's habitual failure

to be anything substantial. Today a blank like color
by numbers, filled in with fog that frames the lake   10
in transient tones. That's the color I mean, some mist
painting the shore pastel and pointillist

rain, painting the shadow between window and light. Today
each hue dissolves in humid air, transparency
I grasp and then let go, clear overflow   15
of waves on gravel. The mist with its single-dipped brush

smears itself across the canvas of the pines.
The pines know no better, run together on a morning
palette. Today the scene's dismantled, that can't be
dismissed. *I once was blind, but now*   20

I see my landscape attenuate itself, drowned lake
of evergreens. On a morning like this with new crayons
I drew a man, that red valentine
in the side. The picture of two hands scrawling the outline

where only one thing's missing; the crayons scattering   25
from childish fingers. Color me or leave me vacant.

8

TALE, TELLER, AND TONE

E very poem begins with a voice, a **speaker,** the person who tells us what
we hear or read. Just as anything can serve as the subject of a poem, so too
anyone or anything can serve as the speaker. A murderous mermaid whose
song seduces sailors into shipwreck speaks in this poem by Amy Gerstler (B. 1956):

 Siren

I have a fish's tail, so I'm not qualified to love you.
But I do. Pale as an August sky, pale as flour milled
a thousand times, pale as the icebergs I have never seen,
and twice as numb—my skin is such a contrast to the rough
rocks I lie on, that from far away it looks like I'm a baby   5
riding a dinosaur. The turn of centuries or the turn
of a page means the same to me, little or nothing.
I have teeth in places you'd never suspect. Come. Kiss me
and die soon. I slap my tail in the shallows—which is to say
I appreciate nature. You see my sisters and me perched   10
on rocks and tiny islands here and there for miles:
untangling our hair with our fingers, eating seaweed.

As the siren talks, she characterizes herself and presents the scene where we find
her stretched out on a rock, munching on seaweed. Her cool diction ("not qualified," "I appreciate nature") supports her cool temperament and temperature. Her
skin is "pale as the icebergs." She matter of factly says, "Kiss me / and die soon,"
a markedly flat, even mechanical phrase, which implies this is the natural order
of things. She knows the deadly task at hand. As such, she fits our assumptions
about sirens, but the details of her portrait—her phrasing, her tail slapping the

[L]ook for a persona and a world...."

—Stephen Burt

water, her disinterest in passing time, her diet—sharpen and complicate the picture.

Think of a poem as a miniature play. The speaker steps out and addresses us, or someone else, and begins to flesh out a character or create a context. Just as when we see a character step onto a stage, when we see a poem on the page our expectations are heightened. We expect that what follows will somehow be significant (even if what's said is simple); we expect a *distillation* of thought, emotion, and events—not merely someone's prosaic ramblings. Even when a poem appears to capture the inner stream of someone's consciousness, the poem presents particular associations of a particular mind at a particular time, not accidental musings. The scene in which we find a speaker can be just as various as a poem's speaker. We may find the complex world of Brigit Pegeen Kelly's "Song" (p. 198), telling the fable of a senseless killing of a goat. Or we find the more direct but mythic circumstances of "Siren." But for the speaker's circumstances to matter to us, something must be at stake. In "Song," the fate of the goat and the little girl who owned the goat are at stake. In "Siren," what's at stake is implicit—the siren will lure in and murder sailors.

Consider the simple yet dynamic circumstances of this emotionally charged poem:

The Hare
HENRI COLE (B. 1956)

The hare does not belong to the rodents;
he is a species apart. Holding him firmly
against my chest, kissing his long white ears,
tasting earth on his fur and breath,
I am plunged into that white sustenance again,   5
where a long, fathomless calm emerges—
like a love that is futureless but binding
for a body on a gurney submerged in bright light,
as an orchard is submerged in lava—
while the hand of my brother, my companion   10
in nothingness, strokes our father,
but no power in the air touches us,
as one touches those one loves, as I
stroke a hare trembling in a box of straw.

No one would mistake this for a Hollywood action flick, but notice that the poem opens dynamically, with a **motivating incident,** something that prompts the poem: stroking a trembling hare, the speaker recalls his father's death.

Look how the circumstances change and how much is at stake though nothing dramatic *happens.* We're presented with an animal and a strained gesture of scientific fact ("The hare does not belong to the rodents"). Yet the powerful tactile experience of touching the animal plunges the speaker into "white sustenance," the stuff of memory, the animal's fur, the particular light around his father's gurney where his brother touched their dying father. Notice the syntax; after one short declarative sentence, the poem unfolds into a very long sentence and moves energetically, following the twists and turns of memory.

Narration, Pacing, and Tense

Many poems are **narratives;** they tell (or imply) stories, albeit in compressed, resonant language. Books of poetry can be novel-like: Robert Browning's crime thriller *The Ring and the Book* (1868–1869), Vikram Seth's *The Golden Gate* (1986), Andrew Hudgins's *After the Lost War* (1988), Mark Jarman's *Iris* (1992), Margaret Gibson's *The Vigil* (1993), Anne Carson's *The Autobiography of Red* (1998), and Rita Dove's *Sonata Mulattica* (2009). And poets have written striking short stories in verse, from Chaucer's tales to Christina Rossetti's "Goblin Market" to Marilyn Nelson's (B. 1946) poem that follows.

 Minor Miracle

Which reminds me of another knock-on-wood
memory. I was cycling with a male friend,
through a small midwestern town. We came to a 4-way
stop and stopped, chatting. As we started again,
a rusty old pick-up truck, ignoring the stop sign,   5
hurricaned past scant inches from our front wheels.
My partner called, "Hey, that was a 4-way stop!"
The truck driver, stringy blond hair a long fringe
under his brand-name beer cap, looked back and yelled,
        "You fucking niggers!"   10
and sped off.
My friend and I looked at each other and shook our heads.
We remounted our bikes and headed out of town.
We were pedaling through a clear blue afternoon
between two fields of almost-ripened wheat   15
bordered by cornflowers and Queen Anne's lace
when we heard an unmuffled motor, a honk-honking.
We stopped, closed ranks, made fists.
It was the same truck. It pulled over.
A tall, very much in shape young white guy slid out: 20
greasy jeans, homemade finger tattoos, probably
Marine Corps boot-camp footlockerful
of martial arts techniques.

"What did you say back there!" he shouted.
My friend said, "I said it was a 4-way stop.   25
You went through it."
"And what did I say?" the white guy asked.
"You said: 'You fucking niggers.'"
The afternoon froze.

"Well," said the white guy,   30
shoving his hands into his pockets
and pushing dirt around with the pointed toe of his boot,
"I just want to say I'm sorry."
He climbed back into his truck
and drove away.   35

Paying attention to the fundamentals of good narrative allows a poet to choose what to include and what to leave out, when to summarize details and when to depict the action moment by moment, all of which contribute to a poem's **pacing**, or the way information and events unfold. Nelson's deft handling of the narrative derives from her pacing, her control of the poem's sense of time. She starts her story within a story, with a memory of an event ("Which reminds me..."). This framing device creates tension, as it both invites the reader into the conversation and pushes us out of the conversation, which apparently was going on before the poem's start. This precarious opening mirrors the tension within the poem's narrative. Nelson quickly moves through the bike ride, while presenting resonant details that create context; we know it takes place in a small Midwestern town at a (symbolically loaded) four-way stop. In terms of pacing, the major confrontation with the driver begins by line 6. When the driver "hurricane[s] past," the action speeds up through strong verbs, imagery, and dialogue. The details grow menacing, then erupt.

After the driver hurls the racial slur at the bikers, Nelson slows the action down again by turning the camera on the countryside, building suspense. In rendering the lush natural world around them—in "writing off the subject," as Richard Hugo called the technique—Nelson sharpens the scene's contrast with the threatening man. The driver seems to intrude upon the peaceful meadows, foreshadowing the amazing transformation of his character. Through stanza breaks and by focusing on details like the pointed toes of the man's boots, Nelson creates suspense and intensifies the man's unexpected apology.

A seemingly unimportant feature, *verb form*, helps control the action. Most of "Minor Miracle" takes place in the simple past tense: "stopped," "started," "yelled," "slid out," "shouted," "climbed back," and "drove away." But the past progressive marks crucial moments; the central story begins with "I was cycling," signaling that the action will soon shift. Look at the point after they remount their bikes: "We were pedaling through a clear blue afternoon...when we heard an unmuffled motor...." (lines 14–17). The use of the past progressive tense indicates something is about to happen. Similarly at the end, we see the man "shoving his hands in his pockets / and pushing dirt" before he apologizes. And did you notice that the entire poem is framed within the present tense, within the phrase, "Which reminds me..."? Such a frame helps supply the poem's motivating incident: Spurred by something in conversation, the speaker recounts the story.

When writing a poem, the writer must handle verb form attentively. As we can see in Nelson's poem, the verbs help us keep track of where the action is going, where it has been, and where it's headed. Use of the past tense indicates completed action; the speaker has had time to reflect, as Wordsworth says, *to recollect in tranquility*, and weigh the events. Nelson's title suggests such reflection: The man's apology was a "Minor Miracle," which years later still inspires awe in the speaker.

For creating immediacy and intensity, the present tense usually works best. You will often find that when a poem *feels* cool and remote, casting it in present tense can warm it up. The present tense also controls the realm of eternal truths, as in Whitman's "A Noiseless Patient Spider" (p. 30), and that of discovered truths, like those of Liz Rosenberg's "The Silence of Women" (p. 79). Gerstler's siren also lives in an eternal, remorseless present.

As we might expect, the future tense belongs to the realms of the imagined and desired; it controls prophetic poems such as Nina Cassian's "Ordeal" (p. 169) and Donald Justice's "Variations on a Text by Vallejo" (p. 182). Carefully handled, verbless fragments can be effective "sentences." Sharon Bryan's "Sweater Weather" strings such fragments into a "Love Song to Language" (p. 3). But use verbless sentences with care. A passage without verbs surrenders a significant marker. As you work on your poems, carefully weigh your decisions about verb form; try out different tenses to see what effect they have on your subject. Consider how "The Hare" cast entirely in the present tense would lose its poignancy, as would "Siren" if cast in the past tense. The skilled writer attends to a poem's tense, its syntax, and its verbs. This layered poem about storytelling makes the point clear:

 Story

STEPHEN DUNN (B. 1942)

A woman's taking her late-afternoon walk
on Chestnut where no sidewalk exists
and houses with gravel driveways
sit back among the pines. Only the house
with the vicious dog is close to the road.   5
An electric fence keeps him in check.
When she comes to that house, the woman
always crosses to the other side.

I'm the woman's husband. It's a problem
loving your protagonist too much.   10

Soon the dog is going to break through
that fence, teeth bared, and go for my wife.
She will be helpless. I'm out of town,
helpless too. Here comes the dog.
What kind of dog? A mad dog, a dog   15
like one of those teenagers who just loses it
on the playground, kills a teacher.

Something's going to happen that can't happen
in a good story: out of nowhere a car
comes and kills the dog. The dog flies   20
in the air, lands in a patch of delphiniums.
My wife is crying now. The woman who hit
the dog has gotten out of her car. She holds
both hands to her face. The woman who owns
the dog has run out of her house. Three women   25
crying in the street, each for different reasons.

All of this is so unlikely; it's as if
I've found myself in a country of pure fact,
miles from truth's more demanding realm.
When I listened to my wife's story on the phone   30
I knew I'd take it from her, tell it
every which way until it had an order
and a deceptive period at the end. That's what
I always do in the face of helplessness,
make some arrangements if I can.   35

Praise the odd, serendipitous world.
Nothing I'd be inclined to think of
would have stopped that dog.
Only the facts saved her.

Persona

The poet's ability to imagine and to project underlies what Keats called **negative capability.** In a letter he described this as the capability "of being in uncertainties, Mysteries, doubts, without any irritable reaching after fact & reason." In another letter he talks about "the chameleon Poet...the most unpoetical of anything in existence, because he has no Identity—he is continually in for [informing] and filling some other Body—The Sun, the Moon, the Sea and Men and Women." Through negative capability poets can suspend their egos and judgment, and so imagine others from the inside out. This act can be liberating for the poet. Free from the fixed self, any character or experience, any spin of the imagination is available to the poet. Keats wrote, "If a sparrow come before my window, I take part in its existence and pick about the gravel," and conceived that "a bil-liard Ball...may have a sense of delight from

Poetry is the supreme fiction.
—Wallace Stevens

its own roundness, smoothness volubility & the rapidity of its motion." Indeed, we imbue jewelry, buildings, hillsides, and all kinds of objects with memories, feelings, and stories.

The following poem shows how the poet can get inside the existence of others and manifest their inner reality. While touring an abandoned coal mine in Wales, the speaker imagines the strange sunless world of the ponies his guide describes. This layered poem about storytelling makes the point clear:

 Pit Pony
WILLIAM GREENWAY (B. 1947)

There are only a few left, he says,
kept by old Welsh miners, souvenirs, like
gallstones or gold teeth, torn
from this "pit," so cold and wet my
breath comes out a soul up   5
into my helmet's lantern
beam, anthracite walls running,
gleaming, and the floors iron-rutted
with tram tracks, the almost pure
rust that grows and waves like   10
orange moss in the gutters of water
that used to rise and drown.
He makes us turn all lights off, almost
a mile down. While children scream
I try to see anything, my hand touching   15
my nose, my wife beside me—darkness palpable,
velvet sack over our heads, even the glow
of watches left behind. This is where
they were born, into this nothing, felt
first with their cold noses for the shaggy   20
side and warm bag of black
milk, pulled their trams for twenty
years through pitch, past birds
that didn't sing, through doors
opened by five-year-olds who sat   25
in the cheap, complete blackness listening
for steps, a knock. And they
died down here, generation after
generation. The last one, when it
dies in the hills, not quite blind, the mines   30

closed forever, will it die strangely? Will it
wonder dimly why it was exiled from the rest
of its race, from the dark flanks of the soft
mother, what these timbers are that hold up
nothing but blue? If this is the beginning   35
of death, this wind, these stars?

The poem moves us from the present to the past, then—as the poet explores the
weird world of creatures shut away from the open air—to the future. By moving
us through three time periods, Greenway gives the impression of having made
a wide sweep through time. He thereby projects dignity to the forgotten ponies.
A poem set only in the past or present tense would not reflect the speaker's
expansive vision or the potential transformation of the exploited animals.

When a poem's speaker is clearly someone other than the poet, such as a
fictional, mythic, historic, or other figure (for example, if "Pit Pony" were written
from the point of view of one of the ponies), it is called a **persona poem**. In the
following persona poem, Louise Glück (B. 1943) depicts the interior life of flowers
with surprising results:

Daisies

Go ahead: say what you're thinking. The garden
is not the real world. Machines
are the real world. Say frankly what any fool
could read in your face: it makes sense
to avoid us, to resist   5
nostalgia. It is
not modern enough, the sound the wind makes
stirring a meadow of daisies: the mind
cannot shine following it. And the mind
wants to shine, plainly, as   10
machines shine, and not
grow deep, as, for example, roots. It is very touching,
all the same, to see you cautiously
approaching the meadow's border in early morning,
when no one could possibly   15
be watching you. The longer you stand at the edge,
the more nervous you seem. No one wants to hear
impressions of the natural world: you will be
laughed at again; scorn will be piled on you.
As for what you're actually   20
hearing this morning: think twice
before you tell anyone what was said in this field
and by whom.

These articulate and daring daisies see through the poet's nervousness and mock her internal struggle: "It is very touching," they sarcastically say. They apparently have recognized that the poet resists them as poetic subject—even though she is drawn to them—because daisies are "not modern enough." The poet feels she "will be / laughed at again; scorn will be piled on" if she presents "impressions of the natural world." The daisies allow the poet to voice the undercurrent of misgivings and expose the tangle of voices in the creative process: "think twice," the daisies advise, "before you tell anyone what was said in this field / and by whom." Glück uses tonal mockery, even aggression, to counter the potential sentimentality of a persona poem written from the point of view of flowers.

In a sense, all poems involve a persona and the perception of a presented character, real or otherwise. Thus, even the poet writing or trying to write in his or her own voice creates a self by presenting a *particular* tone, stance, circumstance, and theme; otherwise, the poem risks seeming generic. In life, we show different faces to different people in different situations; in writing, often without realizing it, we adjust the voice we use, naturally adopting different *personae*. Yeats called such versions of the self the poet's *masks*. In writing a poem, the poet puts on a mask and adopts a persona who speaks the poem. This process of taking on a mask may even amount to exploring one's identity, ethnicity, gender, or heritage and can lead to self-discovery.

Point of View

The angle from which a poem comes to us is its **point of view.** In *first-person* point of view, the "I" or "we" reports what happens; in *second person* the "you" reports; in *third person* "he," "she," or "they" report. Although we use these three general categories, any point of view involves fine gradations. As this devious speaker makes plain, control of the vantage point makes all the difference:

My Last Duchess
ROBERT BROWNING (1812–1889)

That's my last duchess painted on the wall,
Looking as if she were alive. I call
That piece a wonder, now: Frà° Pandolf's hands
Worked busily a day, and there she stands.
Will't please you sit and look at her? I said   5
"Frà Pandolf" by design, for never read

3 Frà: Friar, a monk; Browning has invented a Renaissance painter-monk, like Frà Angelico, for this poem. The sculptor of the poem's last line (Claus of Innsbruck) is also Browning's invention.

Strangers like you that pictured countenance,
The depth and passion of its earnest glance,
But to myself they turned (since none puts by
The curtain I have drawn for you, but I)   10
And seemed as they would ask me, if they durst,
How such a glance came there; so, not the first
Are you to turn and ask thus. Sir, 'twas not
Her husband's presence only, called that spot
Of joy into the Duchess' cheek: perhaps   15
Frà Pandolf chanced to say "Her mantle laps
Over my lady's wrist too much," or "Paint
Must never hope to reproduce the faint
Half-flush that dies along her throat": such stuff
Was courtesy, she thought, and cause enough   20
For calling up that spot of joy. She had
A heart—how shall I say?—too soon made glad,
Too easily impressed; she liked whate'er
She looked on, and her looks went everywhere.
Sir, 'twas all one! My favor at her breast,   25
The dropping of the daylight in the West,
The bough of cherries some officious fool
Broke in the orchard for her, the white mule
She rode with round the terrace—all and each
Would draw from her alike the approving speech,   30
Or blush, at least. She thanked men—good! but thanked
Somehow—I know not how—as if she ranked
My gift of a nine-hundred-years-old name
With anybody's gift. Who'd stoop to blame
This sort of trifling? Even had you skill   35
In speech—which I have not—to make your will
Quite clear to such an one, and say, "Just this
Or that in you disgusts me; here you miss,
Or there exceed the mark"—and if she let
Herself be lessoned so, nor plainly set   40
Her wits to yours, forsooth, and made excuse,
—E'en then would be some stooping; and I choose
Never to stoop. Oh sir, she smiled, no doubt,
Whene'er I passed her; but who passed without
Much the same smile? This grew; I gave commands;   45
Then all smiles stopped together. There she stands
As if alive. Will't please you rise? We'll meet
The company below, then. I repeat,
The Count your master's known munificence

Is ample warrant that no just pretense   50
Of mine for dowry will be disallowed;
Though his fair daughter's self, as I avowed
At starting, is my object. Nay, we'll go
Together down, sir. Notice Neptune, though,
Taming a sea-horse, thought a rarity,   55
Which Claus of Innsbruck cast in bronze for me!

By having this Renaissance duke speak for himself, Browning subtly reveals that within this eloquent, intelligent, cultivated man lurks greed, arrogance, cunning, and ruthlessness. The Duke of Ferrara is addressing a subordinate, an envoy from a count; they are negotiating the terms for the count's daughter to become the next duchess.

Just as he controls who looks at the framed portrait of his last duchess, the duke controls his words, all the while claiming he has no "skill / In speech." With prevaricating smoothness, he reveals that he had her murdered ("I gave commands; / Then all smiles stopped together," lines 45–46) because he felt, among other things, that she did not exhibit a high enough regard for him and his title ("as if she ranked / My gift of a nine-hundred-years-old name / With anybody's gift," lines 32–34). He puts a slick spin on his portrayal of her.

When he comes to the delicate subject of the new dowry from the count's daughter, notice how abstract his diction and how convoluted his syntax become ("no just pretense / Of mine for dowry will be disallowed," lines 50–51). The duke doesn't specify how much of a dowry he expects; instead he compliments the count's generosity and notes the expectations that munificence engenders.

When a character's speech creates a dramatic scene, like the Italian Renaissance world of "My Last Duchess," we often call the poem a **dramatic monologue.** Created by his speech, the duke appears as vividly as a character on stage. Besides monologues, poems can take the forms of letters (called **epistles**), newspaper articles, calendars, definitions—any form that human utterance can take.

The first-person point of view has the advantages of creating immediacy, intensity, and sympathy. Recall the child speaker in "First Death in Nova Scotia" (p. 109). Filtered through the girl's innocence and inexperience, the scene depicts the strangeness and sadness of such a loss, even when the feelings aren't entirely understood by the speaker. Hearing the duke's story from his own mouth in "My Last Duchess" makes him a savvy, powerful, and perversely attractive figure; we hear what he wants the envoy to hear, although we perhaps end up knowing more about his ruthlessness than he intends. The duke's self-disclosure, however, may be a tactic. Is he taking the envoy and thus the count into his confidence, and planting a message for the new bride about his expectations? Perhaps the duke doesn't care how much he reveals; perhaps he is merely relishing his power.

We make out of the quarrel with others, rhetoric, but of the quarrel with ourselves, poetry.
—W. B. Yeats

Like many first-person narrators, the duke is unreliable; the reader must weigh his claims. First-person narrators may have intellectual, psychological, emotional, experiential, or even moral limits that color the picture they present. The duke's arrogance skews his description of his duchess, who apparently is guilty only of having had an easy and open nature. Typically, the more involved a narrator is with the poem's central character, the less reliable that narrator will be, just as the closer we are to an event, the less objective we can be.

The second-person point of view appears more often in poetry than in prose fiction. The second person appears in the direct address of love poems and in imperatives—directions and directives—like Glück's "Daises" (p. 144), which dare the speaker and/or reader to "say what you're thinking" and "think twice." In American English, we often use "you" when the British would use "one" to describe habitual or typical action; such is the case with poems such as Natasha Sajé's "Reading the Late Henry James" (p. 179) and B. H. Fairchild's "The Death of a Small Town" (p. 117). At times "you" may signify "I," as when you mutter to yourself, "You're going to be late for work." When speakers address themselves—advising, blaming, warning, reminding— we glimpse their inner struggle and can feel pulled into sympathy with the speaker:

When Someone Dies Young
ROBIN BECKER (B. 1951)

When someone dies young
a glass of water lives
in your grasp like a stream.
The stem of a flower
is a neck you could kiss.   5
When someone dies young
and you work steadily
at the kitchen table
in a house calmed by music
and animals' breath,   10
you falter at the future,
preferring the reliable past,
films you see over and over
to feel the inevitable
turning to parable, characters   15
marching with each viewing
to their doom.
When someone dies young
you want to make love furiously

and forgive yourself.   20
When someone dies young
the great religions welcome you,
a supplicant begging with your bowl.
When someone dies young
the mystery of your own   25
good luck finds a voice
in the bird at the feeder.
The strict moral lesson
of that life's suffering
takes your hand, like a ghost,   30
and vows companionship
when someone dies young.

The poem's distinctive details—such as working at the kitchen table "in a house calmed by music / and animals' breath"—suggest that the speaker is addressing herself, and yet the poem's entire attitude also includes the reader. In a sense the "you" calls us by name and includes us, helping us remember, or imagine, our own feelings "when someone dies young." The repetition of this subordinate clause forms a rhythm of suspension and release that further involves the reader. At the same time, the "you" may also reveal the speaker's attempt to distance herself from the pain of loss. In either case, the second-person point of view engages the reader; such engagement, through a variety of techniques, is an essential aspect of poetry.

The third-person point of view covers a wide spectrum, from narrow to wide angles of vision, from limited points of view that focus on a single character to wider, all-knowing points of view. *Omniscient* third-person points of view may display god-like powers, jumping around in time and space, shifting from inside one character's consciousness to another's, and understanding events, motives, and circumstances. We see such a wide point of view in Donald Justice's "Variations of a Text by Vallejo" (p. 182) in which Justice predicts how the grave diggers will behave when he is buried.

Tone

When we attempt to describe the **tone** of a poem, we are trying to identify the attitude the poem has toward its subject, including the attitudes of the speaker and the poet. Poetry can range through all human attitudes and so register many tones at once—anger, elation, hysteria, indifference, sorrow, terror, tenderness, anxiety, and silliness, among others. Because poems often deal with moments of heightened awareness and emotional intensity, the poet may take a reader on a roller-coaster ride of feelings. A poet can express any attitude, even contradictory attitudes, in the course of a poem.

Consider the interplay of tones in this poem by Richard Lyons (B. 1951):

 ## Lunch by the Grand Canal

Harry Donaghy, an ex-priest, is telling us
that, after ten rounds, the welterweight was still panting
from a literal hole in his heart.
The fish the waiter lays before me on a white plate
is hissing through its eye, I swear it.   5
Harry spills out a carton of old photos
between the bread & the vials of vinegar.
The people in the pictures are friends of his aunt, whose body

he's signed for & released, now on a jet lifting from Rome.
He says he's always preferred Venice,   10
here a Bridge of Sighs separates this life from the next.
One of the photos, he thinks, is of his aunt,
she's no longer young having dropped a cotton dress at her feet
so the artist at arm's length might see her beauty
as if it had already slipped away. Across from me,   15
Paige Bloodworth is wearing a red hat, which looks good on her,
but she hasn't said a word, so pissed we missed the launch
to San Michele where Pound is buried.

For her, Harry's unidentified relatives
posing on the steps down to the Grand Canal   20
are lifting stones from their pockets
and pelting the poet's coffin as it eases out
on a black boat, chrysanthemums hoarding their perfumes.

I'm stroking the curved prow of a boat as if it were
the neck of a wild stallion rearing close   25
for a hidden cube of sugar or a slice of apple.
Miss Bloodworth's hat becomes a figure in memory's contract
as it lifts over water the color of tourmaline.
Harry's big hands trap all the photos, spilling the wine.
It's the winter of 1980, just warm enough   30
to sit outside as I remember. The rest of that year
no doubt is a lie.

The heterogeneous mix of people, motives, details, and time frames makes for a darkly funny poem with an ironic tone. The speaker seems to feel simultaneously intrigued and appalled by the circumstances he delineates. The aimless trio of Harry, Paige, and the narrator sit around a table, but have little in common, except perhaps a shared annoyance with things that might interrupt their diversions.

Quirky **juxtapositions,** or the grouping together of unlike or loosely associated items, intensify the scene's incongruence. A welterweight boxer with a hole in his heart is set against a fish hissing through its eye (both suggest death and a release of bodily elements). An ex-priest ironically flips through what's left of his aunt's life, including nude photographs of her, at an outdoor café (the intimate, public, and spiritual collide). A woman whose surname is *Bloodw*orth wears a red hat that "looks good on her" even though she is sulking because they missed a boat to see a poet's grave (she might be flushed with anger).

The discordance of these people and their lives seems to be cosmically dismissed when the wind scatters the photographs and carries off the hat. Although Lyons writes the poem in present tense, the scene remains distant; that is, he establishes an ironic distance between himself and the poem's subject.

One feature of tone that deserves elaboration is **irony,** which generally indicates a discrepancy between the author's attitude and the attitude(s) expressed within the poem. The incongruous elements that Lyons assembles imply a critique of the self-centered, dislocated lives we glimpse in the poem. The poem's entire tone is ironic, and in the poem's closing the speaker levels that irony at himself: "The rest of that year / no doubt is a lie." In the last line Lyons shows his hand and reports to us that he made up the entire poem. He had been encouraging his students to feel freer about using lies in their poems and wrote the poem to show how believable an invented story can be.

The term **verbal irony** identifies a discrepancy between what the speaker says and what the speaker means, as, when wrestling with an umbrella in the rain, you say, "What a lovely day." In Gerstler's "Siren" (p. 137), verbal irony occurs when the siren claims: "...I'm not qualified to love you. / But I do." We know this is a ploy to lure in sailors through false affection.

Situational irony occurs when our expectations meet unexpected twists. The deserted church is turned into a liquor store. The "D" math student becomes a physics genius. An example of situational irony occurs in Stephen Dunn's "Story" (p. 141), when a car hits a dog and thereby saves the speakers' wife from being mauled.

Dramatic irony marks a discrepancy between what the author and reader know and what the speaker or characters know. Hamlet does not kill the king when he is at prayer, lest the king in a state of grace go straight to heaven. Hamlet does not know what the audience has seen: that the king is burdened with guilt and unable to pray. In Browning's "My Last Duchess" (p. 145), dramatic irony allows the audience to become the moral voice in the poem when we come to understand the Duke shows no remorse for his wife's murder. Dramatic irony solidifies the relationship between audience and writer, letting readers in on what remains hidden to the characters. Through dramatic irony, we become caught up wondering if the characters will catch on or fall for the trap.

QUESTIONS AND SUGGESTIONS

1. Take a look at C. D. Wright's "Personals" (p. 153) and experiment with writing a poem framed as a personal ad that reveals, through details and irony, unique and quirky qualities about the speaker. What does this character think about, desire, and fear? Is he or she a dog or cat person? Favorite foods? Dream job?

2. Take a poem you are revising and change its point of view. Then change its tense. How does it affect the poem to move from first to third person? How does changing from past to present tense shift the overall tone?

3. Write a poem in which two narratives occur, similar to Henri Cole's "The Hare" (p. 138). What metaphor can trigger the second narrative to unfold? In what ways do the two narratives overlap or remain distinct?

4. Try writing a poem using one of the following as the speaker:

    the dog in Stephen Dunn's poem "Story" (p. 141)
    Kurt Cobain or Elvis in hiding
    one of the boys who kills the goat in Brigit Pegeen Kelly's "Song" (p. 198)
    someone ashamed of a childhood prank
    a servant in the Duke of Ferrara's household
    a flower whose personality is surprising

    What might you need to know, or find out, or invent in order to make the poem convincing and interesting?

5. *For a group:* Experiment with writing a few character-driven "exquisite corpse" poems. Form a circle. On the top of a blank piece of paper, write two lines describing a character (e.g., "A twenty-year-old barista... / who is studying pre-Columbian art..."). Then fold over the first line so only the last of the two lines appears. Pass it to the person to your right, who should write two more lines, fold over the paper so only the very last line shows, and pass it to the next person. Each person should add a further detail about the character or the situation using the last line written by the previous person as a springboard. You can write as many poems as you have people in the group.

POEMS TO CONSIDER

 Personals   1991

C. D. WRIGHT (B. 1949)

> Some nights I sleep with my dress on. My teeth
> are small and even. I don't get headaches.
> Since 1971 or before, I have hunted a bench
> where I could eat my pimento cheese in peace.
> If this were Tennessee and across that river, Arkansas,   5
> I'd meet you in West Memphis tonight. We could
> have a big time. Danger, shoulder soft.
> Do not lie or lean on me. I am still trying to find a job
> for which a simple machine isn't better suited.
> I've seen people die of money. Look at Admiral Benbow. I wish   10
> like certain fishes, we came equipped with light organs.
> Which reminds me of a little known fact:
> if we were going the speed of light, this dome
> would be shrinking while we were gaining weight.
> Isn't the road crooked and steep.   15
> In this humidity, I make repairs by night. I'm not one
> among millions who saw Monroe's face
> in the moon. I go blank looking at that face.
> If I could afford it I'd live in hotels. I won awards
> in spelling and the Australian crawl. Long long ago.   20
> Grandmother married a man named Ivan. The men called him
> Eve. Stranger, to tell the truth, in dog years I am up there.

[writing for a young man on the redline train: "to his boy mistress"]   2004

D. A. POWELL (B. 1963)

> *All the bodies we cannot touch*
> *Are like harps. Toucht by the mind*
>   —Robert Duncan, "Fragments of a Disordered Devotion"

writing for a young man on the redline train: "to his boy mistress"
first to praise his frame: pliable as hickory.   his greasy locks waxy ears
I'll stop the world and melt with you brustling through a nearby headset

if I had time to ride this monster to the end I would: hung by handstraps
jostle through the downtown stations.   each stop bringing us closer   5
to what? gether? perhaps: or that exit of the tunnel where I look back

and *poof*:   no lover.   men have led shameful lives for less proportioned fare
tossing greetings thick as rapunzel's hair: "anybody ever told you that you
[ugh, here it comes lads, stifle those chortles]   resemble a young james dean?"

why *fiddle-dee-dee*, he bats his lids: the fantasy already turning to ruin   10
what if he debarked at my destination of pure coincidence?   followed
through the coppice of the square: fox and hound, fox and hound

I'd lead him on a merry chase: pausing every few: admire a fedora
check the windows of the haberdashers and cruise the sartorial shops
until I felt his winded breathing on my neck: yawned and departed again   15

we could while away the afternoon just so.   but at my back, etc

fresh and sprouting in chestnut-colored pubes is how I'd want him
not after the dregs of cigarettes.   the years of too many scotch sours
why, I wouldn't even know what to say to one who drinks scotch sours

except, "sir."   and "tough luck about those redsox" [which it always is]   20
now I've spent myself in lines and lost.   where is that boy of yesteryear?
let him die young and leave a pretty corpse: die with his legs in the air

 ## Bleeder   1984
STEPHEN DOBYNS (B. 1941)

> By now I bet he's dead which suits me fine,
> but twenty-five years ago when we were both
> fifteen and he was camper and I counselor
> in a straightlaced Pennsylvania summer camp
> for crippled and retarded kids, I'd watch   5
>
> him sit all day by himself on a hill. No trees
> or sharp stones: he wasn't safe to be around.
> The slightest bruise and all his blood would simply
> drain away. It drove us crazy—first
> to protect him, then to see it happen. I   10
>
> would hang around him, picturing a knife
> or pointed stick, wondering how small a cut
> you'd have to make, then see the expectant face
> of another boy watching me, and we each knew
> how much the other would like to see him bleed.   15
>
> He made us want to hurt him so much we hurt
> ourselves instead: sliced fingers in craft class,

busted noses in baseball, then joined at last
into mass wrestling matches beneath his hill,
a tangle of crutches and braces, hammering at   20

each other to keep from harming him. I'd look up
from slamming a kid in the gut and see him watching
with the empty blue eyes of children in sentimental
paintings, and hope to see him frown or grin,
but there was nothing: as if he had already died.   25

Then, after a week, they sent him home. Too much
responsibility, the director said.
Hell, I bet the kid had skin like leather.
Even so, I'd lie in bed at night and think
of busting into his room with a sharp stick, lash   30

and break the space around his rose-petal flesh,
while campers in bunks around me tossed and dreamt
of poking and bashing the bleeder until he
was left as flat as a punctured water balloon,
which is why the director sent him home. For what   35

is virtue but the lack of strong temptation;
better to leave us with our lie of being good.
Did he know this? Sitting on his private hill,
watching us smash each other with crutches and canes,
was this his pleasure; to make us cringe beneath   40

our wish to do him damage? But then who cared?
We were the living children, he the ghost
and what he gave us was a sense of being bad
together. He took us from our private spite
and offered our bullying a common cause: 45

which is why we missed him, even though we wished
him harm. When he went, we lost our shared meanness
and each of us was left to snarl his way
into a separate future, eager to discover
some new loser to link us in frailty again.   50

 ## Winter   1998

MARIE PONSOT (B. 1921)

    I don't know what to say to you, neighbor,
    as you shovel snow from your part of our street
    neat in your Greek black. I've waited for
    chance to find words; now, by chance, we meet.

We took our boys to the same kindergarten,   5
thirteen years ago when our husbands went.
Both boys hated school, dropped out feral, dropped in
to separate troubles. You shift snow fast, back bent,
but your boy killed himself, six days dead.

My boy washed your wall when the police were done.   10
He says, "We weren't friends?" and shakes his head,
"I told him it was great he had that gun,"
and shakes. I shake, close to you, close to you.
You have a path to clear, and so you do.

The Wood-Pile   1914
ROBERT FROST (1874–1963)

Out walking in the frozen swamp one gray day,
I paused and said, "I will turn back from here.
No, I will go on farther—and we shall see."
The hard snow held me, save where now and then
One foot went through. The view was all in lines   5
Straight up and down of tall slim trees
Too much alike to mark or name a place by
So as to say for certain I was here
Or somewhere else: I was just far from home.
A small bird flew before me. He was careful   10
To put a tree between us when he lighted,
And say no word to tell me who he was
Who was so foolish as to think what *he* thought.
He thought that I was after him for a feather—
The white one in his tail; like one who takes   15
Everything said as personal to himself.
One flight out sideways would have undeceived him.
And then there was a pile of wood for which
I forgot him and let his little fear
Carry him off the way I might have gone,   20
Without so much as wishing him good-night.
He went behind it to make his last stand.
It was a cord of maple, cut and split
And piled—and measured, four by four by eight.
And not another like it could I see.   25
No runner tracks in this year's snow looped near it.
And it was older sure than this year's cutting,
Or even last year's or the year's before.

The wood was gray and the bark warping off it
And the pile somewhat sunken. Clematis   30
Had wound strings round and round it like a bundle.
What held it, though, on one side was a tree
Still growing, and on one a stake and prop,
These latter about to fall. I thought that only
Someone who lived in turning to fresh tasks   35
Could so forget his handiwork on which
He spent himself, the labor of his ax,
And leave it there far from a useful fireplace
To warm the frozen swamp as best it could
With the slow smokeless burning of decay.   40

9

THE MYSTERIES
OF LANGUAGE

Mystery lies at the heart of all the arts. Something essential to their power always remains elusive, beyond understanding. In their origins, the arts were primitive and no doubt occult. Julian Jaynes, in *The Origin of Consciousness in the Breakdown of the Bicameral Mind* (1976), argues that poetry was originally the "divine knowledge" or "divine hallucinations" of primitive peoples. "The god-side of our ancient mentality...usually, or perhaps always, spoke in verse.... Poetry then," he adds, "was the language of the gods."

The Greeks explained the magic of poetry through the Muses. Nine goddesses aided and inspired writers and musicians, but the nine were hard to please and had to be courted and seduced. The Christian and Renaissance writers explained the magic through *inspiration* (from Latin, "to be breathed into"). The divine wind blows where it will. The Romantics looked to *genius,* some freak of nature or of the soul. Followers of Freud have regarded the subconscious as the magic's source, a bubbling up from hidden parts of the mind. The Spanish poet Federico García Lorca used the untranslatable term *duende.* It comes to the artist, an old musician told Lorca, not from the artist's conscious control or native talents but "from inside, up from the very soles of the feet." Duende can be found in "the remotest mansions of the blood" and "burns the blood like a poultice of broken glass" to achieve its emotional power and depth. García Lorca's description of duende is in itself a stunning, associative work of art.

Researchers into creativity have found that artists free-associate more easily than those in science and technology, but these psychologists can't identify what qualities of the mind, or the brain, create creativity. Who can explain the complex associations of a well-turned metaphor or of ambiguity? Both invite multiple readings, not in an effort to confuse but to invite possibilities. Even though creativity and mystery often go hand in hand, poets must be cautious of writing poetry that is difficult for difficulty's sake.

Poetry often plays with the unsayable and embodies this struggle with language, as in Robin Becker's "When Someone Dies Young" (p. 148). Poet Lyn Hejinian posits: "Language discovers what one might know, which in turn is always less than what language might say." Being conscious of the limitations of language need not fill writers with anxiety. Rather, it can inspire us to explore, take literary risks, and push language, craft, and form beyond our own limits.

The Sense of Nonsense

At times we may get so bogged down in pondering the imponderabilities of language we forget what any nursery rhyme, like this one, reminds us.

> Bat, bat,
> Come under my hat,
> And I'll give you a slice of bacon;
> And when I bake,
> I'll give you a cake
> If I am not mistaken.

5

Nonsense is fun. Part of the magic of words stems from how often and how easily words give us pleasure without asking us to pay dues. A killjoy might ask why such incongruous images as "bat" and "bacon" appear in this verse. We're not irresponsible if we answer simply: because the words *sound good* together. What a delight to be led along by the string *bat–hat–bacon–bake–cake–mistaken*, all the more fun because the elements are incongruous. In a post-Freudian, post-Marxist era, theorists might reason some hidden political and sexual agenda in phrases such as "the cow jumped over the moon" and "the dish ran away with the spoon." But nonsense wiggles out of the bonds of reason—and more important, it's fun. Why write, why practice any art, if fun isn't fundamental?

As you read this familiar example of nonsense poetry by Lewis Carroll (1832–1898), relax with its weirdness as you stay alert to how it affects you.

 Jabberwocky

> 'Twas brillig, and the slithy toves
>   Did gyre and gimble in the wabe;
> All mimsy were the borogoves,
>   And the mome raths outgrabe.

"Beware the Jabberwock, my son!   5
    The jaws that bite, the claws that catch!
Beware the Jubjub bird, and shun
    The frumious Bandersnatch!"

He took his vorpal sword in hand:
    Long time the manxome foe he sought—   10
So rested he by the Tumtum tree,
    And stood awhile in thought.

And as in uffish thought he stood,
    The Jabberwock, with eyes of flame,
Came whiffling through the tulgey wood,   15
    And burbled as it came!

One, two! One, two! And through and through
    The vorpal blade went snicker-snack!
He left it dead, and with its head
    He went galumphing back.   20

"And hast thou slain the Jabberwock?
    Come to my arms, my beamish boy!
O frabjous day! Callooh! Callay!"
    He chortled in his joy.

'Twas brillig, and the slithy toves   25
    Did gyre and gimble in the wabe;
All mimsy were the borogoves,
    And the mome raths outgrabe.

In *Through the Looking Glass,* Humpty Dumpty heightens the poem's absurdity by informing Alice that "slithy" means "lithe and slimy," "mimsy" means "flimsy and miserable." And "toves" are "something like badgers…something like lizards—and…something like corkscrews" that "make their nests under sundials" and "live on cheese."

Though the words are nonsense, the story of "Jabberwocky" comes through clearly enough: A boy quests after the dreaded Jabberwock, slays it with his sword, and is hailed for his deeds. The story is archetypal, like the story of David and Goliath or Luke Skywalker and Darth Vadar. An **archetype** is a story, setting, character type, or symbol that recurs in many cultures and eras. Because we recognize the archetypal pattern, we don't much concern ourselves with who the "beamish boy" is or that the "Jubjub bird" and "Bandersnatch" still lurk out there. While cueing us into the familiar, the poem can carry us through the unfamiliar and celebrate language: its inventiveness, its whimsical sounds, its Jabberwock that "Came whiffling" and "burbled as it came."

Ride the music.…
            —Steve Orlen

Like riddles, jokes, and other word games, nursery rhymes and poems like "Jabberwocky" remind us of the deep roots that join poetry—and all of the arts—to play. After all, the common word for a dramatic composition is a *play;* we *play* musical instruments, and literary devices such as metaphors and puns *play on* words. The play of language juxtaposes all sorts of things from the palpably untrue to the delectably outrageous. The impossible happens. Grammatically, one noun can substitute for another so that "The cow jumps over the fence" becomes "The cow jumps over the moon." The syntax of a sentence may seem to be clear while its meaning remains murky; the linguist Noam Chomsky offers this example: "Colorless green ideas sleep furiously." Poets need to balance their engagement with the mysteries of language with generosity for the reader and be cautious of obscurity, even in the midst of play. After all, poetry is an art of communication, and you don't want to leave your readers behind.

Creating art certainly requires work. In poetry, this means draft after draft after draft. We speak of the finished product as a *work* of art, but we must also keep in mind that art grows out of play—free-associating, experimenting, being willing to discover, and moving beyond our usual tropes and forms. If we read the following poem by James Tate (B. 1943) as a kind of game, we can avoid troubling ourselves too much about what it means and appreciate what it does—how it plays with patterns of words and phrases, shuffling them to create new patterns.

 ## A Guide to the Stone Age
—*for Charles Simic*

A heart that resembles a cave,
a throat of shavings,
an arm with no end and no beginning:

How about the telephone?
—Not yet.   5

The cave in your skull,
a throat with a crack in it,
a heart that still resembles a cave:

How about the knife?
—Later.   10

The fire in the cave of your skull,
a beast who died shaving,
a cave with no end and no beginning:

A big ship!
—Shut up.   15

Instructions which ask you to burn other instructions,
a circle with a crack in it,
a stone with an arm:

A hat?
—Not the hat.   20

A ship with a knife in it,
a telephone with a hat over it,
a cave with a heart:

The Stone Age?
—There is no end to it.   25

Despite the poem's strangeness, the poem shrewdly controls form: twenty-five lines of alternating three- and two-line stanzas. Each stanza type serves a different function. The tercets offer a kind of list; the couplets offer a question and an answer. Each element in the first stanza reappears at least once in combinations with new items in the following tercets; for instance the parts of line 1, "A heart that resembles a cave," reappear in "The cave in your skull" (line 6), "a heart that still resembles a cave" (line 8), "The fire in the cave of your skull" (line 11), and "a cave with a heart" (line 23). The last line reverses the order of the first line. Clearly, there is an order to the disorder, an effective counterbalance to the weird subject.

A colon closes each tercet and introduces the couplet that apparently proposes some item to be included (e.g., line 4: "How about the telephone?"). At first, each possibility (telephone, knife, ship, hat) is rejected; then in the final tercet all the rejected items are included in the first two lines while its last line rearranges the items of line 1. The final couplet echoes the title and reflects on the poem itself: "—There is no end to it"; that is, the process of combining and recombining could go on endlessly, though indeed it does end, albeit ironically.

The poem takes care that we appreciate its jocularity. The Abbott and Costello bantering in the couplets seems to come to a head with the central couplet (lines 14–15). "A big ship!" the interjector proposes. And the respondent, as if out of exasperation, rejoins with a half-rhyme, "Shut up!" The deflation of the tone alerts us we are not meant to take the whole poem seriously, despite its often grim imagery of warfare and brutality. And it's that very tension that lends the poem its odd, associative power. The two speakers are humorously at odds, while ruin and chaos are close at hand.

The poem's meaning—which sometimes is a limiting way to approach a poem—may be unclear, but Tate's intentions aren't. The poem uses the elements of a game. When a poem indicates we should approach it as a game, we begin to ask ourselves where the game begins and ends, if our sense of its rules are correct, and if the payoff is worth our effort. A poem should *not* be a riddle, though it can use the qualities of a riddle for a specific effect. A poem needs to rise above its own cleverness and offer something else, be it interesting language, imagery, sound, form, or better yet, a combination of these elements.

The "Guide to the Stone Age" seems to mock the need for a rule book, as one speaker asks the other which elements fit the game and which don't. The poem doesn't so much guide us as deflate the efficacy of any guide (much less one to a prelinguistic era). The poem seems to be an instance of "Instructions which ask you to burn other instructions," an unending cycle.

Poems such as Tate's have an ancestor in the work of Gertrude Stein (1874–1946), an expatriate American who has been called the "Mama of Dada." Stein spent most of her adult life in Paris as a central part of that city's great artistic and intellectual community; her circle included Pablo Picasso, Henri Matisse, Ernest Hemingway, Mina Loy, Djuna Barnes, and Alfred North Whitehead. She described her writing as a "disembodied way of disconnecting something from anything and anything from something." Here is an excerpt from "A Valentine for Sherwood Anderson."

Very fine is my valentine.
Very fine and very mine.
Very mine is my valentine very mine and very fine.
Very fine is my valentine and mine, very fine very mine and mine is my valentine.

Later in the "Valentine" Stein asks, "Why do you feel differently about a very little snail and a big one?", emphasizing her interest in how words affect readers. In writing such as Stein's and Tate's, and in many more poems, such as Sharon Bryan's "Sweater Weather" (p. 3) and Williams's "The Red Wheelbarrow" (p. 82), words, phrases, images, and whole passages are used as objects for their tone and color, rather than for their representation or "meaning." Many avant-garde writers have experimented with ways of stripping fixed meanings from language and reinvigorating it.

Since the nineteenth century, the avant-garde has constantly wrestled with notions of "meaning" and "reality." One wave of experimentation has followed another, challenging the notions of some generations while adopting and adapting techniques of others to create their own innovations. Some of the movements in poetry include Symbolism, Imagism, Modernism, Surrealism, Dadaism, Futurism, Objectivism, Projectivism, Post-Modernism, Beat poetry, the New York School, and L=A=N=G=U=A=G=E poetry.

By tapping into the potential of language, poets can suppress the ordinary conscious workings of the mind and allow the profound, subliminal effects of sound, image, and metaphor to confront the reader directly—without a concern for a poem's explicit "meaning." T.S. Eliot describes the assumptions behind such poems:

The chief use of the "meaning" of a poem, in the ordinary sense, may be (for here... I am speaking of some kinds of poetry and not all) to satisfy one habit of the reader, to keep his mind diverted and quiet, while the poem does its work upon him: much as the imaginary burglar is always provided with a bit of nice meat for the house-dog. This is a normal situation of which I approve. But the minds of all poets do not work that way; some of them, assuming that there are other minds like their own, become impatient of this "meaning" which seems superfluous, and perceive possibilities of intensity through its elimination.

Eliot's *The Waste Land* is an early example of experimental poetry; it challenges meaning by suppressing the "habits" of narrative and logical argument in favor of a succession of characters, voices, scenes, fragments of scenes, images, quotations, allusions, and snippets. The process of creating meaning unveils itself and, at times, breaks down. The poem is as much about what it says as how it says it. Indeed, much of contemporary poetry is as much about *how* it is written as *what* it says.

Like paintings, sculptures, houses, and vases, poems are, first of all, *things* made of other *things* (that is, words). We rob poetry of its power when we forget that and tie it solely to the mast of preconceived meanings. Sometimes, intention must be left at the door. Archibald MacLeish concurs in his poem "Ars Poetica": "A poem should not mean / But be." If the "how" of a poem—the way it is made—is carefully and deliberately crafted, then it will nevertheless succeed on many levels and offer the reader another kind of experience.

The Logic of the Analogic

Among its more ordinary—even traditional—functions, the nonrational in literature undermines the barriers normally erected between the normal and abnormal, the real and imaginary, the logical and illogical.

In the following poem, Dara Wier (B. 1949) uses the archetype of the journey to play with the nature of contradiction:

 Daytrip to Paradox

> Just as you'd expect
> my preparations were painstaking
>   and exact. I took two
>
> butane lighters and a cooler
>   of ice. I knew the route   5
> had been so well-traveled
>
>   there'd be a store for necessities
> and tobacco and liquor and axes.
>   And near the Utopian village of Nucla
>
>   three Golden Eagles watched me   10
> from a salt cedar tree. One of them
>   held its third talon hard in the eye

of a white Northern Hare. Audubon
   couldn't have pictured it better.
      Everything was perfect. Naturally   15

   it made me think of Siberia,
the bright inspirational star
      that's handed down the generations,

and the long, terrible nights
      of the pioneers' journey to paradise.   20
   The valley on the way to Paradox

   was flat, there would be no choice,
nothing to get me lost.
      Cattleguards, gates and fencing

bordered the open range. Of course   25
   I crossed a narrow bridge
      to get into Paradox proper.

   In the store that doubled
as town hall and post office
      there was an account book for everybody   30

laid square on the counter.
   No one was expected to pay
      hard cold cash in Paradox apparently.

Wier takes us on a journey to **Paradox,** which is a contradictory but true state-ment. The poem's journey is metaphoric, and in order to arrive at Paradox we must pass through contradictions. The speaker's preparations are "painstaking / and exact," and yet consist of taking only "two / butane lighters and a cooler / of ice." But perhaps she needs them for the "tobacco and liquor" she will apparently pick up at the store, which strangely doesn't seem to carry lighters or ice. The speaker claims the harsh scenery, which includes a Golden Eagle with its "third talon hard in the eye / of a white Northern Hare," is "perfect," then tells us it makes her think of Siberia. The valley is also paradoxical; "Cattleguards, gates and fencing" define the "open range." A "narrow bridge" leads to "Paradox proper," *proper* as if it were a large town, though its small size is evident by the town hall that simultaneously acts as a post office and general store.

The speaker seems appropriately skeptical. It's only a "Daytrip," a place to visit, not stay. Nor does she seem persuaded by what she finds: "No one was expected to pay / hard cold cash in Paradox apparently." By connecting the sounds of the final two words, "Paradox apparently," Wier registers irony. What seems to be ap-parent is that Paradox deceives.

The fluid form supports the poem's wit. Wier deploys the poem in three-line stanzas, but of four different shapes. The pattern of indentations of stanza 1 is repeated in stanzas 6, 8, and 10; that of stanza 2 repeats in stanza 7; that of stanza 3 repeats in stanza 4; and that of stanza 5 repeats in stanzas 9 and 11. The appearance is of logical order and exactness, but the differing stanza patterns fall in place more or less randomly. They seem to point right (stanzas 2 and 7), left (stanzas 3, 4, 6, 8, and 10), and often both ways or neither (stanzas 1, 5, 9, and 11). The shifting pattern is never resolved; the impression seems finally to point every which way at once—suggesting the experience of a paradox.

The commonplace framework of narrative or argument can offer steady support to a structure built of nonlogical components. Consider the following poem by John Ashbery (B. 1927), for instance:

At North Farm

Somewhere someone is traveling furiously toward you,
At incredible speed, traveling day and night,
Through blizzards and desert heat, across torrents, through narrow passes.
But will he know where to find you,
Recognize you when he sees you,   5
Give you the thing he has for you?

Hardly anything grows here,
Yet the granaries are bursting with meal,
The sacks of meal piled to the rafters.
The streams run with sweetness, fattening fish;   10
Birds darken the sky. Is it enough
That the dish of milk is set out at night,
That we think of him sometimes,
Sometimes and always, with mixed feelings?

The framework allows this poem to sound as though it makes literal sense. The end-stopped lines suggest a series of factual assertions. The vivid imagery creates a convincing world that is subject to cold, heat, floods, and farm products. But what do the assertions add up to? In the speedy first stanza, where "someone is traveling furiously toward you," how can he move toward you if he's not sure where to find you? Will he not be able to recognize you because he hasn't met you or because you have changed? And is this "thing" he has for you something real and tangible, such as a car, bouquet of flowers, or a hug? Possibilities resound, but so do tonal anxiety and, surprisingly, warmth. In the world of the poem, someone is coming toward us and working with great energy to overcome opposition, which may, ironically, be our own resistance.

The second stanza suddenly slows down; clauses pile up like the abundance they describe, and the point of view becomes specified as "we." We cannot infer from the poem who "you," "he," or "we" signify, so we float in their indeterminacy.

Certainly we feel somehow generally included in this "we," because when we finish the poem we, too, have "mixed feelings." We simultaneously imagine the scene of plenty ("meal piled to the rafters"), while we ponder its source because "Hardly anything grows here." We wonder how the dish is relevant, set out as if for a cat. Is the dish for "him"? "Is it enough / That we think of him" because *thinking* of someone is enough to satisfy him or ourselves? Is thinking "Sometimes and always" the nature of all imagining, paradoxically sporadic and constant because we think on many levels at once? And what are those mixed feelings? Sadness and love? Regret and joy? The poem resists our questions and expectations, but allows for a satisfying ambiguity through its layered imagery and rich tone. The poem's pastoral title, "At North Farm," belies the poem's tone, at once anxious and filled with longing.

Ashbery has cited music as analogous to his purposes:

> I feel I could express myself best in music. What I like about music is its ability of being convincing, of carrying an argument through successfully to the finish, though the terms of this argument remain unknown quantities. What remains is the structure, the architecture of the argument, scene or story. I would like to do this in poetry.

Just as we can string together a perfectly regular, syntactic sequence with nonsense parts ("the cow crawled to conclusions"), so, too, can poets take the framework of story, description, or argument, but avoid logical components. As Paul Carroll suggests in an essay on Ashbery, "Multiple combinations of words and images (islands of significance) continually form, dissolve, and reform." Because meaning is not fixed, such poems invite the reader to help create the poem. They are analogous to abstract art, where a streak of red seems to confront a field of green paint. Such paintings aren't about the realistic rendering of reality but about form, shape, color, and paint itself, and what the viewer brings to the art.

Ordinary Strangeness

Our most everyday—or everynight—experience of the nonrational comes in dreams. Our dreaming minds seem to translate our conscious experiences and obsessions into a host of symbols and situations. While immersed in dreams, we accept them and feel their significance, but when we wake and try to sort through them, we often are baffled while still feeling their deep relevance. Certainly life itself can be as strange as a dream. Consider reality television, the latest weather catastrophe, or your neighbor down the street. The surrealist photographer Brassai agreed: "there is nothing more surreal than reality itself."

Our senses help us test whether what we are experiencing is really happening. "Pinch me," we might say when something seems incredible. But our senses don't always tell the truth. Optical illusions prove that. In our dreams we can experience sensations of waking life—and respond with a racing heart. A dream experience can be so convincing and a waking experience so strange that we might ask, as Keats does at the end of "Ode to a Nightingale," "Do I wake or sleep?"

In this passage from his *Leaves of Grass* (1855), Whitman captures the frantic energy and heaving confusion of dreams where the divisions between the real and unreal break down, and weird, often erotic, images erupt in our heads:

> O hotcheeked and blushing! O foolish hectic!
> O for pity's sake, no one must see me now!...my clothes were stolen
>   while I was abed,
> Now I am thrust forth, where shall I run?
>
> Pier that I saw dimly last night when I looked from the windows,
> Pier out from the main, let me catch myself with you and stay... I will
>   not chafe you;   5
> I feel ashamed to go naked about the world,
> And am curious to know where my feet stand...and what is this flooding me,
>   childhood or manhood...and the hunger that crosses the bridge between.
>
> The cloth laps a first sweet eating and drinking,
> Laps life-swelling yolks...laps ear of rose-corn, milky and just ripened:
> The white teeth stay, and the boss-tooth advances in darkness,   10
> And liquor is spilled on lips and bosoms by touching glasses, and the best
>   liquor afterward.

Asleep and dreaming, we assume the genuineness of our fantastic experiences. Images and events open seamlessly into one another. Poems such as Whitman's operate through associations. In flash after flash, one image suggests another, and the images in their sequence replace rational and discursive ways of saying something. When the method fails and the poet has not arranged the images so that a reader's responses can glide along with them, obscurity results. When association succeeds, it produces poems of great compressive power.

Whitman's dream-vision resists a rational approach. Readers cannot simply look for its meaning, because its meaning lies beyond interpretation; it lies within our response to the sensual, frenetic images and within the frenzied pace of its sentences. It recalls to us our own wonderfully bizarre and embarrassing dreams, where each element harbors a powerful significance that is often beyond our powers to define. The force of Whitman's images seems primitive. The landscape is biological, the self is alone, thrust out naked on a mysterious pier, with slippery footing, and with the orgiastic imagery of yolks, milky rose-corn, teeth, and liquor.

The poet lives in a daydream that is awake, but above all, his daydream remains in the world, facing worldly things.

—Gaston Bachelard

In both our waking and dreaming lives, our bodies act and react without our conscious control; this is perfectly normal. Our lungs expand and contract, our blood circulates, and our synapses fire. We're not aware of these autonomic responses until something out of the ordinary happens, and even then our bodies do most of their work outside our consciousness. After narrowly avoiding a head-on collision, you realize your heart is pounding, your lungs are straining, your skin is sticky with sweat. However, you still aren't aware of how often you blink your eyes or how your pancreas is operating. This immense nonconscious activity of our bodies—which constitutes what being alive literally means—forms the basis of this poem by Nina Cassian (B. 1924):

 Ordeal

Translated from the Romanian by Michael Impey and Brian Swann

I promise to make you more alive than you've ever been.
For the first time you'll see your pores opening
like the gills of fish and you'll hear
the noise of blood in galleries
and feel light gliding on your corneas   5
like the dragging of a dress across the floor.
For the first time, you'll note gravity's prick
like a thorn in your heel,
and your shoulder blades will hurt from the imperative of wings.
I promise to make you so alive that   10
the fall of dust on furniture will deafen you,
and you'll feel your eyebrows like two wounds forming
and your memories will seem to begin
with the creation of the world.

The eerie power of "Ordeal" recalls primitive spells devised for a particular person or situation. The poem's intimate tone suggests the speaker knows the person addressed. She promises to "make you more alive than you've ever been," a promise suggestive of the expansive claims a lover, or torturer, makes. On another level, of course, the poem addresses us. Notice how the intense imagery throughout the poem traps us in its embrace.

Through metaphor, imagery, and a form of **synesthesia** (a mixing of the senses), Cassian creates the ordeal, carrying us into a world so minute that the senses seem to blur and explode. The speaker promises "you" will be able to see your pores opening "like the gills of fish," hear the noise of blood, and feel light as it glides across the cornea "like the dragging of a dress across the floor." By magnifying autonomic responses, the speaker implies that the "you" will not only become acutely aware of the microscopic processes of the body but also feel a great and perhaps terrifying awakening. Line 9, "...your shoulder blades will hurt from the imperative of wings," implies that the aching is caused by one's need to be more than human, to be divine. Cassian strategically avoids defining the ordeal at hand and instead invites the reader to decide, while offering us a sensory feast.

Translation

One powerful and timeless way poets have delved into language's mysteries is through translating poems. Chaucer was fascinated by his Italian contemporary Petrarch's work with the sonnet, and a few generations later so were the Renaissance poets Wyatt and Surrey. T. S. Eliot looked to nineteenth-century French Symbolist poets, and Ezra Pound went further afield to eleventh-century Provencal and ancient Chinese poetry. Frost was a Latin scholar. Anglo-Saxon, Spanish, Latin American, Russian, Polish, Scandinavian, Japanese, Vietnamese, Persian, Cherokee, Urdu—poetry in English of the twentieth and twenty-first centuries has continually found new resources in the languages of other peoples.

When we try to carry the meaning of one language into another, we are *translating*. The word comes from the Latin *transfer*. We might easily think of translation as related to the word *metaphor* (from the Greek for "transference"). In trying to keep the sense, spirit, and sound of an original, translators of poetry must weigh literal meanings against considerations of connotation, idiom, form, sound, and rhythm. In the following poem, notice how Paul Éluard (1895–1952) creates a Surrealist poem that nevertheless employs familiar modes of logical argument. (Surrealism, an early twentieth-century movement, aimed to discover the artistic applications of the unconscious.) The first stanza poses a question, and the rest of the poem sets out to answer it.

 The Deaf and Blind

Translated from the French by Paul Auster

Do we reach the sea with clocks
In our pockets, with the noise of the sea
In the sea, or are we the carriers
Of a purer and more silent water?

The water rubbing against our hands sharpens knives.   5
The warriors have found their weapons in the waves
And the sound of their blows is like
The rocks that smash the boats at night.

It is the storm and the thunder. Why not the silence
Of the flood, for we have dreamt within us   10
Space for the greatest silence and we breathe
Like the wind over terrible seas, like the wind

That creeps slowly over every horizon.

The practice of translation, even for fun, opens up rich networks of language. For example, the phrase that Auster translates as "with clocks / In our pockets" (lines 1–2) in the original poem is *"avec des cloches / Dans nos poches,"* literally, "with bells in our pockets." "Cloche" means the large bell found, for instance, in a belfry; the French words for smaller bells are *clochette* and *sonnette*. We derived our English word *clock* from *cloche;* the earliest clocks—often placed on the town hall—rang out the hour. Sailors still use "bells" to measure time, and when we're "saved by the bell," we're saved by time running out (itself a phrase from the hourglass and its sands).

> *True art can only spring from the intimate linking of the serious and the playful.*
>
> —J. W. Goethe

The translator's choice of "clocks" is shrewd. To the Surrealists, a poem's sounds often matter more than one particular meaning. "Clocks" permits an internal rhyme with "pockets," registering Éluard's internal rhyme ("cloches," "poches") while retaining the absurdity and lucidity of Éluard's first image. Our pockets can't hold something as huge as a town bell or a clock (we carry watches in our pockets). On a metaphoric level, however, we might carry along to the sea the weight of regulation, time, and social order, which town bells and clocks imply. As the scholar Richard Stroik points out, the French have a phrase for parochialism that makes this point: *esprit de clocher,* literally, "spirit of the bell tower." Part of the Surrealist agenda is to strip away layers of received social attitudes to create a fresh realization of language, self, and reality.

Éluard's poem doesn't so much dismiss the rational as transcend or absorb it. The question–answer structure suggests a rational approach toward understanding while the terms of Éluard's argument shift and change, much as the time and the sea do. The sea, the various silences, and the flood seem simultaneously to refer to reality *and* to act as metaphors for our complex experience of that reality. In effect, Éluard makes us question the divisions between the rational and nonrational, between the reality that exists independently of our senses and the reality we know through our senses. The title helps posit these questions. We know the sea through sight and sound, but how do the deaf and blind experience the sea? When they touch it and feel its coldness, might they think of knives? No matter who observes it, the sea is itself; it exists apart from human perception of it.

The poem also suggests that we may be deaf and blind in a metaphoric sense—blinded and deafened by our knowledge and preconceptions. Conversely, the poem may imply an inverse reading: Is the knowledge we carry in ourselves "purer and more silent," perhaps more "real" than the reality we experience around us? Our experience of reading the poem imitates what it seems to be about: the multiplicity, fluidity, and mysteriousness of physical and metaphysical existence; it makes us feel this mystery, its masterful craft.

QUESTIONS AND SUGGESTIONS

1. Write a dream resume. That is, write a poem in which you combine several of your most vivid dreams. You might incorporate your most vivid dreams from your childhood or keep pen and paper by your bed. As soon as you wake up, write down everything you can remember—in detail—for a period of two weeks. Choose your most promising material, and arrange it into a poem.

2. Imagine you are a zipper, a brick in a chimney, a country on a map, a basketball, or another inanimate object. What might you feel as that thing? Experiment with synesthesia. What sensory information would you be especially aware of? Write a poem in the first person, speaking as that object, and adopting an attitude.

   Here's an example:

 Moon at the Mirror

MICHELLE BOISSEAU (B. 1955)
Location, location, location.
Even when I'm a slivered wafer
blanked out by the big guy, I got pull.

Just a shiny rock? So what. I'm close.
Others triumph in looks and power   5
but watch them fade as darkness brightens—

the big brassy moment I show up
(I adore being a blond), entrancing
homesick soldiers and drowning poets.

3. Take a poem you are revising and experiment with the $n + 7$ exercise developed by the mathematically inclined Oulipo poets. First, circle all the nouns in your poem. Then get a dictionary and open it up to any page. Find a noun on that page, then skip ahead seven more nouns, and insert the seventh noun into your poem. This playful revision exercise can be used to replace verbs or adjectives as well and invite unexpected surprises into your poems.

4. Take a look at "Ordeal" (p. 169) by Nina Cassian, "The Moon" (p. 176) by Jamie Sabines, or "Hunger" (p. 173) by Yasser Abdel-Latif. Choose one of these translations and write a poem inspired by the translation that acknowledges the challenge of translation and the slipperiness of language.

5. Experiment with writing a phonetic translation. That is, find a piece of writing in another language and rewrite it by using similar sounding words

in English. Don't worry about your poem making sense. Just explore the
sounds as a compositional device until you complete a first draft. You can
always revise later, or simply use your best lines to start a new poem.

POEMS TO CONSIDER

Hunger   2010
YASSER ABDEL-LATIF (B. 1969)
Translated by Yasser Abdel-Latif and Erica Mena-Landry

> Why don't I eat something new
> like the map of Sudan, for example
> or the Egyptian delta
> in a longitudinal slice
> from split branches to mouth   5
> a million generations of built up silt
> or eat a vast library
> full of immense books on the soul
> or a French dictionary
> until letters stream from my eyes   10
> Why don't I eat an extremely beautiful woman
> raw save for her femininity
> Why don't I eat a whole warehouse
> of steel nuts for high-octane trucks
> Why don't I eat a Communist Party   15
> or a whole town, maybe Damascus
> Why don't I eat something like Sayyed Darwish Hall
> at the Academy of Arts
> Why don't I eat something forgotten in one dream
> and sought in vain in the next   20
> Hunger devours me
> and still I travel
> indifferent to what you're eating…

Remember the Trains?   1998
MARTHA COLLINS (B. 1940)

> The friendly caboose. The whistle
> at night, the light across the field.
>
> Not a field: her yard,
> its little fountain. Not

a fountain: cattle cars crammed   5
with people. Cattle grazed in the field

of the friendly farmer across the road.
The farmer remembers everything.

She remembers counting the cars,
they were filled with cattle, coal,   10

it would fall on the tracks. The cattle
cars were crammed, he could see the faces

through the cracks, he could hear them cry
for the water he wasn't supposed to give.

She remembers waving, the engineer   15
who waved, the tracks behind her house.

He remembers the bodies, he saw them leap
from the windows, he heard the shots,

and the cars returning, empty,
not a whistle, the single light.   20

The cries she heard were children
at play, friendly children, except the boys

who turned the hose in her face, they said
Come look! she'd almost forgotten.

And the trains kept coming, full,   25
empty, full again, while the fountain

rose like a flower in the yard that was not
a field and the farmer worked

in the field while they wept,
they waited, they asked for water—   30

A Hunger So Honed   2003
TRACY K. SMITH (B. 1972)

Driving home late through town
He woke me for a deer in the road,
The light smudge of it fragile in the distance,

Free in a way that made me ashamed for our flesh—
His hand on my hand, even the weight   5
Of our voices not speaking.

I watched a long time
And a long time after we were too far to see,
Told myself I still saw it nosing the shrubs,

All phantom and shadow, so silent   10
It must have seemed I hadn't wakened,
But passed into a deeper, more cogent state—

The mind a dark city, a disappearing,
A handkerchief
Swallowed by a fist.   15

I thought of the animal's mouth
And the hunger entrusted it. A hunger
So honed the green leaves merely maintain it.

We want so much,
When perhaps we live best   20
In the spaces between loves,

That unconscious roving,
The heart its own rough animal.
Unfettered.

        The second time,   25
There were two that faced us a moment
The way deer will in their Greek perfection,

As though we were just some offering
The night had delivered.
They disappeared between two houses,   30

And we drove on, our own limbs,
Our need for one another
Greedy, weak.

Everything   2004
SRIKANTH REDDY (B. 1973)

She was watching the solar eclipse
through a piece of broken bottle

when he left home.
He found a blue kite in the forest

on the day she lay down   5
with a sailor. When his name changed,

she stitched a cloud to a quilt
made of rags. They did not meet,

so they could never be parted.
So she finished her prayer,   10

& he folded his map of the sea.

The Moon   2007
JAIME SABINES (1926–1999)
Translated by Philip Levine and Ernesto Trejo

You can take the moon every two hours
either with a tablespoon or in capsules.
It works as a tranquilizer and a sedative
and it also relieves
a hangover from OD-ing on philosophy.   5
In your pocket a ray of moonlight
is a surer charm than a rabbit's foot:
with it you'll find the beloved
or get secretly rich
and avoid doctors and clinics.   10
It calms and sweetens children
who can't fall asleep,
and a few drops of the moon in the eyes of the old
can help them find a good death.

Put a fresh leaf of the moon   15
under your pillow
and you'll see whatever you want to see.
Always carry a small flask of moon air
to breathe when you go under,
and donate the key to the moon   20
to prisoners and the others without hope.
For anyone condemned to death,
for anyone condemned to life
there's no better medicine than the moon
taken regularly in the prescribed dose.   25

PART

III

PROCESS

10

FINDING THE POEM

How do you start a poem? Where does it come from? Like the confluence of streams flowing into a river, many sources flow together to create a poem. Often the sources are hidden, subterranean, difficult to trace. Wade into a river and try to pinpoint where its waters originated. Writing a poem involves finding something to say and finding the best way to say it.

Many beginning poets start a poem burning to express something, such as heartbreak, the death of a grandparent, or the perils of climate change. The urge to write *about* something often gives the poet the first impulse. But poetry isn't primarily "about" something. If it were, a prose summary could excite us as much as a poem. Poet Louis Simpson cautions: "Most bad poetry is written because somebody sat down with an idea....Somebody has an idea and sits down and writes it out in lines, and maybe rhymes, but it's all from a very shallow level of the mind. The thing that comes *at* you, when you don't expect it, is the thing you really love."

When writing a poem, you want to go where the words themselves take you: the unexpected connection, the intriguing sentence, the resonant metaphor, the striking image. You will discover the most promising poems usually don't start as an idea or a feeling but more as a kind of potential, an urge to discover what the poem will reveal through language. "You don't make a poem with ideas, but with words," asserted the French symbolist poet Stephen Mallarme. Let language itself guide you. Yes, it feels fantastic to get off our chests what we truly care about, though writing with such heavy intention may be more appropriate for an essay, editorial, or diary entry. Poetry needs to make *its readers* care through its intense engagement with language, as this poem does by Natasha Sajé (B. 1955):

 Reading the Late Henry James

is like having sex, tied to the bed.
Spread-eagled, you take whatever comes,

179

trusting him enough to expect
he'll be generous, take his time. Still
it's not exactly entertainment: 5
Page-long sentences strap
your ankles and chafe your wrists.
Phrases itch like swollen bee stings
or suspend you in the pause
between throbs of a migraine,   10
the pulsing blue haze
relieved. You writhe and twist—
if you were split in half,
could he get all the way in?
When you urge him to move faster,   15
skim a little,
get to the good parts, he scolds,
"It's all good parts."
Then you realize you're bound
for disappointment, and you begin   20
to extricate yourself,
reaching past his fleshy white fingers
for a pen of your own.

Sajé's irreverence for a master writer and her playful language instigates the poem's fun and immediately pulls the reader in through its energetic **running title** (a title that syntactically continues into the first line). Sajé connects James's congested syntax with bondage and continues to develop that metaphor throughout the poem ("tied to the bed," "chafe your wrists," "you're bound," etc.). James often is referred to as "The Master," which is yet another deepening of the bondage metaphor. And just look at Sajé's visceral verbs ("chafe," "itch," "writhe," "twist," etc.), which seem to wriggle off the page.

As painters work with paint, and filmmakers with film, poets work with language—thankfully, our medium is plentiful and free. We feel our way into poems word by word, groping for the right sentence, the magic metaphor—step by step, into the stream.

Imitation and Models

The best advice a beginning poet can get is the simplest: READ. Poet Ted Kooser has told his students to read 100 poems for every one they write. Most of the poems beginning poets have read are tame ones approved by school boards or the predictable lyrics of popular music that are supported by driving rhythms of drums, guitars, and keyboards. But poetry isn't tame, predictable, or dependent on a band. Poetry is what disturbs through language, although it may be subtle as a gust that sweeps over a pond and troubles the cattails. Your work as a poet includes knowing how other

Imitation, conscious imitation, is one of the great methods, perhaps the method of learning to write.

—Theodore Roethke

poets have used language; reading their works shows you new ways to imitate it, use it, and keep language fresh, particularly if you're aware of what has already been written. Find poems that captivate you. The more you read, the more you'll realize where your own poems might go.

Without your being aware, you already have been influenced by an ocean of voices. These may include an intoxicating line by Emily Dickinson, Natasha Sajé, or Henri Cole. The danger lurks not in being too much influenced by powerful poems but in being influenced too little. "Originality is not the denial of origins," insists Dean Young. Rather, you can learn from "the masters" (however you define them) and from that knowledge choose the best options for the poem at hand. Read Shakespeare, Baudelaire, Lorca, and Glück. Read literary journals and search out poems of other ages and cultures. Read poems in translation. The more you soak up, the less likely you'll fix on a single mentor, voice, method, or theory. Beware of theories: It is *poems* you want.

Look for the poems and the poets who really speak to you. Find poems that make you feel, as Emily Dickinson said, as if physically the top of your head were taken off. Find one poet you love, then find another. Look their books up in the library, the bookstore, and on the Internet. Memorize their poems, learn them *by heart*—with all of that phrase's connotations. Make them part of yourself, and you will gain what Robert Pinsky calls the "pleasure of possession—possession of and possession by" another poet's words. These poems will be your models, after which you'll fashion your own poems.

Rather than being a problem, *imitation* makes poets. Art students copy paintings by Degas and Renoir. College basketball players study the reverse layups of the pros. Medical residents stand at the elbows of attending physicians. Apprentice poets—all poets—read. As a student, you may write Dickinson poems, Yeats poems, Frost poems, Bishop poems, any number of other poets' poems. This is essential exercise. As you discover and absorb possibilities, the poems you write will begin to be in your own voice, not in Ginsberg's or Plath's. Don't worry about finding your own voice. The many poems you discover and absorb will gradually come together to help you create your particular voice, approach, and vision, which will likely change as your work continues to develop. Often, a poet's love for other poems engenders new poems; Homer inspired Virgil, who inspired Dante, who inspired Petrarch, who inspired Sidney, who inspired Herbert, who inspired Dickinson, who herself inspired generations of poets. Here, Donald Justice (1925–2004) takes off on

"Piedra negra sobre una piedra blanca," a poem by the Peruvian poet César Vallejo (1892–1938):

Variations on a Text by Vallejo

> *Me morirá en Paris con aguacero...*

I will die in Miami in the sun,
On a day when the sun is very bright,
A day like the days I remember, a day like other days,
A day that nobody knows or remembers yet,
And the sun will be bright then on the dark glasses of strangers   5
And in the eyes of a few friends from my childhood
And of the surviving cousins by the graveside,
While the diggers, standing apart, in the still shade of the palms,
Rest on their shovels, and smoke,
Speaking in Spanish softly, out of respect.   10

I think it will be on a Sunday like today,
Except that the sun will be out, the rain will have stopped,
And the wind that today made all the little shrubs kneel down;
And I think it will be a Sunday because today,
When I took out this paper and began to write,   15
Never before had anything looked so blank,
My life, these words, the paper, the gray Sunday;
And my dog, quivering under a table because of the storm,
Looked up at me, not understanding,
And my son read on without speaking, and my wife slept.   20

Donald Justice is dead. One Sunday the sun came out,
It shone on the bay, it shone on the white buildings,
The cars moved down the street slowly as always, so many,
Some with their headlights on in spite of the sun,
And after a while the diggers with their shovels   25
Walked back to the graveside through the sunlight,
And one of them put his blade into the earth
To lift a few clods of dirt, the black marl of Miami,
And scattered the dirt, and spat,
Turning away abruptly, out of respect.   30

Justice's variations on Vallejo's poem—his repetition of phrases, syntax, images, words—create a wholly new poem, but also honor the poem that inspired him. As you look at Vallejo's poem, consider how the poems are related:

Piedra negra sobre una piedra blanca

> Me morirá en Paris con aguacero,
> un día del cual tengo ya el recuerdo.

Me morirá en Paris—y no me corro—
tal vez un jueves, como es hoy, de otoño.

Jueves será, porque hoy, jueves, que proso   5
estos versos, los húmeros me he puesto
a la mala y, jamás como hoy, me he vuelto,
con todo mi camino, a verme solo.

César Vallejo ha muerto, le pegaban
todos sin que ál les haga nada;   10
le daban duro con un palo y duro

tambián con una soga; son testigos
los días jueves y los huesos húmeros,
la soledad, la lluvia, los caminos...

Vallejo's first line gave Justice his epigraph, which can be translated, "I will die in Paris in a downpour"; Justice adapts the line to fit his own imagined circumstances: "I will die in Miami in the sun." He imagines his death as a returning to his hometown, where the sun shines "on the bay" and "on the white buildings," whereas Vallejo pictures his death far from his native Peru; he will die a stranger.

Vallejo's is a spare sonnet-length poem of two quatrains and two tercets with rhyming end words (even if you don't speak Spanish, scan the last word in each line, and you'll see the rhyme pattern). Justice's poem is longer, denser in detail, and made up of three ten-line stanzas. Justice and Vallejo may not have actually written their poems about their own deaths on a stormy day (or in Justice's case, with his dog quivering at his feet), but it *sounds* as though they did. Both poems begin with the future tense and strategically shift to the past tense at about two-thirds into the poems, after the equivalent phrases, "César Vallejo ha muerto" and "Donald Justice is dead." Both poems repeat phrases that include the anticipated death day ("jueves" means "Thursday") and the words *day* and *today* ("día" and "hoy").

In Justice's poem the grave diggers, who wait for the funeral party to be off, speak the Spanish of the Peruvian poet as if Vallejo's spirit presided over the funeral. The repetitions sound an incantory tone—apropos for someone imagining his own funeral. "Variations on a Text by Vallejo" illustrates how many streams flow together in a poem—one's imagination, intuition, ear for language, technical mastery, and knowledge of other poems.

Because reading other poets is such a strong stimulus for writing poems, many poets begin writing sessions by reading poems for an hour or so, or until some line, image, or rhythm launches them into a poem's (often provisional) beginning. Many poets also read while they revise, which helps them find the right word or form.

Try not to mistake conscious re-creations such as Justice's "Variations" with **parody,** a deliberate, exaggerated imitation of another work or style. Parodies are a form of criticism, exposing weaknesses in the original whereas writing a rigorous imitation—following the form, syntax, or subject matter of another poet, such as Whitman's catalogues or Dickinson's darting dashes—can let you absorb what another poet has to teach you.

Sources and "Truth"

As you start a poem, stay open to opportunities; allow early impulses to shift and meander. Maxine Kumin says, "You write a poem to discover what you're thinking, feeling, where the truth is. You don't begin by saying, now this is the truth" and then start writing about it. Often your first notions aren't the richest—they're merely the first. If you stubbornly stick to them, you may miss a more tantalizing direction. Maybe you first thought of a cross-country car trip with your family. Don't let your memory of how bored you were keep you from writing about the graffitied water tower you saw in Iowa or the kid from Hattiesburg you met in a motel pool. Maybe you weren't as bored as you thought. Follow the most intriguing and resonant phrases and images, but don't try to record the entire trip.

Keeping yourself open to sources means keeping your imagination open, too. Obviously, Justice doesn't *know* he'll die in Miami—in fact, he died in Iowa City—and that's not the point. The poet's first loyalty is to making the best possible poem and exploring the reaches of the imagination in service of the poem. Just because something happened a particular way in life doesn't mean it should happen that way in a poem. Poems have their own realities and their own truths. Ask yourself what your poems need, not what you do.

The rich imagery in this poem by Yusef Komunyakaa (B. 1947) suggests it rose from multiple, even contradictory, sources:

 Sunday Afternoons

They'd latch the screendoors
& pull venetian blinds,
Telling us not to leave the yard.
But we always got lost
Among mayhaw & crabapple.   5

Juice spilled from our mouths,
& soon we were drunk & brave
As birds diving through saw vines.
Each nest held three or four
Speckled eggs, blue as rage.   10

Where did we learn to be unkind,
There in the power of holding each egg
While watching dogs in June
Dust & heat, or when we followed
The hawk's slow, deliberate arc?   15

In the yard, we heard cries
Fused with gospel on the radio,
Loud as shattered glass

In a Saturday-night argument
About trust & money.   20

We were born between Oh Yeah
& Goddammit. I knew life
Began where I stood in the dark,
Looking out into the light,
& that sometimes I could see   25

Everything through nothing.
The backyard trees breathed
Like a man running from himself
As my brothers backed away
From the screendoor. I knew   30

If I held my right hand above my eyes
Like a gambler's visor, I could see
How their bedroom door halved
The dresser mirror like a moon
Held prisoner in the house.   35

The children are shut out of the house and shut in the yard, caught in the middle, between the private world of the parents and the dangerous one beyond the yard. They are powerless to enter either, though what holds them is flimsy: only a latched screen door and parental orders. Komunyakaa intensifies the power the parents hold over the children by identifying them only as "they": the others, the adults, the all-powerful enemies.

> *I think I knew very early on that if I knew how a poem was going to end, that poem was not going to be very good.*
> —Michael Ondaatje

Every detail here probably did not occur in Komunyakaa's childhood precisely as the poem lays it out. The poem is not a report. Rather, the chosen details evoke the children's pain and confusion. The image of the robin's eggs may have flowed into the poem from another day or another experience. Nevertheless, Komunyakaa decided that this image of beauty, fragility, and violence ("blue as rage") was an appropriate metaphor. The vandalism of the bird nests implies the boys' anger and perplexity over their parents' vacillating intimacy and fights. In this emotional universe, feelings of entrapment spread. Komunyakaa ends the poem with a simile that compares the speaker's obstructed view to the moon being held prisoner. Both speaker and moon are pinned to space and unable to see or move due to other forces (parents and gravity). The simile reflects the speaker's powerlessness and isolation.

In starting poems, stay receptive to everything. Let impressions, ideas, metaphors, half-forgotten memories, and the rhythms of a well-loved poem stream into your poem, enrich your original inspiration, and surprise you—and your readers. As Frost put it, no surprise for the poet, no surprise for the reader. When something odd or outrageous enters your poem, allow it to register, to grow and deepen. The analytical faculty can help you revise, but don't turn it on too early. When writing a first draft, you want to rouse that part of your brain that says, "What if?" and remain open to possibility.

Emotion and Thought

Every poem has a speaker and a voice, even if that voice is disembodied or personified. Every voice expresses a tone, an attitude toward the subject. Therefore all poems express some emotion, even if unstated or matter-of-fact. Handling emotion can be challenging for any poet. In the earliest stages of writing poems, particularly those poems whipped up in an emotional storm, achieving a degree of detachment is essential, though that detachment may not come until the revision stage.

When the heat of your emotions has cooled, you'll be able to see more clearly and ask yourself honestly what is or isn't working in your poem. As Wordsworth notes, poetry

> takes its origin from emotion recollected in tranquillity; the emotion is contemplated till, by a species of re-action, the tranquillity gradually disappears, and an emotion, kindred to that which was before the subject of contemplation, is gradually produced, and does itself actually exist in the mind. In this mood successful composition generally begins.

Wordsworth described the writing process as "emotion *recollected* in tranquility." When writing, we regather the emotion and re-experience it; we re-vision, we re-see. When revising, you don't stop feeling what's driving you to write, but your relationship to your emotions changes. Poems, of course, are more than feelings. As you revise, you'll be able to do *more* than feel—you can explore, imagine, discover, and discriminate.

In the earliest drafts of bringing a powerful emotion to the page, get down those words that are bubbling forth, and be open to any image or metaphor that arises. At first you might start with the obvious: flat assertions and clichés, such as "You make me so happy" or "My heart is heavy as lead." Such generalities offer a kind of shorthand to our feelings; we use them without considering what they really mean or what our *particular* feeling is.

Don't be dismayed if your early drafts are riddled with generalities and clichés. If you find yourself drawn to a particular cliché, try delving into it, exploding it, and tweaking it in some way. You may find a way of bringing the dead metaphor inside back to life, as Emily Dickinson does in "After great pain, a formal feeling comes—":

After great pain, a formal feeling comes—
The Nerves sit ceremonious, like Tombs—
The stiff Heart questions was it He, that bore,
And Yesterday, or Centuries before?

The Feet, mechanical, go round—   5
Of Ground, or Air, or Ought—
A Wooden way
Regardless grown,
A Quartz contentment, like a stone—

This is the Hour of Lead—   10
Remembered, if outlived,
As Freezing persons, recollect the Snow—
First—Chill—then Stupor—then the letting go—

Out of frustration to describe the pain we suffer, we talk about our heavy hearts, how we can't breathe, how we feel made of stone. But all these feelings remain abstract to someone else and won't affect an objective reader. Beware of sentimentality and overblown emotion that tell your reader how to feel. Instead, use metaphor, imagery, resonant details, and fresh language to spark a response in your reader.

Dickinson's poem makes pain vivid by revisiting and revising clichés. Lead, that deadly and heavy element, aptly describes how grief weighs on us. But feeling "heavy as lead" isn't a particularly fresh or evocative phrase. Instead Dickinson uses lead to depict the eerie sense of timelessness that pain creates. It shuts us in an eternity where the days blur; we exist in an "Hour of Lead." Dickinson's image of lead also excites other senses; we can almost taste the dull metal on our tongues. Such particular imagery reveals that Dickinson moved beyond clichés to write about an emotionally charged subject. But how can writers accomplish this?

One way of achieving critical distance from a subject is to consider that the speaker of a poem isn't you, the living poet, but a version of you, an invented *persona*. You might even experiment with shifting from first to third-person point of view. When we begin a poem, we put on the poet's mask that Yeats talks about to see beyond the emotional muddle we find ourselves in and gain insight into ourselves and humanity. In the space of their poems, poets become noble, brave, brilliant, and generous—better people than they normally are. And they can become worse—bitter, jealous, and vindictive. The speaker you create for your poems might be a terrible person, which is fine if that's what the poem demands.

Using a persona can help you explore your feelings by focusing on another character in the situation. William Carlos Williams (1883–1963) expresses his concern for his newly widowed mother by writing in her voice:

 ## The Widow's Lament in Springtime

Sorrow is my own yard
where the new grass
flames as it has flamed
often before but not
with the cold fire   5
that closes round me this year.

Thirtyfive years
I lived with my husband.
The plumtree is white today
with masses of flowers.   10
Masses of flowers
load the cherry branches
and color some bushes
yellow and some red
but the grief in my heart   15
is stronger than they
for though they were my joy
formerly, today I notice them
and turn away forgetting.
Today my son told me   20
that in the meadows,
at the edge of the heavy woods
in the distance, he saw
trees of white flowers.
I feel that I would like   25
to go there
and fall into those flowers
and sink into the marsh near them.

Williams writes the poem from the point of view of a widow and mother, showing the depths of her grief. To her, the gorgeous spring day loses its luster. The blades of new grass and the plum and cherry blossoms don't touch her; she wants to leave it all. His efforts to cheer her up with tales of flowering trees only make her long for her own demise. Williams allows readers to re-experience deep grief through the lens of the inconsolable widow-mother. We not only feel her pain, but the helplessness of her son who is unable to comfort her. This poem is more than a self-enclosed expression solely intended for Williams and his mother. Notice the open-ended title (as opposed to calling it "My Mother" or "My Father's Death") and the luminous details that invite the reader in, regardless of the poem's particular origin.

What might it feel like for another person to feel what you're feeling? Invent a situation, emotionally similar to yours, and speak through that situation. Or become another character entirely, such as the mermaid Amy Gerstler creates (p. 137) or the field of daisies Louise Glück uses as speakers (p. 144). These poets use their understanding of human emotion to create unexpected characters and situations to affect their readers. The emotion and the scene must be re-created for the reader, not merely referred to. In your poems, you want to create a three-dimensional world for your readers, a dynamic world they can also inhabit.

Using raw emotions risks **sentimentality:** writing that doesn't earn—through imagery, metaphor, and detail—the emotion it asks a reader to feel; writing burdened with clichés; writing more interested in self-expression than in making a poem. Most often sentimentality is merely simplistic, cheap, easy: the schmaltz of little girls in rags and starving puppies. At its worst, sentimentality masks the truth, especially from the writer. If a writer depicts a ragged child as cute, how much of the child's actual situation has the writer really imagined? Will we be likely to see that child as a real human being instead of merely as a category? This sort of writing lacks consideration for language and the reader. Instead, it delivers banal familiarity and clichés of thought.

Attendant with sentimentality is **overstatement,** or **hyperbole;** whenever used (which should be shrewdly), it must seem appropriate to the situation and grounded through particulars. Hyperbole opens up the Dickinson poem we discussed earlier in this chapter: "After great pain, a formal feeling comes—". However, Dickinson grounds this grand statement through surpising and effective particulars, including wood, quartz, lead, and snow. The widow in Williams's poem claims, "Sorrow is my own yard," and then shows the circumstance which justifies her claim.

The calm, detached, or numb quality of **understatement** carries an air of authenticity, like Dickinson's deft touch in depicting death by exposure: "First—Chill—then Stupor—then the letting go—." Understatement has an effective edge when used to inscribe crisis or trauma, and your readers won't miss, or need, the syrupy emotion. In the small violence of the following poem, notice how the scene's quietness makes it all the more affecting:

The Hawk
MARIANNE BORUCH (B. 1950)

He was halfway through the grackle
when I got home. From the kitchen I saw
blood, the black feathers scattered
on snow. How the bird bent
to each skein of flesh, his muscles   5
tacking to the strain and tear.
The fierceness of it, the nonchalance.
Silence took the yard, so usually
restless with every call or quarrel—
titmouse, chickadee, drab   10
and gorgeous finch, and the sparrow haunted
by her small complete surrender
to a fear of anything. I didn't know
how to look at it. How to stand
or take a breath in the hawk's bite   15

and pull, his pleasure
so efficient, so *of course, of course,*
the throat triumphant,
rising up. Not
the violence, poor grackle. But the   20
sparrow, high above us, who
knew exactly.

The speaker admits she "didn't know / how to look" at the hawk eating the grackle and doesn't ask us to feel more about this scene than it merits. Nature doesn't sentimentalize its creatures; people do. One task of Boruch's poem includes seeing the predator and prey "exactly," with respect for the precision of the predator, sympathy for the "poor grackle," and acknowledgment that the sparrow's fears were accurate.

Boruch's poem might offend some readers because it depicts the violent death of an animal. Keep in mind that a poem that takes no risks is probably not worth writing. Marvin Bell offers this advice: "Try to write poems at least one person in the room will hate." Not that you need be cruel, but don't try to win a popularity contest. A poem burdened with trying not to offend can harbor little of poetry's power.

Getting into Words

Wherever it originates, the poem begins when the poet becomes aware of the possibility of a poem. Sometimes the seed can be another poem—as with "Variations on a Text by Vallejo." Some poets begin by writing randomly, capturing in a notebook or on a computer whatever swims into their heads: phrases, rhymes, ideas, images, lists, weird words. Random writing can serve as a writer's exercise, just as the baseball player slugs away in the batting cage or the pianist plays scales.

Poems often begin in the head and continue to develop there in the relatively free-floating mixture of thought, memory, and emotion. Putting something down on paper tends to fix it (although, of course, you can revise it later). Words that feel full and wonderful in the mind or mouth may look spindly and naked on the page. All that blankness can be intimidating, swallowing up the handful of words that try to break the silence. Some poets compose scores of lines in their heads before taking up the pen or turning on the computer. Other poets need to get words down early, when a sentence, line, or phrase seems strong enough to withstand the scrutiny of the page.

Consistently writing in a notebook—which Billy Collins calls "keeping a log of the self"—can help you keep track of your ideas until you have time for them. Then later, you'll have something to begin with instead of an oppressive blank page staring back at you. For the earliest, sloppiest stages of writing, the notebook has many advantages: It's portable, accessible, and usable during a thunderstorm.

Also, unlike the computer that obliterates deletions, the notebook allows you to reconstruct what you've crossed out.

The poet Richard Hugo in *The Triggering Town* advises student poets to use number 2 pencils, to cross out instead of erase, and "to write in a hard-covered notebook with green lined pages. Green is easy on the eyes.... The best notebooks I've found are National 48–81." That's what worked for him, and every poet will find a particular system that feels right. Experiment with many methods, drafting poems on the computer, with paper and pencil, with lined and unlined pages, etc. Be adventurous. Poets have written while nursing a baby, by flashlight on an army footlocker after lights-out, and under odder conditions. But the poet is entitled to work wherever it feels right: a coffeeshop, a restaurant, or in bed.

Discipline is key, as any working writer will tell you. Set up a work schedule and stick with it. Try to fence off a particular time of day for writing. When you sit down at your scheduled time, your mind will be alert to poems—your unconscious will have already begun getting you ready. Be protective of your writing schedule. Shut off your phone, wake up before anyone else, or stay up after they've turned in. Discipline may not be a substitute for talent (however one defines that), but talent evaporates without it.

Most writers go through dry spells. Even the most disciplined writers come to a point where the well seems empty. Instead of moping or getting frustrated, feed your imagination. Go for a drive, wander around a museum, or page through a book of photographs, and you may find a way to get started. Or try one of the writing exercises in this book's "Questions and Suggestions" sections. When a writing method begins to seem stale, try something else. Just as any athlete or musician will tell you, practice helps; practice your art regularly, whether you feel inspired or not. And revise, revise, revise.

Keeping a Poem Going

When the poem is coming, when the wind is in your sails, go for it. "And the secret of it all," Whitman says, "is to write in the gush, the throb, the flood, of the moment—to put things down without deliberation—without worrying about their style." Writing the first draft all in one sitting, filling up the page from top to bottom, pushing onward when you feel the growing poem resist, can give a poem coherence and clarity, for you are writing under the influence of a single mood, following the notions of a particular time. Getting a whole first draft early, even if sketchy, sloppy, and wordy, will give you material to work on later.

Talking to yourself, *literally*, may also help a poem along. Brainstorming can allow you to evaluate and explore phrases or images. In the early stages when you don't know what angle your poem will take (unlike, say, the writer of an editorial), literally talking through your choices can guide you toward a solution. Ask yourself questions (who, what, where when, why), or try using the questions for revision in Appendix I.

At some stage in the process, seeing the words on the page becomes crucial. You might mark key words and see if those words open up other associations. Because we read poems in print, seeing a draft of a poem on the page can also help you see clearly how it *looks*. Lines will be longer or shorter than you imagined, for instance, and the poem skinnier or chunkier or more graceful.

Considering its form, even if tentative and provisional, can also help coax out the poem. The very first line you write may provide a norm to build the poem around, even if you cut it later. You will be looking to discover what visual form the poem will take: A narrow ribbon? A squat, solid poem? Staggered loosely across the page? Determining line and form may open up a stuck poem. Simlarly altering the form of a stuck poem can invite different words, even entire stanzas, into your poems. Try switching a prose poem into couplets and see how it helps you compress your language. Try shifting your couplets into a prose poem and see what opportunities for narrative arise.

From these loose impressions that he recorded after a visit in 1929 with Olivia Shakespeare (with whom he had been in love as a young man), W. B. Yeats (1865–1939) began to lure the poem out:

Your hair is white
My hair is white
Come let us talk of love
What other theme do we know
When we were young
We were in love with one another
And then were ignorant

The lines and phrases he began trying out were equally sketchy (and thin). Here are bits of them over several drafts:

Your other lovers being dead and gone
Those other lovers being dead and gone

friendly light
hair is white

Upon the sole theme of art and song
Upon the supreme theme of art and song
Upon the theme so fitting for the aged; young
We loved each other and were ignorant

Once more I have kissed your hand and it is right
All other lovers estranged or dead

The heavy curtains drawn—the candle light
Waging a doubtful battle with the shade

Gradually Yeats began to find the poem in his phrases and arrived at eight lines of iambic pentameter, rhyming *abba cddc*. The image of the white hair didn't last, but it lead to a rhyme (*right, night*), which became the opening argument of the final poem:

 After Long Silence

Speech after long silence; it is right,
All other lovers being estranged or dead,
Unfriendly lamplight hid under its shade,
The curtains drawn upon unfriendly night,
That we descant and yet again descant   5
Upon the supreme theme of Art and Song:
Bodily decrepitude is wisdom: young
We loved each other and were ignorant.

Writing even a few lines may be a mingling of a hundred creative and critical acts in rapid-fire. You will find it useful to list several alternatives to a sentence or a word in the margin. You might try keeping a word-bank at hand as you write and revise. Is the tulip *scarlet, ruby streaked, deflated, smiling,* or *gulping?* As the poem starts to materialize on the page, listen to it, and follow where it wants to lead you.

> *The more art is controlled, limited, worked over, the more it is free.*
>
> —Igor Stravinsky

Put your ear to the poem, too. When a poem seems to peter out, try saying aloud what you have so far so you can hear the awkward and graceful parts. Copying out by hand and retyping word by word can help, too. Repeating the poem from the beginning will improve the continuity and can allow the poem's original energy to refuel it, providing the momentum to get across a hard spot.

To clarify the poem's intentions, try challenging your word choices. Turn negative phrases into positives, positives into negatives. For instance, if you've written, "I loved him the first night," try, "I wouldn't love him the first night" or "No one loved him at first." If the peacock's feathers were "oily swirls," try them out as "beaten metal." By challenging your initial impulse, you will test your commitment to your words and may find the opposite assertion a more resonant, beautiful, or accurate choice.

When a poem knots up and won't spool out, you may have before you two or more poems. A poem can set off in almost any direction, and in many directions at once. Ask yourself if the poem's directions support each other or crowd each other out. "Kill your darlings," Faulkner advised. You must often excise those parts most precious to you before the whole can flourish. You can always recycle phrases or even entire stanzas and use them for another poem.

Look for the central thrust of the poem. Find the poem's central time and place, its key voice. Ask yourself: Who is speaking? To whom? Why? When? Where? Bring the possibilities into focus and cut or replace whatever word or gesture isn't working. As Yeats drafted "After Long Silence," he sketched out the scene with Olivia Shakespeare—the lamplight, the drawn curtains, and a context ("other lovers being dead and gone")—and gradually arrived at the final version.

Every poem develops from a unique set of sources and a unique application of tools. Even if the first draft comes in a rush, it will need you to go through it step by step, weighing each word. If the poem comes slowly, nail by nail and board by board, try working out a new draft in one swift torrent. A strategy that launches one poem may not work for another. Be elastic in your approach. Writing from formulas will likely give you formulaic poems.

Every poet has times when, after hours of hard work, the poem flops. Put it aside; you may resuscitate it next week or next month. Or maybe not. Let it go. You have other poems to write. The adventure—and the frustration—begins all over with each poem. But each time you'll have more options to choose from, more experience, and more skills to apply to your poems.

QUESTIONS AND SUGGESTIONS

1. Keep an inspiration or idea notebook. Write down favorite lines from poems you admire; tape in images you find compelling, fortunes from fortune cookies, newspaper articles, phrases you cut from your own poems but hope to recycle, and anything else that inspires you. Whenever you feel stuck, use your idea notebook to help you get going.

2. Use a line by another poet as inspiration for a poem of your own, similar to Adrian Blevins (p. 195). You can use the line as a title, a first line, or imbed it in the body of the poem, as Hadara Bar-Nadav (B. 1973) does in the following poem:

 ## I Dreaded that First Robin, So

Title and italics after Emily Dickinson

That willful singing. Blare of arrival and ache of thaw. My hands ringing with blood-heat. I preferred fingers of ice fringing the windows and doors. Fringes made pear-yellow in the sun, so the world is tinted distant soft. The roads untouched. The grass asleep. No note rippling the landscape. Mind filling with wind. A timeless now—a pause here that resists spin. *I dared not meet the Daffodils.* Those bile-yellow skirts shock the eyes from reverie. All morning, the robin's rust-red cry, too eager for its season. Relentless trumpet, trumpet, twitter. Face of a trollop, voice like tin. This garish onslaught of spring.

3. With Brigit Pegeen Kelly's "Song" (p. 198) in mind, write a poem-fable. You might research fables from your childhood or from various cultures, and reimagine them in a poem. Could Hansel and Gretel eat the witch? What would their house need to look like in order to lure her in?

4. Go to a café, train station, or any place where people gather and talk. Then eavesdrop, write down what you hear, and use that language to create a poem. Will you use dialogue in the poem? What new words and ideas can you incorporate?

5. Translate one of your own poems (or a classmate's) into another language using a translation dictionary or one of the many translation dictionaries available online (such as Babel Fish). Then translate your poem back into English. How has the language or syntax changed? What words seem untranslatable? Are there particular lines or phrases in the second language you used that are particularly striking, sonorous, or rhythmic that you should keep in that language?

POEMS TO CONSIDER

The Other Cold War   2003
ADRIAN BLEVINS (B. 1964)

> *I am the girl who knows better but.*—John Berryman

If you want to know what my lousy childhood was like
and how my parents were occupied and all before they had me

and all that [defunct, whiney, Anne Sexton] *kind of crap,*
I don't mind, I'm not shy, I'll tell you. But first let me say

I was born as mute as a white Dixie cup in a cattle-pissing stream   5
with just my eyes for talking, with just my cotton pout of a mouth.

But then something snapped and I'm not saying the vocal chords.
I'm not saying worries in the rain like *does he love me, does he not.*

I'm talking a much more foremost evil ambition—
talking the sway that spawned in my crotch   10

and rose through my belly and climbed up my throat
to shape the vowels that to the boys said *yes.*

I'm talking the feigned plea of the blink and put-on lick of the kiss
that would trigger the kick of bowling them over.

I'm talking the chief assault of the pubescent trot,   15
the poor moon through the window, the bites on my lip.

I'm talking the violence and the violation of the say-so and the clout
since it got me their anguish once I said we were over—

that rancid begging of *please, more trouble*—
that reduction of them to nothing but rubble.   20

 Realism   1994
CZESLAW MILOSZ (1911–2004)

Translated from the Polish by the author and Robert Hass

We are not so badly off if we can
Admire Dutch painting. For that means
We shrug off what we have been told
For a hundred, two hundred years. Though we lost
Much of our previous confidence. Now we agree   5
That those trees outside the window, which probably exist,
Only pretend to greenness and treeness
And that the language loses when it tries to cope
With clusters of molecules. And yet this here:
A jar, a tin plate, a half-peeled lemon,   10
Walnuts, a loaf of bread—last, and so strongly
It is hard not to believe in their lastingness.
And thus abstract art is brought to shame,
Even if we do not deserve any other.
Therefore I enter those landscapes   15
Under a cloudy sky from which a ray
Shoots out, and in the middle of dark plains
A spot of brightness glows. Or the shore
With huts, boats, and, on yellowish ice,
Tiny figures skating. All this   20
Is here eternally, just because once it was.
Splendor (certainly incomprehensible)
Touches a cracked wall, a refuse heap,

The floor of an inn, jerkins of the rustics,
A broom, and two fish bleeding on a board.   25
Rejoice! Give thanks! I raised my voice
To join them in their choral singing,
Amid their ruffles, collets, and silk skirts,
One of them already, who vanished long ago.
And our song soared up like smoke from a censer.   30

 ## Off-Season at the Edge of the World   1994
DEBORA GREGER (B. 1949)

We have crawled on our fins
from the sea into the sandy sheets
of the Holiday Inn.
How late we are to rise, how civilized,

who put on the furs of animals   5
against the seasonable chill.
Who walk on two legs down Commercial Street
past the petrified saltwater taffy,

the shops gaily boarded up.
By then it is midafternoon   10
at the end of the world, near dark,
time for a drink. The nights are long,

these the ones the ancients measured
fourteen fingers deep by water clock.
The room's a postcard, the view a stamp.   15
The ancients were right,

the earth's just driftwood, a slab of wood
adrift in a bowl of dishwater
under an overturned sky.
You empty your pockets: 20

from a two-fisted hourglass,
a little dune spills on the bed,
the racket immense,
grain against grain, wave after wave.

Parts rubbing each other wrong,   25
resistance wearing resistance down,
how civil we are to each other,
who have laid bare the law of friction,

skin sliding against skin
slick with the rigors of inventing pleasure.   30
I love you as I love salt, the ancients said.
Everywhere I lick you, you taste of it.

Visitation   2002
KATHY FAGAN (B. 1958)

An hour before dusk on a Tuesday, mid-November—
sunstruck clouds with winter in them,
beeches, sycamores, white with it too.
Blue sky. Also
an aroma of blue   5
sky, bell-clear, hard as a river
in your lungs, which is why you're
breathless again, grateful,
as if it were the banks of the Seine
you strolled on and not   10
the mastodon back of the Midwest,
gray unraiseable thing like a childhood
slept through, and past.
On the horizon now a kind of golden
gate of sunset. To visit   15
means to both comfort and afflict,
though neither lasts long.
That charm of finches lifting from a ditch
can surprise you with a sound like
horselips, and paddle toward the trees   20
beautifully, small,
brown, forgettable as seeds,
but they, too, must sing on earth unto the bitter death—

Song   1995
BRIGIT PEGEEN KELLY (B. 1951)

Listen: there was a goat's head hanging by ropes in a tree.
All night it hung there and sang. And those who heard it
Felt a hurt in their hearts and thought they were hearing
The song of a night bird. They sat up in their beds, and then
They lay back down again. In the night wind, the goat's head   5
Swayed back and forth, and from far off it shone faintly
The way the moonlight shone on the train track miles away

Beside which the goat's headless body lay. Some boys
Had hacked its head off. It was harder work than they had imagined.
The goat cried like a man and struggled hard. But they   10
Finished the job. They hung the bleeding head by the school
And then ran off into the darkness that seems to hide everything.
The head hung in the tree. The body lay by the tracks.
The head called to the body. The body to the head.
They missed each other. The missing grew large between them,   15
Until it pulled the heart right out of the body, until
The drawn heart flew toward the head, flew as a bird flies
Back to its cage and the familiar perch from which it trills.
Then the heart sang in the head, softly at first and then louder,
Sang long and low until the morning light came up over   20
The school and over the tree, and then the singing stopped....
The goat had belonged to a small girl. She named
The goat Broken Thorn Sweet Blackberry, named it after
The night's bush of stars, because the goat's silky hair
Was dark as well water, because it had eyes like wild fruit.   25
The girl lived near a high railroad track. At night
She heard the trains passing, the sweet sound of the train's horn
Pouring softly over her bed, and each morning she woke
To give the bleating goat his pail of warm milk. She sang
Him songs about girls with ropes and cooks in boats.   30
She brushed him with a stiff brush. She dreamed daily
That he grew bigger, and he did. She thought her dreaming
Made it so. But one night the girl didn't hear the train's horn,
And the next morning she woke to an empty yard. The goat
Was gone. Everything looked strange. It was as if a storm   35
Had passed through while she slept, wind and stones, rain
Stripping the branches of fruit. She knew that someone
Had stolen the goat and that he had come to harm. She called
To him. All morning and into the afternoon, she called
And called. She walked and walked. In her chest a bad feeling   40
Like the feeling of the stones gouging the soft undersides
Of her bare feet. Then somebody found the goat's body
By the high tracks, the flies already filling their soft bottles
At the goat's torn neck. Then somebody found the head
Hanging in a tree by the school. They hurried to take   45
These things away so that the girl would not see them.
They hurried to raise money to buy the girl another goat.
They hurried to find the boys who had done this, to hear
Them say it was a joke, a joke, it was nothing but a joke....
But listen: here is the point. The boys thought to have   50

Their fun and be done with it. It was harder work than they
Had imagined, this silly sacrifice, but they finished the job,
Whistling as they washed their large hands in the dark.
What they didn't know was that the goat's head was already
Singing behind them in the tree. What they didn't know   55
Was that the goat's head would go on singing, just for them,
Long after the ropes were down, and that they would learn to listen,
Pail after pail, stroke after patient stroke. They would
Wake in the night thinking they heard the wind in the trees
Or a night bird, but their hearts beating harder. There   60
Would be a whistle, a hum, a high murmur, and, at last, a song,
The low song a lost boy sings remembering his mother's call.
Not a cruel song, no, no, not cruel at all. This song
Is sweet. It is sweet. The heart dies of this sweetness.

11

DEVISING AND REVISING

The secret to writing is rewriting. To paraphrase W. H. Auden, literary composition in the beginning of the twenty-first century A.D. remains pretty much what it was in the early twenty-first century B.C.: "Nearly everything has still to be done by hand," word by word and page by page. Technique brings inspiration to life; craft makes the magic. "Writing is like evolution," says Forrest Gander, "in that poems are invented...as they develop in the act of writing." The first draft of a poem is just the lump of clay; revision shapes the material into the poem.

For most poems, the process takes many drafts. Elizabeth Bishop's "The Moose" took twenty-six years from first draft to finished poem. Richard Wilbur reports that he waited fourteen years, occasionally jotting down a phrase "that might belong to a poem," before he started to write "The Mind-Reader"; he took another three years to finish the poem. Asked how long he was likely to work on a poem, he said, "Long enough."

Nothing in a poem should seem accidental. As you revise, consider and reconsider every mark on the page for its potential effect. Each word is an opportunity to create a poem *as a system* with all its parts working together.

> *It is no accident that book, sentence, and pen are the terms not only of artistic profession, but of penal containment.*
>
> —Heather McHugh

Exploring

First drafts often mean exploration. The poet creates a sketch of a few ideas or impulses. How can the poem grow out of these notions? How should it begin? Hopeless blunders usually mix with useful clues, and by writing them down you sort them out like an explorer charting new territories.

Let's take a look at an early draft of the poem that became Whitman's "A Noiseless Patient Spider" (which we talked about in Chapter 2).

The Soul, Reaching, Throwing out for Love

The Soul, reaching, throwing out for love,
As the spider, from some little promontory, throwing out filament after
    filament, tirelessly out of itself, that one at least may catch and form
    a link, a bridge, a connection,
O I saw one passing along, saying hardly a word—yet full of love I detected
    him, by certain signs,
O eyes wishfully turning! O silent eyes!
For then I thought of you o'er the world,   5
O latent oceans, fathomless oceans of love!
O waiting oceans of love! yearning and fervid! and of you sweet souls
    perhaps in the future, delicious and long:
But Death, unknown on the earth—ungiven, dark here, unspoken, never born:
You fathomless latent souls of love—you pent and unknown oceans of love!

Whitman transforms the material of this early draft into an entirely new poem:

A Noiseless Patient Spider

A noiseless patient spider,
I marked where on a little promontory it stood isolated,
Marked how to explore the vacant vast surrounding,
It launched forth filament, filament, filament, out of itself,
Ever unreeling them, ever tirelessly speeding them.   5

And you O my soul where you stand,
Surrounded, detached, in measureless oceans of space,
Ceaselessly musing, venturing, throwing, seeking the spheres to connect them,
Till the bridge you will need be formed, till the ductile anchor hold,
Till the gossamer thread you fling catch somewhere, O my soul.   10

The early draft, "The Soul, Reaching, Throwing out for Love," offers Whitman many clues to his final poem. In the opening lines, he stumbles upon the primary metaphor of the poem, making the connection between the spider's flinging out of filaments and the soul's groping. The earlier draft doesn't yet tap the metaphor's full potential, but in coming back to this draft, Whitman must have begun to see—to have "re-visioned"—the possibilities of the spider–soul analogy.

In the draft printed here, retitled "A Noiseless Patient Spider," Whitman re-shapes this spider–soul analogy to make it the poem's motivating incident and suggests that one day, the speaker came upon a spider at work. This revision deftly resolves the overwrought sentimentality of the original draft's opening line ("The Soul, reaching, throwing out for love") and replaces it with concrete imagery and resonant details. After seeing the spider, the speaker "marked where on a little promontory it stood isolated," carefully observes it, then compares it to his own soul "Ceaselessly musing, venturing, throwing, seeking."

In the early draft, the motivating incident seems to be something entirely different. After addressing the soul, the speaker says he first saw a person "passing along, saying hardly a word—yet full of love I detected him." The speaker describes this person's eyes, thinks of "you o'er the world" (whoever "you" is), then drifts through abstract references: "oceans of love" and "souls of love." Whitman let go of his abstract first notions and allowed the poem to develop in a more fruitful direction.

Both poems have about the same number of lines, though the first weighs in at 125 words and the final poem is a tighter 87 words. While Whitman jettisons "eyes," "sweet," "delicious," "future," "Death," and "love," he keeps "oceans of" along with a few other words and phrases—"little promontory," "filament," "tirelessly," "bridge," and "catch"—that lead him to the poem's final discoveries. For instance, "filament" is echoed in "ductile anchor" and "gossamer thread"; the phrases "latent oceans," "fathomless oceans of love," and "waiting oceans" develop into the philosophic "measureless oceans of space," akin to the "vacant vast surrounding" in which the spider finds itself. Whitman further develops this water motif with "launched" and "unreeling," words that help ground the less concrete acts of "musing, venturing, throwing, seeking." These gerunds (nouns ending in *-ing*) stem from the original draft, although in it Whitman does not yet recognize the gerunds' deeper implications, how they celebrate process, activity, and exploration itself. Gerunds, like any word in a poem, must be deliberately and consciously chosen. Overuse of them can deaden their effect (especially if used to create too-easy rhymes).

Appreciating the potential of the spider-soul analogy from his first draft also helped Whitman refine the physical shape of the poem. The two five-line stanzas of "A Noiseless Patient Spider" create a parallel structure that subtly affirms the connection between spider and soul. By pursuing this analogy, the poem comes to be about our struggle to be connected and to make connections—how we venture, reach out, and hope to connect to something in the "measureless oceans of space" around us—which is very like the process of writing: We try and try again.

Early stages of writing often involve looking for clues. Before a passage can sound right and words click into place, your own dissatisfaction—the cranky sense that something remains vague, weak, or flat—can spur your revision. Trust that internal editor, and use it to help you strengthen your poems.

Focusing

When we read poems, we want them brought into clear focus. Sharpening fuzzy spots—unintentional ambiguity, exaggerations, private meanings, confusing omissions, and especially purple (or overblown) passages—is part of the poet's job in revising. Poets' initial drafts often capture their struggle to zoom in on the poem. Manuscripts and drafts by hundreds of poets, from Alexander Pope to Julia Alvarez, are reproduced in *The Hand of the Poet: Poems and Papers in Manuscript* (the originals are in the Berg collection at the New York City Public Library). On page after page we see the scrawlings and scratchings of poets working to focus the draft at hand. For instance, in the first draft of "Variations on a Text by Vallejo" (discussed in Chapter 10), written out on a legal pad sheet, we can see Donald Justice teasing the poem from his first notions. The draft has the title from the start and a good feel for the beginning of the poem (Justice started with "I will die in Miami in the sunlight" instead of "sun"), but the draft shows him feeling his way into what became the second stanza. Lines 14 through 17 of the finished poem read

And I think it will be a Sunday because today,
When I took out this paper and began to write,
Never before had anything looked so blank,
My life, these words, the paper, the gray Sunday

Justice first wrote these lines:

                                    because today
When I got up from my nap & reached for paper
I could think of nothing else, I could only think
of how I have been sick for five or six weeks,

He then crossed out "I could only think / of how I have been sick for five or six weeks" and replaced it with "I coughed and could think of nothing else." In the end, Justice cut both of these lines and focused the stanza around the larger metaphysical concern of blankness and of trying to write. This astute revision is less self-enclosed and more intriguing.

*[P*oetry*] aims—never mind either communication or expression—at the reformation of the poet, as prayer does.*

—John Berryman

At times, the smallest tinkerings with a poem allow for a brilliant stroke that otherwise might never have come to the poet. Consider the fourth stanza of a 1924 revision of Marianne Moore's "My Apish Cousins," which she retitled in 1935:

The Monkeys

winked too much and were afraid of snakes. The zebras, supreme in
their abnormality; the elephants with their fog-colored skin
  and strictly practical appendages
    were there, the small cats; and the parakeet
      trivial and humdrum on examination, destroying   5
    bark and portions of the food it could not eat.

I recall their magnificence, now not more magnificent
than it is dim. It is difficult to recall the ornament,
   speech, and precise manner of what one might
      call the minor acquaintances twenty   10
         years back; but I shall not forget him—that Gilgamesh among
      the hairy carnivora—that cat with the

wedge-shaped, slate-gray marks on its forelegs and the resolute tail,
astringently remarking, "They have imposed on us with their pale
   half-fledged protestations, trembling about   15
      in inarticulate frenzy, saying
         it is not for us to understand art; finding it
      all so difficult, examining the thing

as if it were inconceivably arcanic, as symmet-
rically frigid as if it had been carved out of chrysoprase   20
   or marble—strict with tension, malignant
      in its power over us and deeper
         than the sea when it proffers flattery in exchange for hemp,
      rye, flax, horses, platinum, timber, and fur."

Whether ordinary, odd, or noble, the zoo animals are handled affectionately. The admired big cat seems a Gilgamesh—that is, like the Babylonian epic hero.

At line 14 the poem takes a stunning leap, for the cat is suddenly **anthropomorphized** (given human qualities) and summarizes the paralyzing attitudes of certain art critics. The speaker's admiration for the cat reveals her allegiances and aligns her with the common readers whose portraits she has been amusedly sketching in the guise of zoo creatures. The poem argues against the notion that aesthetic experience and life itself are "not for us to understand" and "inconceivably arcanic." As the speaker and zoo-readers imply, we ourselves can choose how to appreciate a poem, an aesthetic experience, or the natural world.

Moore's poem first appeared in 1917 with this fourth stanza:

As if it were something inconceivably arcanic, as
Symmetrically frigid as something carved out of chrysoprase
Or marble—strict with tension, malignant
   In its power over us and deeper
   Than the sea when it proffers flattery in exchange for hemp,
Rye, flax, horses, platinum, timber and fur."

Besides dropping the lines' formal initial capitals, Moore's only change occurs in lines 19 and 20. Especially after "thing" in line 18, the repetition of "something" in both lines no doubt seemed redundant. Because the poem is in syllabics, she couldn't simply drop "something." Moore's solution repairs the syllable count of line 20 by inserting "if it had been" and moving the first two syllables of "symmetrically" up to restore the syllable count of line 19. She trades the off-rhyme of "as-chrysoprase" for the enactment of crabby rigidity itself, ironically dividing the word "symmet- / rically." Moore's careful tinkering leads to a moment of wit.

Shaping

Another essential part of composition is *shaping*. As the words of a poem come, they must be deployed into lines. Sometimes the earliest verbalization carries with it an intuitive sense of form—as Whitman's earlier draft was similar in length and number of lines to his final "A Noiseless Patient Spider." But often the first phrases are a scattering in a notebook or on a napkin. As a poem grows, the poet opts for some possible form, however tentative, which can be tested and altered from draft to draft. Meter? Rhyme? Free verse? Longer lines? Stanzas? The initial preference may be habitual, as Dickinson or William Carlos Williams instinctively worked in very short lines, or Whitman in very long lines. But a given poem may want a different sort of form, which the poet must be open to trying. In "The Yachts," for instance, Williams elected to write in lines much longer than was his custom: "Today no race. Then the wind comes again. The yachts // move, jockeying for a start, the signal is set...." He thereby creates a more satisfying sense of the wind, the current, and the floating boats.

In choosing stanzaic forms, whether in free verse or in meter, the poet looks for a pattern that can be used throughout and perhaps altered once or twice within a poem for strategic effect. Keep in mind that selecting a pattern for your poems doesn't always happen at a poem's start. Robert Lowell recalled that his well-known "Skunk Hour" was "written backwards," the last two stanzas first, then the next-to-last two, and finally the first four in reverse order.

Along with a tentative choice of form, shaping involves the experimental sculpting or fitting of parts into the poem's design. In the published versions of Marianne Moore's "The Fish," we can trace her shaping her poem to its final form. Here is an early version that appeared in a magazine in 1918:

 The Fish

Wade through black jade.
Of the crow-blue mussel-shells, one
Keeps adjusting the ash-heaps;
Opening and shutting itself like

An injured fan.   5
The barnacles undermine the
Side of the wave—trained to hide
There—but the submerged shafts of the

Sun, split like spun
Glass, move themselves with spotlight swift-   10
Ness, into the crevices—
In and out, illuminating

The turquoise sea
Of bodies. The water drives a
Wedge of iron into the edge   15
Of the cliff, whereupon the stars,

Pink rice grains, ink-
Bespattered jelly-fish, crabs like
Green lilies and submarine
Toadstools, slide each on the other.   20

All external
Marks of abuse are present on
This defiant edifice—
All physical features of

Accident—lack   25
Of cornice, dynamite grooves, burns
And hatchet strokes, these things stand
Out on it; the chasm side is

Dead. Repeated
Evidence has proved that it can   30
Live on what cannot revive
Its youth. The sea grows old in it.

As usual, Moore has devised a poem with an inventive form. Unmistakable rhyme-pairs (*wade–jade, keeps–heaps, an–fan*, and so on) begin and end lines 1 and 3 of each stanza. Tightly laced, these lines seem to resist the otherwise fairly straightforward movement of the sentences, so that the poem alternates between the rigidity of rhyme and the fluidity of enjambment (even over stanza breaks), mimicking the push and pull of water.

But Moore was dissatisfied with the poem's shape. Over several years, she recast the form and indented the lines, coming to this version published in 1935:

 ## The Fish

wade
through black jade.
   Of the crow-blue mussel-shells, one keeps
   adjusting the ash-heaps;
      opening and shutting itself like   5

an
injured fan.
   The barnacles which encrust the side
   of the wave, cannot hide
      there for the submerged shafts of the   10

sun,
split like spun
   glass, move themselves with spotlight swiftness
   into the crevices—
      in and out, illuminating   15

the
turquoise sea
   of bodies. The water drives a wedge
   of iron through the iron edge
      of the cliff, whereupon the stars,   20

pink
rice grains, ink-
   bespattered jelly-fish, crabs like green
   lilies, and submarine
      toadstools, slide each on the other.   25

All
external
   marks of abuse are present on this
   defiant edifice—
      all the physical features of   30

ac-
cident—lack
   of cornice, dynamite grooves, burns and
   hatchet strokes, these things stand
      out on it; the chasm side is   35

dead.
Repeated
   evidence has proved that it can live
   on what cannot revive
      its youth. The sea grows old in it.   40

Moore sharpens her images with two verbal changes: the line "The barnacles *undermine* the / Side of the wave—trained to hide..." becomes "The barnacles *which encrust* the side / of the wave, *cannot* hide..." The physical image of encrusting is an ingenious choice and clearly reverses the usual way of seeing barnacles as belonging to or being attached to rocks; the barnacles are given agency and activity.

In stanza 4, "Wedge of iron *into* the edge" becomes "wedge / of iron *through* the iron edge...." "Wedge" by itself on a line animates the word; its placement wedges into the next line. Moreover, the repetition of "iron" makes the opposing forces of sea against cliff equal; the denser sound suggests iron's heaviness.

The most dramatic change, of course, is visual: Moore opens up the earlier boxy stanzas and devises a pattern of staggered indentation. Each flush-left rhyme has a subsequent line of its own, which underscores the dynamic sea, seething with its own life force. "An injured fan" becomes "an / injured fan." This slight adjustment makes both words *an* and *fan* end-rhymes and suggests the opening and shutting of mussel shells. Moore also varies the indented rhymed and unrhymed line pairs throughout the poem, and thereby creates a more flexible stanza shape that moves in and out like the sea against the shore. As a result, "The Fish" of 1935 exemplifies great fluidity through its form and great rigidity through its unvaried syllabics and unremitting rhyming (which incorporates any word, however unimportant). This tension makes the poem vibrate. Moore's acute attention to rhyme, diction, and form is an excellent example of the rigours of revision and its many rewards.

Creating Community

Respect for the poem includes finding for it readers who complete the equation. Later, as you grow as a poet, you may think of submitting your work to magazines and journals, or even gathering your poems into a book. For now, though, your audience is your workshop group or poetry class. In effect, your poems are published—made public—as soon as the class reads them. Proofread carefully to prevent mistakes that derail your poems. A grammatical error, mispunctuation, cloudy syntax, or a typo will cost your poem your reader's attention and undercut your credibility. In general, avoid odd typefaces or colors, use standard one-inch margins, and include a title.

When you discuss another poet's work in class, give the poem and the discussion your honest attention. You will learn by listening to others talk about a fellow poet's work and by trying to articulate your response to it. Read the poem on its own terms. (A list of questions to guide the discussion and revision of poems appears in Appendix I.) What is the poem trying to do? How is it working? Be specific, offer suggestions, and ask questions, but never be cruel or patronizing. Speaking about *the poem* instead of *the poet*, and using "I" instead of "you" statements can help the student whose work is under discussion maintain a critical distance and be receptive to your comments. Your responsibility as a poet-reader means you respect and trust the poet's effort. At the same time, when your poem comes up for discussion, listen to what people are saying. What a gift to have readers who can enable you to revise your poems! Don't rush to explain or defend during workshop; a poem that needs explaining isn't doing its job.

Because the poem that seems great today can seem dumb tomorrow and wonderful again the day after, poets need honest, thoughtful readers: other members of a writing class, other poets, and eventually editors. Good readers aren't those who love everything you write (or who love you!), nor are good readers those who merely slash your poems to ribbons. It is helpful to know what a poem's strengths are and why a particular line or phrase works, but if a reader only praises, you will feel reluctant to listen to other suggestions or to your internal editor.

Your class will likely act as one of your earliest readers. Before the term finishes, trade e-mail addresses and continue exchanging poems with the best critics in your class. You may also find fellow poets in the community around you. Check local and regional universities, newspapers, and websites for writing groups and literary readings—you'll find them in bars, coffee shops, museums, bookstores, and beyond. Regularly attending poetry readings will put you in contact with a variety of poetry and poets out there.

Besides the writing programs at local colleges and universities, many cities and towns have literary centers and libraries that hold workshops, sponsor readings, publish literary calendars, and provide space for poets to meet. These centers often rely on the help of volunteers. Active citizenship in your writing community is a great way to meet like-minded individuals and support the community that supports you.

Since the development of the Internet, you also can access readers all over the globe. You can find poetry chatrooms at many sites, from small groups that started in a college writing class to groups allied with large literary organizations. To find them, you might start surfing Poets and Writers (www.pw.org), Poetry Society of America (www.poetrysociety.org), the Association of Writers and Writing Programs (awpwriter.org), the Academy of American Poets (www.poets.org), and the Poetry Foundation (www.poetryfoundation.org).

Submitting Your Work

When should a beginning poet start sending poems to magazines? If your school has a literary magazine, start readying a group of poems now—apply the finishing touches, check the journal's deadlines—and away they go! How about national journals? As soon as you have three or four good, polished poems and know several magazines or journals that would be appropriate, send your poems to them. Stick to magazines you have read and admire. If you like the poems in a magazine, odds are that you and the editors have similar taste.

Your first task is getting acquainted with literary journals that publish poetry, both in print and online (we offer a list of some titles in "Questions and Suggestions," p. 213). You might get ideas for literary journals by checking the acknowledgments page of your favorite books of poetry. You can also browse titles at the library, check out your local bookstore, surf the Internet, and subscribe to a few journals that feature work you like. Literary magazines remain some of the great bargains on the planet, and your support can sustain them.

Writer's Digest Books publishes *Poet's Market*, an annual publication that lists about two thousand periodicals and presses and specifies their submissions guidelines. The journals *Poets & Writers* and *The Writer's Chronicle* include calls for journals and publishers seeking poetry. If you can't find a particular magazine at a bookstore or library, go online and purchase a sample copy.

Once the poet has properly embodied his most fleeting emotion in the most appropriate words, then this emotion will continue to live on through these words for millennia and will flourish anew in every sensitive reader.

—Arthur Schopenhaur

Create a list of ten journals you admire and believe might publish your work. When you are ready, send your work to the first few magazines on your list, and make sure to check their websites for the latest submission information. In general, submit no more than four poems. If you are sending a paper submission, each poem should appear cleanly typed, single-spaced on one side of a sheet of 8½-by-11-inch paper, with your name, address, phone number, and e-mail address in the upper right corner. Include a brief cover letter thanking the editor for his/her consideration, and *always* enclose a self-addressed, stamped envelope (SASE) for a response. If you want your poems back, include enough postage for their return; otherwise, ask the editors to recycle them. Address the packet to the editor by name if you know it, or to the Poetry Editor. Keep a log of your poems, the date you submitted them, and, later, the responses. Several journals, including print journals, have begun to accept only electronic submissions, so be sure to check the individual guidelines.

Practice patience. Editors of small journals receive thousands of submissions a year. On average, expect to wait from six months to a year. The probability, at least in the beginning, is rejection. And the rejection will probably be a short form letter. Even very good poets receive enough rejection slips to wallpaper a den. But don't be discouraged. Read the poems over again as objectively as you can. New ways to revise might now become clear. If the poems still look good to you, put them in another envelope and ship them off to the next magazine on your list. Sooner or later, a rejection slip will carry a scribbled "Sorry" or "Came close." And perhaps a letter of acceptance will arrive and, in the words of poet and editor Richard Howard, you'll receive "an infinitesimal check." Usually, journals pay in copies of the issue in which your work appears or sometimes with a subscription.

If anyone wants money to publish or consider your poems, beware. Odds are, unless you know the journal or press to be reputable, it is a scam. Several publishers offer grand prizes for winning poems. Once you enter, they will send you a letter celebrating your poem's acceptance and offering you the chance to send them money for the hardcover book where you can see your poem in print. Don't be impressed. They often take anything sent to them and make a profit with those they've seduced.

Recent copyright law gives copyright protection to a work created since 1978 for the author's lifetime plus seventy years. That protection begins with its creation, so the penciled poem on your desk is included. The publisher of any reputable periodical or book will register the work upon publication. Even though the registration is made in the publisher's or magazine's name, the copyright belongs to the author, unless there is a written agreement to the contrary. In the absence of such a written agreement, a magazine acquires only the right to initial publication in one issue (and possibly reprint rights on its website or in an anthology). The author retains copyright and full control. If in doubt, consult a teacher or someone you trust in the field.

Very few poets earn a living through poetry. Williams was a doctor, Moore a librarian and editor, and Stevens an attorney for an insurance company. Today, many poets teach, and many others are park rangers, attorneys, maids, ranchers, nurses, therapists, journalists, and just about anything else. Writing poetry does not in itself pay the bills.

More important than money, though, is freedom. In our society, poetry doesn't pay much, but poets are free to write, engage their imaginations, and engage the world. When we're writing, we join a community of writers that includes William Shakespeare, Emily Dickinson, Rita Dove, and you.

QUESTIONS AND SUGGESTIONS

1. Write an **ars poetica** (a poem about poetry). In the "Poems to Consider" section, consider the various ways Dana Gioia, Kim Addonizio, and other poets approach this. What images and metaphors might you use to help you make a poetic statement about writing or reading poetry?

2. Visit an art museum or gallery. If you can't get to one, look through a book of art and find a piece of art that really strikes you. Write a poem about the work of art. Consider all of your senses (what might the work smell, taste, and feel like?). Also consider ways to look at art that might inform your poem, such as color, texture, shape, value, point of view, and subject. As you revise, feel free to go wherever the images in your poem take you.

3. Try your hand at an **abecedarian,** a poem in which each line begins with a letter of the alphabet. Copy the letters of the alphabet down the left side of a blank page, and begin filling in the lines using each next letter as a clue for what might come next. Following is an example of a brief abecedarian by Robert Pinsky (B. 1940).

ABC

Any body can die, evidently. Few
Go happily, irradiating joy,
Knowledge, love. Many
Need oblivion, painkillers,
Quickest respite.   5
Sweet time unafflicted,
Various world:
X = your zenith.

You also can try writing a sestina, pantoum, or other poetic form that
appears in Appendix II.

4. In this "poetry recycling" activity, look at a few of your "failed" poems. Pull
   out your favorite lines and see if you can collage together a new draft. You can
   play around with the order and add or delete lines as needed. You might also
   use your best recycled lines as titles to kick-start new poems. Wallace Stevens
   kept a notebook full of inspirational titles for poems he hoped to write.

5. *For a group*: Have each person in the group do research on three literary
   journals. Visit a bookstore or library and browse the poetry in magazines,
   including such titles as *Agni, American Poetry Review, Beloit Poetry Journal,
   Callaloo, Colorado Review, Crab Orchard Review, Iowa Review, Fence, Georgia
   Review, Kenyon Review, Memorious* (online), *New Letters, Octopus* (online),
   Pleiades, Ploughshares, Poetry, Quarterly West, Southern Review, Tin House, and
   Yale Review. Make sure each person in the group provides complete submissions guidelines and an overview of the journal's aesthetic. Create a list of
   journals you would like to submit to and send out your poems. Make sure
   to record the journal titles, what poems you submitted, what date you
   submitted them, and the results.

POEMS TO CONSIDER

Workshop   1995
BILLY COLLINS (B. 1941)

I might as well begin by saying how much I like the title.
It gets me right away because I'm in a workshop now
so immediately the poem has my attention,
like the ancient mariner grabbing me by the sleeve.

And I like the first couple of stanzas,   5
the way they establish this mode of self-pointing

that runs through the whole poem
and tells us that words are food thrown down
on the ground for other words to eat.
I can almost taste the tail of the snake   10
in its own mouth,
if you know what I mean.

But what I'm not sure about is the voice
which sounds in places very casual, very blue jeans,
but other times seems standoffish,   15
professorial in the worst sense of the word
like the poem is blowing pipe smoke in my face.
But maybe that's just what it wants to do.

What I did find engaging were the middle stanzas,
especially the fourth one.   20
I like the image of clouds flying like lozenges
which gives me a very clear picture.
And I really like how this drawbridge operator
just appears out of the blue
with his feet up on the iron railing   25
and his fishing pole jigging—I like jigging—
a hook in the slow industrial canal below.
I love slow industrial canal below. All those *l*'s.

Maybe it's just me,
but the next stanza is where I start to have a problem.   30
I mean how can the evening bump into the stars?
And what's an obbligato of snow?
Also, I roam the decaffeinated streets.
At that point I'm lost. I need help.

The other thing that throws me off,   35
and maybe this is just me,
is the way the scene keeps shifting around.
First, we're in this big aerodrome
and the speaker is inspecting a row of dirigibles,
which makes me think this could be a dream.   40
Then he takes us into his garden,
the part with the dahlias and the coiling hose,
though that's nice, the coiling hose,
but then I'm not sure where we're supposed to be.
The rain and the mint green light,   45
that makes it feel outdoors, but what about this wallpaper?
Or is it a kind of indoor cemetery?
There's something about death going on here.

In fact, I start to wonder if what we have here
is really two poems, or three, or four,   50
or possibly none.

But then there's that last stanza, my favorite.
This is where the poem wins me back,
especially the lines spoken in the voice of the mouse.
I mean we've all seen these images in cartoons before,   55
but I still love the details he uses
when he's describing where he lives.
The perfect little arch of an entrance in the baseboard,
the bed made out of a curled-back sardine can,
the spool of thread for a table.   60
I start thinking about how hard the mouse had to work
night after night collecting all these things
while the people in the house were fast asleep,
and that gives me a very strong feeling,
a very powerful sense of something.   65
But I don't know if anyone else was feeling that.
Maybe that was just me.
Maybe that's just the way I read it.

 ## Immediate Revision   2005
CHASE TWICHELL (B. 1950)

I love milkweed, especially
summer's taut linen pods
just splitting, reluctant to part
with the white silk, the seeds.
And then the bits of cirrus   5
snagged in the field.

The sky I'm trying to paint
changes fast, keeps fooling me,
slurring the intermarriages of clouds,
hemorrhaging darkness and chill,   10
banking the fire on Pitchoff's rocky spine.
My painting ends up a night sky,
so I add a couple of constellations,
sketching in the star-beasts.

Such carnage of ferns,   15
clanging and male shouts
from the work site—
they're dredging coal tar

from the brook. Big machines
root around in the woods.   20
But in moonlight the toxic trees
look heaped with snow,
so profuse are their flowers.

Muse   2009
KIM ADDONIZIO (B. 1954)

When I walk in,
men buy me drinks before I even reach the bar.

They fall in love with me after one night,
even if we never touch.

I tell you I've got this shit down to a science.   5

They sweat with my memory,
alone in cheap rooms they listen

to moans through the wall
and wonder if that's me,

letting out a scream as the train whines by.   10

But I'm already two states away, lying with a boy
I let drink rain from the pulse at my throat.

No one leaves me, I'm the one that chooses.
I show up like money on the sidewalk.

Listen, baby. Those are my high heels dangling from the phone wire.   15

I'm the crow flapping down,
that's my black slip

you catch sight of when the pain
twists into you so deep

you have to close your eyes and weep like a goddamned woman.   20

The Next Poem   1985
DANA GIOIA (B. 1950)

How much better it seems now
than when it is finally done—
the unforgettable first line,
the cunning way the stanzas run.

The rhymes (for, yes, it will have rhymes)   5
almost inaudible at first,
an appetite not yet acknowledged
like the inkling of a thirst.

While gradually the form appears
as each line is coaxed aloud—   10
the architecture of a room
seen from the middle of a crowd.

The music that of common speech
but slanted so that each detail
sounds unexpected as a sharp   15
inserted in a simple scale.

No jumble box of imagery
dumped glumly in the reader's lap
or elegantly packaged junk
the unsuspecting must unwrap.   20

But words that could direct a friend
precisely to an unknown place,
those few unshakeable details
no confusion can erase

And the real subject left unspoken   25
but unmistakable to those
who don't expect a jungle parrot
in the black and white of prose.

How much better it seems now
than when it is finally written.   30
How hungrily one waits to feel
the bright lure seized, the old hook bitten.

Winter Conception   2004
ELEANOR WILNER (B. 1937)

Silence in the forest's heart, and snow.
Palimpsest of trees, centuries of winter text—

bare twigs that interlock in blurred white
air, as one thought leads to the next,

half-obscured in snowy veils,   5
no end, though, to their reach or

to the snow; flakes thicken, the silence
deepens as they fall, lint from the pockets

of the cold, whirled to a dizziness
of white; the blizzard swallows back   10

the view, and every syllable of sound;
even the creaking of wood in wind

is silenced by the snow.
The wind breathes in and out

in clouds of white, the snow pure   15
kindness after so much noise,

so long a war of elements, of jarring
things whose natures clash, spring

back or shatter—the clang of armored
flesh, desire's fangs, the shouts   20

of dying men, bombed cities full
of burning souls, as Semele

who asked to see her god unveiled
saw only fire, and was consumed—

the unborn Dionysus brought to term   25
in the thigh of Olympian Zeus.

In whose loins will the drunken
force of life grow now, concealed

inside the falling snow, this wood
of birch and ash, as, veiled again,   30

the god, aroused, moves toward
another bed, and time folds back

its long white sheets of snow.

QUESTIONS FOR DISCUSSING

AND REVISING POETRY

The following questions are designed to support a poetry workshop, creative writing class, or an individual poet drafting and revising. The best conversations about poetry are those that cannot be outlined or predicted: They're collaboratively, even spontaneously, tailored to fit the particular poem, the particular poet, and the particular group. Nevertheless, these questions can provide you with a concrete starting point. In general, when discussing another poet's poem, train your attention on the words on the page—not the person who wrote the poem—and give the poem a fair and rigorous reading. Look up words you're unfamiliar with. Take time to re-read and re-consider. Be generous.

The following questions can help you gain critical distance from a poem so you can focus on specific features to revise, such as abstract language, murky imagery, clichés, awkward phrasing, inattentive lineation, or clunky sounds. Depending on the poem, certain questions will undoubtedly be more applicable than others. Ultimately, you can develop your own list of useful questions that will help you push each draft further along.

Approach

1. Who is speaking? Where? What is the situation presented?
2. What is the point of view, and how does it support the poem? Would another point of view be more appropriate or effective?
3. Is the poem in past, present, or future tense? Does the tense change or seem inconsistent? How does the choice of tense support the poem?
4. If the poem tells a story, what information has been left out? Are these omissions effective?
5. Is there something a reader needs to know that is not yet present in the poem?

Form

1. What is the poem's shape on the page? Stanzas? Couplets? Quatrains?
2. How does the shape support or obstruct the content?
3. How does the poem handle line breaks? Are strong words at the ends of lines?
4. Is there a combination of end-stopped and enjambed lines, and do they appropriately support the poem's content?
5. Do the line breaks suggest an undercurrent of meaning?

Imagery and Metaphor

1. What imagery does the poem present? What can you see, hear, smell, feel, and taste?
2. How does the imagery support the poem? What other imagery might be more effective?
3. Where can imagery be developed to replace the abstractions?
4. What is implied by the metaphors?
5. Do the metaphors throughout the poem work together to create a system, or do they compete with one another and seem inconsistent?

Diction and Syntax

1. Where is the language fresh and intriguing and where is it dull and cliché?
2. Are there instances of obscurity? Are the sentences clear?
3. Where can the poem be compressed? Are there moments of flat or prosy language or places where modifiers (for example, adjectives and adverbs) overtake the poem?
4. Are the verbs varied and strong, or does the poem rely on flat verbs (*is, were, seem, look, have,* etc.)?
5. Could active voice be used instead of passive voice?
6. Are the sentences tight or loose? Does the syntax create tension? How do the sentences work with the lineation?
7. What choices have been made regarding punctuation? Is the punctuation consistent and effectively deployed?

Sound and Rhythm

1. What words support or obstruct overall sound patterns?
2. Does the poem use alliteration, assonance, or other sound devices? Where do the sounds of the poem create an undercurrent of meaning?
3. If the poem uses rhyme, is it fresh and surprising, or does it seem forced and obvious?

4. Where else in the poem would slant-rhyme, alliteration, onomatopoeia, or other devices of sound be effective?
5. Do the variations in stresses per line support the poem's content? Do monosyllabic words create a flat rhythm? Where would rephrasing or relining create a more compelling rhythm?

Tone

1. Describe the tone. How does it support the content?
2. Are there places where the tone is inconsistent and does not seem to support the poem's content?
3. Does the tone seem complex or one-dimensional? How might the tone be enriched to enliven the poem?

Mystery and Imagination

1. Does the poem seem to have something yet to discover? Does it deliver on its promises?
2. Is the poem larger than the sum of its parts? Does it engage mystery? Does it overexplain or become obscure?
3. What about the poem prompts you to re-read and enjoy it?

APPENDIX II

A BRIEF GLOSSARY OF FORMS

See also the Index of Terms for items defined within the text.

abecedarian A variant of the acrostic in which each line begins with a successive letter of the alphabet. Robert Pinsky's "ABC" (p. 213) is a variant whose words are alphabetical: "Anybody can die, evidently," the poem opens.

accentual-syllabic verse See syllable-stress verse.

acrostic A poem in which the initial letters of each line spell out a name or message.

ballad A narrative poem typically written in stress meter in quatrains of 4/3/4/3 beats with an exact or slant rhyme on the second and fourth lines (*a b c b*). Keats ("La Belle Dame Sans Merci"), Coleridge ("The Rime of the Ancient Mariner"), and poets such as Dudley Randall and Marilyn Nelson have written successful literary ballads, but most ballads were anonymous creations.

ballade A form developed in medieval France of three eight- or ten-line stanzas followed by an **envoy,** or short concluding stanza, usually dedicated to an important person. The last line of the first stanza acts as a refrain in a typical rhyme scheme of *a b a b b c b C,* with the envoy rhyming *b c b C* (the uppercase letter indicates the refrain). The ten-line version rhymes *a b a b b c c d c D,* and the envoy *c c d c D.*

ballad stanza A quatrain in stress verse of 4/3/4/3 beats with an exact or slant rhyme on the second and fourth lines (*a b c b*), or, in syllable-stress verse, in alternating tetrameter and trimeter lines, a stanza popular with Dickinson.

blank verse Unrhymed iambic pentameter. Since the seventeenth century, it has been a formal workhorse for longer poems, including Shakespeare's tragedies, Milton's *Paradise Lost,* Wordsworth's *The Prelude,* and Browning's and Frost's dramatic monologues. Henry Taylor's "Barbed Wire" (p. 9) is written in blank verse.

couplet   A two-line stanza; when rhymed *a a* it is called a **heroic couplet.** Flexible, it has served for narrative (Chaucer's *The Canterbury Tales*), but is also capable of succinctness and punch, as in Spencer Reece's "Chrysanthemums" (p. 115).

feet   A unit of syllables containing one or more stresses. A foot may occur over more than one word or in the middle of a word. Following are the most common types of feet in English based on the number of feet per line:

monometer: one foot	**pentameter**: five feet
dimeter: two feet	**hexameter**: six feet
trimeter: three feet	**heptameter**: seven feet
tetrameter: four feet	**octameter**: eight feet

ghazal   From the Arabic, a lyric poem composed of at least five closed couplets that rhyme *aa ba ca,* etc., and often at the end, in the penultimate line, include the poet's name. Ghazals are popular in Persian, Urdu, Hindi, Turkish, Pashto, and other languages, like Spanish, that have Arabic influences. Ghazals are often sung at public gatherings. When the form is translated into English, the scheme often involves repeating the final word of the opening couplet as the last word of the succeeding couplets and an internal monorhyme in the couplets' second line.

haiku (hokku)   A Japanese syllabic form composed of three lines of five, seven, and five syllables. The essence of the haiku, however, is not its syllabic form (which is virtually meaningless in English), but its tone or touch, influenced by Zen Buddhism. Haiku are, in general, very brief natural descriptions or observations that carry some implicit spiritual insight. Robert Bly captures this insight (but not in syllabics) in his translation of a haiku by Kobayashi Issa (1763–1827):

> The old dog bends his head listening...
> I guess the singing
> of the earthworms gets to him.

meter   The pattern of stressed and unstressed syllables in a poem. Following are the most common types of metrical feet in English, but remember, meter is determined by the context in which the syllables appear (see Chapter 3):

> **iamb:** an unaccented syllable followed by an accented syllable, as in *a-BOVE* or *the DOOR.*

> **trochee:** an accented syllable followed by an unaccented syllable, as in *SNEAK-er* or *SNEAK in.*

> **anapest:** two unaccented syllables followed by an accented syllable, as in *un-a-BRIDGED* or *on the BRIDGE.*

> **dactyl:** one accented syllable followed by two unaccented syllables, as in *MUR-mur-ing* or *JOAN is a....*

pyrrhic: two unstressed syllables, as in *with the* or *in the.*

spondee: two stressed syllables, as in *HOT CAKES* or *TAKE CHARGE.*

nonce stanza   A stanza created for a particular poem, like that invented by Marianne Moore for "The Fish" (p. 207) or by George Herbert for "Easter Wings" (p. 82). The challenge is to repeat the form naturally and effectively throughout the poem.

ottava rima   An eight-line stanza, *a b a b a b c c,* adopted from Italian and used most memorably, and comically, by Byron in *Don Juan.*

quatrain   In general, a stanza of four lines, but the term often implies a rhymed stanza. Rhyme schemes include *a b c b* (often used in ballads, hymns, and popular songs); *a a b b; a b a a* (Erin Belieu's "Her Web," p. 57); *a b a b* (Gjertrud Schnackenberg's "Signs," p. 56); and *a b b a* (when written in iambic tetrameter, also called the "In Memoriam" stanza after Tennyson's use of it in that elegy).

pantoum   A Malayan form; an indefinite number of *a b a b* quatrain stanzas, with this restriction: Lines 2 and 4 of each stanza become lines 1 and 3 of the following stanza, and so on. The carry-over lines are called *repetons.* The poem ends with a quatrain whose repetons are lines 1 and 3 of the first stanza in reversed order.

rime royal   A seven-line stanza of iambic pentameter, *a b a b b c c,* used by Chaucer, Shakespeare, and occasionally modern and contemporary poets.

sestina   A French form of six, six-line stanzas and an envoy of three lines. Instead of rhyme, the *six words* at the ends of lines in the first stanza are repeated in a specific, shifting order as line-end words in the other five, six-line stanzas. Then all six words are used again in the final triplet, three of them at line ends, three of them in midline. The order of the line-end words in the stanzas may be transcribed this way: 1-2-3-4-5-6, 6-1-5-2-4-3, 3-6-4-1-2-5, 5-3-2-6-1-4, 4-5-1-3-6-2, 2-4-6-5-3-1; and in the triplet (2)-5-(4)-3-(6)-1. Poets in English since Sir Philip Sidney have explored the sestina's potential, notably Elizabeth Bishop, Anthony Hecht, Marilyn Hacker, David Lehman, James Cummins, and Weldon Kees in "After the Trial" (p. 93).

sonnet   A poem typically written in fourteen lines of iambic pentameter (see also the discussion on p. 49). The **Shakespearean** (or **English**) **sonnet** is commonly rhymed in three quatrains and a couplet: *a b a b, c d c d, e f e f, g g.* Shakespeare's Sonnet 73 (p. 28) is a good example in which the sense corresponds to the four divisions. The **Italian** (or **Petrarchan**) **sonnet** is typically rhymed in units of eight (**octave**) and six lines (**sestet**): *a b b a a b b a, c d e c d e* (or *c d c d c d*). The sense, statement, and resolution usually conform to this division. Poets have worked any number of successful variations on the rhyme schemes of both kinds of sonnets.

stress verse   Metrical verse that controls the number of stresses per line. In general, this is the most common meter in English: the meter of song, ballad, and rap.

Spenserian stanza   A nine-line stanza, eight lines in iambic pentameter and the last line in iambic hexameter, *a b a b b c b c c;* Spenser developed it for *The Fairie Queen,* and Keats mastered it in "The Eve of St. Agnes."

syllabics   A poem that counts the number of syllables in each line. Syllabics can offer a poet limitations in which to deploy the poem and create tension. See Marianne Moore's "The Fish" (p. 207).

syllable-stress verse   Metrical verse in which both stress and syllable are regular and controlled. The most common types of syllable-stress verse in English poetry are iambic tetrameter and iambic pentameter.

tercet   A stanza of three lines, sometimes called a **triplet,** which can rhyme *a a a, a b b, a b a,* or *a a b.*

terza rima   An Italian form of interlocking tercets (three-line stanzas) following an *a b a* scheme and using the unrhymed line for the double rhymes of the next stanza: *a b a, b c b, c d c,* and so on. The form is most closely associated with Dante's *Divine Comedy.* Familiar examples in English are Shelley's "Ode to the West Wind" and Frost's "Acquainted with the Night." See Molly Peacock's "Putting a Burden Down" (p. 124).

villanelle   From the French, a poem of six stanzas—five triplets and a quatrain. It employs only *two* rhymes throughout: *a b a, a b a, a b a, a b a, a b a, a b a a.* Moreover, the first and third lines are repeated entirely, three times, as a refrain. Line 1 appears again as lines 6, 12, and 18. Line 3 appears as lines 9, 15, and 19. Dylan Thomas's "Do Not Go Gentle" and Elizabeth Bishop's "One Art" (p. 58) are famous examples.

ACKNOWLEDGMENTS

Yasser Abdel-Latif, "Hunger," translated by Yasser Abdel-Latif and Erica Mena-Landry, from *PEN America: A Journal for Writers and Readers* 12 (2010): 99. Reprinted with the permission of the author.

Kim Addonizio, "Muse" from *What Is This Thing Called Love*. Copyright © 2004 by Kim Addonizio. Used by permission of W. W. Norton & Company, Inc.

Deborah Ager, "Night in Iowa" from *The Georgia Review* (Fall 2000). Reprinted with the permission of the author.

Pamela Alexander, "Look Here" from *The Atlantic* (1994). Copyright © 1994 by Pamela Alexander. Reprinted with the permission of the author.

John Ashbery, "At North Farm" from *A Wave* (New York: Viking, 1984). Copyright © 1981, 1982, 1983, 1984 by John Ashbery. Used by permission of Georges Borchardt, Inc. for the author.

David Baker, "Unconditional Election" from *Changeable Thunder*. Copyright © 2001 by David Baker. Reprinted with the permission of the University of Arkansas Press, www.uapress.com.

Hadara Bar-Nadav, "I Dreaded that First Robin, So" from *A Glass of Milk to Kiss Goodnight*. Reprinted with the permission of MARGIE/The American Journal of Poetry.

Robin Becker, "When Someone Dies Young" from *All-American Girl*. Copyright © 1996 by Robin Becker. Reprinted by permission of the University of Pittsburgh Press.

Erin Belieu, "Her Web" (originally titled "Brown Recluse") from *One Above & One Below*. Copyright © 2001 by Erin Belieu. Reprinted with the permission of Copper Canyon Press, www.coppercanyonpress.org.

Frank Bidart, "Song" from *Star Dust*. Copyright © 2005 by Frank Bidart. Reprinted by permission of Farrar, Straus & Giroux, LLC.

Elizabeth Bishop, "One Art" and "First Death in Nova Scotia" from *The Complete Poems: 1927–1979*. Copyright © 1979, 1983 by Alice Helen Methfessel. Reprinted by permission of Farrar, Straus & Giroux, LLC.

Adrian Blevins, "The Other Cold War" from *The Brass Girl Brouhaha*. Copyright © 2003 by Adrian Blevins. Reprinted with the permission of Copper Canyon Press, www.coppercanyonpress.org.

Deborah Bogen, from "Ghost Images" in *Let Me Open You a Swan*. Originally published (as "What We Know About Ghost Images") in *Crazyhorse* 74 (Fall 2008). Reprinted with the permission of Elixir Press, Denver.

Michelle Boisseau, "Moon at the Mirror" from *Trembling Air*. Copyright © 2003 by Michelle Boisseau. Reprinted with the permission of the University of Arkansas Press, www.uapress.com.

Marianne Boruch, "The Hawk" from *A Stick That Breaks and Breaks*. Copyright © 1997 by Marianne Boruch. Reprinted with the permission of Oberlin College Press.

Geoffrey Brock, "Abstraction" from *Weighing Light*. Copyright © 2005 by Geoffrey Brock. Reprinted with the permission of Ivan R. Dee, Publisher.

Gwendolyn Brooks, "the rites for Cousin Vit" from *Blacks*. Copyright © 1987 by Gwendolyn Brooks. Reprinted by consent of Brooks Permissions.

Sharon Bryan, "Sweater Weather: A Love Song to Language" from *Flying Blind*. Copyright © 1996 by Sharon Bryan. Reprinted with the permission of Sarabande Books, www.sarabandebooks.org.

Nina Cassian, "Ordeal," translated by Michael Impey and Brian Swann, from *An Anthology of Contemporary Romanian Poetry*. Copyright © 1976 by Michael Impey and Brian Swann from *An Anthology of Contemporary Romanian Poetry*. Reprinted by permission of Michael Impey.

Victoria Chang, "Eva Braun at Berchtesgaden" from *Circle*. Copyright © 2005 by Victoria Chang. Reprinted with the permission of Southern Illinois University Press.

Henri Cole, "The Hare" from *Middle Earth*. Copyright © 2004 by Henri Cole. Reprinted by permission of Farrar, Straus & Giroux, LLC.

Billy Collins, "Workshop" from *The Art of Drowning*. Copyright © 1995 by Billy Collins. Reprinted by permission of the University of Pittsburgh Press.

Martha Collins, "Remember the Trains?" from *Some Things Words Can Do* (Bronx: Sheep Meadow Press, 1998). Copyright © 1998 by Martha Collins. Reprinted with the permission of the author.

Emily Dickinson, "A Bird came down the Walk," "I heard a fly buzz—when I died—," and "After great pain, a formal feeling comes—" from *The Poems of Emily Dickinson*, edited by Thomas H. Johnson. Copyright © 1951, 1955, 1979, 1983 by the President and Fellows of Harvard College. Reprinted by permission of The Belknap Press of Harvard University Press and the Trustees of Amherst College.

Stephen Dobyns, "Bleeder" from *Velocities: New and Selected Poems*. Copyright © 1994 by Stephen Dobyns. Used by permission of Penguin, a division of Penguin Group (USA) Inc.

Rita Dove, "A Hill of Beans" from *Thomas and Beulah* (Pittsburgh: Carnegie Mellon University Press, 1986). Copyright © 1986 by Rita Dove. "The House Slave" from *Yellow House on the Corner* (Pittsburgh: Carnegie Mellon University Press, 1989). Copyright © 1989 by Rita Dove. Both reprinted by permission of the author.

Nancy Eimers, "A Night without Stars" from *No Moon* (West Lafayette, IN: Purdue University Press, 1997). Copyright © 1997 by Nancy Eimers. Reprinted with the permission of the author.

Paul Éluard, "The Deaf and the Blind," translated by Paul Auster, from Paul Auster, ed., *The Random House Book of Twentieth Century French Poetry* (New York: Random House, 1982). Copyright © 1982 by Paul Auster. Reprinted with the permission of the author, c/o Carol Mann Agency.

Lynn Emanuel, "The White Dress." Copyright © 1998 by Lynn Emanuel. Reprinted with the permission of the author.

Kathy Fagan, "Visitation" from *The Charm* (Omaha: Zoo Press, 2002). Copyright © 2002 by Kathy Fagan. Reprinted with the permission of the author.

B. H. Fairchild, "The Death of a Small Town" from *The Art of the Lathe*. Copyright © 1998 by B. H. Fairchild. Reprinted with the permission of Alice James Books, www.alicejamesbooks.org.

Robert Frost, "Out, Out–," "After Apple-Picking," and "The Wood-Pile" from *The Poetry of Robert Frost*, edited by Edward Connery Lathem. Copyright © 1944, 1951 by Robert Frost. Copyright © 1916, 1923, 1930, 1939, 1969 by Henry Holt and Co., Inc. Copyright © 1967 by Leslie Frost Ballantine. Reprinted by permission of Henry Holt and Company, LLC.

Amy Gerstler, "Siren" from *Bitter Angel* (New York: North Point Press, 1990). Copyright © 1990 by Amy Gerstler. Used by permission of the author.

Dana Gioia, "The Next Poem" from *Poetry* (1985). Later in *The Gods of Winter* (St. Paul: Graywolf Press, 1991). Copyright © 1985, 1991 by Dana Gioia. Reprinted with the permission of the author.

Louise Glück, "The Racer's Widow" (1968). Copyright © 1968 by Louise Glück. Reprinted with the permission of the author. "Daisies" from *The Wild Iris*. Copyright © 1992 by Louise Glück. Reprinted by permission of HarperCollins Publishers.

Rigoberto González, "The Guides." Reprinted with the permission of the author.

Jorie Graham, "The Way Things Work" from *Hybrids of Plants and of Ghosts*. Copyright © 1980 by Princeton University Press. Reprinted by permission of Princeton University Press.

William Greenway, "Pit Pony" from *Where We've Been* (Portland, Oregon: Breitenbush Books, 1987). Copyright © 1987 by William Greenway. Reprinted with the permission of the author.

Debora Greger, "Off-Season at the Edge of the World" from *Off-Season at the Edge of the World*. Copyright © 1994 by Debora Greger. Used with the permission of the poet and the University of Illinois Press.

Paul Guest, "My Arms" from *My Index of Slightly Horrifying Knowledge*. Copyright © 2008 by Paul Guest. Reprinted by permission of HarperCollins Publishers.

Thom Gunn, "The Beautician" from *Collected Poems*. Copyright © 1994 by Thom Gunn. Reprinted by permission of Noonday Press, a division of Farrar, Straus & Giroux, LLC and Faber & Faber, Ltd.

Jeffery Harrison, "Rowing" from *Feeding the Fire*. Copyright © 2001 by Jeffrey Harrison. Reprinted with the permission of the author and Sarabande Books, www.sarabandebooks.org.

Robert Hayden, "Those Winter Sundays" from *The Collected Poems of Robert Hayden*, edited by Frederick Glaysher. Copyright © 1966 by Robert Hayden. Used by permission of Liveright Publishing Corporation.

Terrance Hayes, "Mule Hour" from *Lighthead*. Copyright © 2010 by Terrance Hayes. Used by permission of Penguin, a division of Penguin Group (USA) Inc.

Bob Hicok, "See Side" from *Words for Empty and Words for Full*. Copyright © 2010 by Bob Hicok. Reprinted by permission of the University of Pittsburgh Press.

Marc Jarman, "Ground Swell" from *Questions for Ecclesiastes*. Copyright © 1991 by Mark Jarman. All rights reserved. Reprinted with the permission of the author.

Robinson Jeffers, "People and a Heron" from *The Collected Poetry of Robinson Jeffers, Volume 1, 1920–1928*, edited by Tim Hunt. Copyright © 1938 and renewed © 1966 by Donnan Jeffers and Garth Jeffers. All rights reserved. Used with the permission of Stanford University Press, www.sup.org.

Donald Justice, "Variations on a Text by Vallejo" from *Collected Poems*. Copyright © 2004 by Donald Justice. Reprinted with the permission of the author.

Brigit Pegeen Kelly, "Song" from *Song*. Copyright © 1995 by Brigit Pegeen Kelly. Reprinted with the permission of BOA Editions Ltd., www.boaeditions.org.

Carolyn Kizer, "Bitch" from *Cool, Calm, and Collected: Poems 1960–2000*. Copyright © 2001 by Carolyn Kizer. Reprinted with the permission of Copper Canyon Press, www.coppercanyonpress.org.

Yusef Komunyakaa, "Sunday Afternoons" from *Magic City* (Middletown, Conn.: Wesleyan University Press, 1992). Copyright © 1992 by Yusef Komunyakaa. Reprinted with the permission of the author.

Richard Lyons, "Lunch by the Grand Canal" from *The Paris Review* (1998). Copyright © 1998 by Richard Lyons. Reprinted with the permission of the author.

Cate Marvin, "Dear Petrarch" from *World's Tallest Disaster*. Copyright © 2001 by Cate Marvin. Reprinted with the permission of Sarabande Books, www.sarabandebooks.org.

William Matthews, "Men at My Father's Funeral" from *Time and Money*. Originally from *The Ohio Review*. Copyright © 1995 by William Matthews. Reprinted with the permission of Houghton Mifflin Company. All rights reserved.

Heather McHugh, "Form" from *Hinge & Sign*. Copyright © 1994 by Heather McHugh. Reprinted by permission of Wesleyan University Press, www.wesleyan.edu/wespress.

Wayne Miller, "Reading Sonnevi on a Tuesday Night" from *Only the Senses Sleep*. Copyright © 2006 by Wayne Miller. Reprinted with the permission of New Issues Poetry & Prose.

Czeslaw Milosz, "Realism," translated by Robert Hass, from *The New Yorker* (1994). Copyright © 1994 by Czeslaw Milosz. Reprinted with the permission of Robert Hass.

Marianne Moore, "To a Steam Roller," "The Monkeys," and "The Fish" from *Collected Poems of Marianne Moore*. Copyright © 1941 and renewed © 1969 by Marianne Moore. Reprinted with the permission of Scribner, a division of Simon & Schuster, Inc. All rights reserved.

Simone Muench, "1: the fever (starring kristy b)" from "Orange Girl Cast" from *Orange Crush*. Copyright © 2010 by Simone Muench. Reprinted with the permission of Sarabande Books, Inc., www.sarabandebooks.org.

Marilyn Nelson, "Minor Miracle" from *The Fields of Praise*. Copyright © 1997 by Marilyn Nelson. Reprinted with the permission of Louisiana State University Press.

Howard Nemerov, "Power to the People" from *The Collected Poems of Howard Nemerov* (Chicago: The University of Chicago Press, 1977). Copyright © 1958, 1962, 1967, 1973 by Howard Nemerov. Reprinted with the permission of Margaret Nemerov.

Aimee Nezhukumatathil, "What the Mosquito Gives" from *At the Drive-In Volcano*. Copyright © 2007 by Aimee Nezhukumatathil. Used with the permission of Tupelo Press.

Naomi Shihab Nye, "Famous" from *Words Under the Words: Selected Poems*. Copyright © 1995 by Naomi Shihab Nye. Reprinted with the permission of the author.

Mary Oliver, "Music at Night" from *The Night Traveler*. Copyright © 1978 by Mary Oliver. Reprinted with the permission of Bits Press and the author.

Molly Peacock, "Putting A Burden Down" from *Cornucopia: New and Selected Poems 1975–2002*. Copyright © 2002 by Molly Peacock. Used by permission of W. W. Norton & Company, Inc.

Robert Pinsky, "ABC." Copyright © 1999 by Robert Pinsky. Reprinted with the permission of the author.

Sylvia Plath, "Balloons" from *Ariel*. Copyright © 1965 by Ted Hughes. Reprinted by permission of HarperCollins Publishers and Faber and Faber, Ltd.

Marie Ponsot, "Winter" from *The Bird Catcher*. Copyright © 1998 by Marie Ponsot. Used by permission of Alfred A. Knopf, a division of Random House, Inc.

D. A. Powell, ["writing for a young man on the redline train: 'to his boy mistress'"] from *Cocktails*. Copyright © 2004 by D. A. Powell. Reprinted with the permission of Graywolf Press, www.graywolfpress.org.

Kevin Prufer, "The Empire in the Air" from *Fallen from a Chariot*. Copyright © 2005 by Kevin Prufer. Reprinted with the permission of Carnegie Mellon University Press.

Claudia Rankine, "The Man. His Bowl. His Raspberries" from *Nothing in Nature is Private* (Cleveland: Cleveland State University Poetry Center, 1994). Copyright © 1994 by Claudia Rankine. Reprinted with the permission of the author.

Srikanth Reddy, "Everything" from *Facts for Visitors*. Copyright © 2004. Reprinted with the permission of the University of California Press.

Spencer Reece, "Chrysanthemums" from *A Clerk's Tale*. Copyright © 2004 by Spencer

Reece. Reprinted by permission of Houghton Mifflin Harcourt Publishing Company. All rights reserved.

Theodore Roethke, "My Papa's Waltz" from *The Collected Poems of Theodore Roethke.* Copyright © 1942 by Hearst Magazines, Inc. Used by permission of Doubleday, a division of Random House, Inc.

Liz Rosenberg, "The Silence of Women" from *Children of Paradise.* Copyright © 1994 by Liz Rosenberg. Reprinted by permission of the University of Pittsburgh Press.

Mary Ruefle, "Do Not Disturb" from *Tristimania.* Copyright © 2004 by Mary Ruefle. Reprinted with the permission of Carnegie Mellon University Press.

Kay Ryan, "Don't Look Back" from *Say Uncle.* Copyright © 2000 by Kay Ryan. Reprinted by permission of Grove/Atlantic, Inc.

Jaime Sabines, "The Moon" from *Tarumba: The Selected Poems of Jaime Sabines,* edited and translated by Philip Levine and Ernesto Trejo. Copyright © 2007 by Philip Levine and Ernesto Trejo. Reprinted with the permission of Sarabande Books, Inc., www.sarabandebooks.org.

Natasha Sajé, "Reading the Late Henry James" from *Red Under the Skin.* Copyright © 1994 by Natasha Sajé. Reprinted by permission of the University of Pittsburgh Press.

Gjertrud Schnackenberg, "Signs" from *Supernatural Love: Poems 1976–1992.* Copyright © 2000 by Gjertrud Schnackenberg. Reprinted by permission of Farrar, Straus & Giroux, LLC.

Ravi Shankar, "Barter" from *AGNI 70* (2009). Reprinted with the permission of the author.

Reginald Shepherd, "Blue" from *Angel, Interrupted.* Copyright © 1996 by Reginald Shepherd. Reprinted by permission of the University of Pittsburgh Press.

Richard Siken, "Meanwhile" from *Crush.* Copyright © 2005 by Yale University. Reprinted with the permission of Yale University Press.

Tracy K. Smith, "A Hunger So Honed" from *The Body's Question.* Copyright © 2003 by Tracy K. Smith. Reprinted with the permission of Graywolf Press, www.graywolfpress.org.

Cathy Song, "Primary Colors" from *Picture Bride.* Copyright © 1983 by Cathy Song. Reprinted with the permission of Yale University Press.

Elizabeth Spires, "Letter in July" from *Poetry* (July 1992). Copyright © 1992 by Elizabeth Spires. Reprinted with the permission of the author.

William Stafford, "Traveling through the Dark" from *The Way It Is: New and Selected Poems.* Copyright © 1962, 1977, 1991, 1998 by the Estate of William Stafford. Reprinted with the permission of Graywolf Press, www.graywolfpress.org.

Ruth Stone, "A Pair" from *In the Next Galaxy.* Copyright © 2002 by Ruth Stone. Reprinted with the permission of Copper Canyon Press, www.coppercanyonpress.com.

James Tate, "A Guide to the Stone Age" from *Selected Poems.* Copyright © 1991 by James Tate. Reprinted with the permission of the Wesleyan University Press, www.wesleyan.edu/wespress.

Henry Taylor, "Barbed Wire" from *The Flying Change.* Copyright © 1985 by Henry Taylor. Reprinted with the permission of Louisiana State University Press.

Jean Toomer, "Reapers" from *Cane.* Copyright © 1923 by Boni & Liveright, renewed © 1951 by Jean Toomer. Used by permission of Liveright Publishing Corporation.

Chase Twichell, "Immediate Revision" from *Dog Language.* Copyright © 2005 by Chase Twichell. Reprinted with the permission of Copper Canyon Press, www.coppercanyonpress.org.

Charles Harper Webb, "Charles Harper Webb" from *Shadow Ball: New and Selected Poems.* Copyright © 2001, 2009 by Charles Harper Webb. Reprinted by permission of the University of Pittsburgh Press.

Stefi Weisburd, "Behind My Ear Is a Little Palace in Broad Daylight" from *The Wind-Up Gods* (Black Lawrence Press, 2007). Copyright © 2007 by Stefi Weisburd. Reprinted with the permission of the author.

Dara Wier, "Daytrip to Paradox" from *The Book of Knowledge.* Copyright © 1988 by Dara Wier. Reprinted with the permission of Carnegie Mellon University Press.

William Carlos Williams, "Pastoral," "Poem" ["As the cat..."], "The Red Wheelbarrow," and "The Widow's Lament in Springtime" from *The Collected Poems of William Carlos Williams, Volume I, 1909–1939,* edited by Christopher MacGowan. Copyright © 1938 by New Directions Publishing Corp. Reprinted by permission of New Directions Publishing Corp.

Eleanor Rand Wilner, "Winter Conception" from *The Girl with Bees in Her Hair.* Copyright © 2004 by Eleanor Rand Wilner. Reprinted with the permission of Copper Canyon Press, www.coppercanyonpress.org.

Christian Wiman, "Pos̄tolka (Prague)" from *Hard Night* (Port Townsend: Copper Canyon Press, 2005). Originally from *The Atlantic Monthly* (2002). Copyright © 2002 by Christian Wiman. Reprinted with the permission of the author.

INDEX OF AUTHORS AND TITLES

INDEX OF TERMS